P9-BJM-768

THE COMMONWEALTH IN THE WORLD

BY THE SAME AUTHOR:

AUSTRALIAN GOVERNMENT AND POLITICS. Third Edition 1964.
THE NATURE OF POLITICS. 1962.

THE COMMONWEALTH IN THE WORLD

By

J. D. B. MILLER
Professor of International Relations, Australian National University

THIRD EDITION

HARVARD UNIVERSITY PRESS
CAMBRIDGE, MASSACHUSETTS
1967

First published in 1958
Second Edition 1960
Third Edition 1965
Reprinted 1967

To

K. B. S.

Printed in Great Britain

CONTENTS

PREFACES 7

INTRODUCTION 9

Part I

THE GROWTH OF THE COMMONWEALTH

Chapter

I BEFORE WORLD WAR I 22

II FROM 1914 TO 1939 31

III FROM 1939 TO 1964 45

IV CONTEMPORARY INSTITUTIONS 56

Part II

INTERESTS AND POLICIES OF COMMONWEALTH MEMBERS

V THE RELATIONSHIP OF INTERESTS AND POLICY . . 83

VI THE WORLD OF STATES SINCE 1945 93

VII BRITAIN 102

VIII CANADA 118

IX INDIA 135

X AUSTRALIA AND NEW ZEALAND 157

XI THE COMMONWEALTH IN AFRICA 186

XII PAKISTAN, CEYLON AND MALAYSIA 208

XIII CYPRUS, THE WEST INDIES AND THE PACIFIC . . 226

Part III

THE NATURE AND FUNCTION OF COMMONWEALTH RELATIONS

XIV THE COMMONWEALTH IN ACTION 239

XV FUTURE POSSIBILITIES 272

CONCLUSION 297

INDEX 300

Cartoons by DAVID LOW

"SEPARATE TABLES" 59

"A LITTLE DIFFERENCE IN TIMING" 95

"BEHIND THE DOOR" 162

"CLEAR OUT, YOU LOT! THE COMPOUND IS ROUND THE CORNER" 201

PREFACE TO FIRST EDITION

An Australian living in England is naturally drawn towards interest in the Commonwealth and its future. He cannot help asking himself what those around him mean when they talk of "the Commonwealth", and how this connects with what is meant by people in his own country and in others which are members of the Commonwealth. From such questions it is only a short step to asking why the Commonwealth exists and what sort of political entity it is.

My debts in this enterprise are many. I cannot say how much I owe to Professors Sir Keith Hancock and Nicholas Mansergh; their writings and conversation have informed and stimulated me to a point where, although they may disagree with a good deal of what I say, they will recognize their influence in some of the remainder. Similarly, I owe much to the members of seminars which I attended for four years at the Institute of Commonwealth Studies in the University of London. My colleagues, Professor A. G. Pool and Mr. C. A. Fisher, have pointed out many mistakes in the manuscript, but must not be held accountable for those which remain in this book. My wife has sternly supervised my use of the English language, and encouraged me in difficult times; my debt to her is inexpressible. Mr. David Low has kindly allowed me to use four of his drawings as illustrations.

Leicester,
April 1958.

J. D. B. M.

PREFACE TO THIRD EDITION

For this edition I have attempted to bring details up to date, and to take account of significant changes in such fields as the Sterling Area (with which I have had the invaluable help of Mr. D. M. Bensusan-Butt), Britain's attempt to enter EEC, and the problems of Malaysia. Chapters XI and XIII are entirely new; changes in Commonwealth membership have created new situations in Africa and elsewhere.

Canberra,
December 1964.

J. D. B. M.

INTRODUCTION

THIS book is about the Commonwealth of Nations in the world of sovereign states. It is concerned with the nature and status of the Commonwealth as an international entity, and with the policies of its members towards one another and towards countries outside the Commonwealth. Since the members are treated in their capacity as sovereign states, there is little or no reference to their internal constitutional development, although there is some discussion of how they came to exercise the rights of sovereign states in the field of foreign policy.

Treatment such as this is appropriate to the present stage of Commonwealth development, but it may still be strange to those people in Britain and in other parts of the Commonwealth who do not separate the "sovereign" from the "colonial" elements in Commonwealth affairs. Because all the other Commonwealth members used to be British dependencies, and because Britain still has a number of dependencies to be granted self-government, it is natural that many British people should not recognize the profound difference in status between the sovereign states which, with Britain, make up the Commonwealth, and the colonies which are still Britain's responsibility. An Australian and a Dominican, a Canadian and a Rhodesian, are often treated without distinction: they all come from "the Commonwealth". Of course, there is something to be said for this treatment. The dependencies of Commonwealth members are included in the circle of the Commonwealth by virtue of their metropolitan country's membership; this applies to Papua and the Territory of New Guinea, which are an Australian dependency, as much as to the British colonies. But in political terms the difference between the relationship in which Australia as a country stands to Britain, and that in which colonial territories stand, is very great. Britain's fellow-members in the Commonwealth have wills of their own and the opportunity to exert those wills; they have foreign policies which Britain must take into account. A colony, on the other hand, cannot have a foreign policy; no matter how rich or populous it may be, and no matter how much discretion is delegated to its administrators, it is inevitably subject to the guidance and control of the colonial power.

Unless this difference is kept in mind, public discussion in Britain is apt to overlook the developing national interests of the other members of the Commonwealth, and the fact that those other members are in a position to make their own policies for themselves. They are sovereign states; it is useless to expect them to behave like colonies. The Commonwealth is "a free association of sovereign, independent states . . . together with certain dependencies".[1] It is better to treat it as a novel kind of international association, and ask what holds it together, than to assume that the members' previous dependence upon Britain will explain all their actions and provide them with a guide to policy in all situations. As we shall see, their former colonial status and the British influence which went with it are factors of great importance; but they are not the only factors deciding the policies of Commonwealth members.

I am attempting here to show that the Commonwealth is a body different in kind from the British Empire; to explain how the difference has developed; to discuss the ways in which past association with Britain affects the policies of the overseas members; to examine the Commonwealth's institutions, and speculate about why they continue in being; to show how each member has developed its own national interests; and to ask what future possibilities the Commonwealth has. The method throughout is empirical, in that the emphasis is thrown upon the actual relations between members and upon the policies which they pursue, rather than upon the relations which one might expect them to have if one assumed in advance that the Commonwealth was a particular kind of international body. It is assumed that countries are members of the Commonwealth for particular reasons, and that their membership is neither simply fortuitous nor an historical hangover; the aim is to discover those reasons and see how they operate.

Before discussing the growth of the Commonwealth in detail, however, it is advisable to consider certain questions of nomenclature. Much change has taken place in Commonwealth language in recent years; inevitably, it has not proceeded at the same speed in every part of the Commonwealth, and there has been much misunderstanding about the content of particular terms. In this

[1] *What is the Commonwealth?* Central Office of Information Reference Pamphlet No. 15 (H.M.S.O., 1956), p. 1.

book I have committed myself to certain usages to describe the institutions of the present time. My justification for them follows, in the form of answers to three questions: What is the relation of "the British Empire" to "the Commonwealth"? Why use "Commonwealth of Nations", and not "*British* Commonwealth of Nations"? What is meant by "a member" of the Commonwealth?

In 1926 it was stated in the Balfour Report that the British Commonwealth of Nations (members of which were Britain, Canada, Australia, New Zealand, the Irish Free State, South Africa and Newfoundland) was a part of the British Empire, which was held to consist of three sections: the British Commonwealth of Nations, India and (by implication) the colonial territories. This broad interpretation of "the British Empire" continued at least until 1939, and was presumably the reason why the Royal Institute of International Affairs entitled a work published in 1937 *The British Empire*, and included in it consideration of all three sections just mentioned. Yet at the same time another usage of the term "empire" was developing. Some people began to reserve it for the colonial territories which were not self-governing, and to associate with it ideas of subordination and inequality while preserving those of liberty and equality for the "Commonwealth". Thus, at one and the same time, men were using the same word to describe both a whole and a part of that whole. Confusion obviously resulted, and efforts were made to resolve it.

One of these (and among the most influential) was that of Sir Keith Hancock in the first volume of the *Survey of British Commonwealth Affairs*, which he published in 1937. His argument was as follows:[1]

> "There was . . . insufficient ground for adopting this antithesis between empire and commonwealth. Life within the Empire was flowing too vigorously to let itself be congealed in two separate seas. . . . It is best to regard the British Commonwealth, not as part of the British Empire, but as the whole British Empire, viewed in the light of [experiment in the art of 'the government of men by themselves']. In this view, the British Commonwealth is nothing else than the 'nature' of the British Empire defined, in Aristotelian fashion, by its end. This is the best way of making sense out of official documents and the speeches of

[1] W. K. Hancock, *Survey of British Commonwealth Affairs*, Vol. I, Problems of Nationality 1918–1936 (London, 1937), pp. 60–1.

> statesmen. It depends upon a speaker's mood and temperament and train of thought, upon conditions of time and place, upon the character of his audience, whether or not he speaks of the British Empire or the British Commonwealth. The two names jostle each other in a competition which is perhaps symbolical of the struggle between liberty and necessity, ideal and fact, aspiration and limiting condition—a struggle which is fought continuously in every creative society."

This view gave reasons for using both "empire" and "commonwealth" to describe the whole of what had previously been the British Empire, but saw the Commonwealth as the end sought and the Empire as the developing organism whose nature was to become the Commonwealth. Perhaps something like this was in the mind of Mr. Attlee, in 1949, when he answered a question in the House of Commons with the following:[1]

> "Terminology, if it is to be useful, keeps step with developments without becoming rigid or doctrinaire. All constitutional developments in the Commonwealth, the British Commonwealth, or the British Empire—I use the three terms deliberately—have been the subject of consultation between His Majesty's Governments, and there has been no agreement to adopt or to exclude the use of any one of these terms, nor any decision on the part of His Majesty's Government in the United Kingdom to do so. . . . Opinions differ in different parts of the British Empire and Commonwealth on this matter, and I think it better to allow people to use the expression they like best."

I am not aware that any legal decision has been taken, or any statute passed, since 1949, to change the vague position described by Mr. Attlee. But it is plain that since then the terms "British Empire", "Empire" and "Imperial" have almost ceased to exist as active elements in speech and writing. Reference to the *Commonwealth Relations Office List*, 1960, shows that nearly all the official and semi-official bodies for co-operation had changed their titles from "Empire" or "Imperial" to "Commonwealth". Some of the private bodies preserve the old word; but these have also been getting fewer. The general tendency is to use the term "the Commonwealth" to cover both member-countries and British dependencies. Sir Winston Churchill and Her Majesty the Queen sometimes used the term, "the Commonwealth and Empire", implying a distinction of the kind which Sir Keith

[1] May 2, 1949. Quoted in Nicholas Mansergh, *Documents and Speeches on British Commonwealth Affairs, 1931–1952* (London, 1953), Vol. II, p. 1211.

Hancock attacked in 1937 between the free and unfree, the equal and the unequal. But it is noticeable that Sir Keith himself, in his Cust Foundation Lecture of 1956, used the term "the British Colonial Empire" to describe the colonies;[1] and from this I draw the conclusion that he now considers that, if "Empire" should be used at all, it should be related specifically to Britain and the British colonies.

My own view is that we should drop the term "Empire" altogether. By no stretch of the imagination can it be given its 1926 meaning of an all-encompassing entity within which the Commonwealth finds a place; such a meaning would be rejected out of hand by Canada and the Asian and African members, and would be admitted only in the maziest sentimental sense by some Australians and some New Zealanders. The only possible use of it is in some such phrase as "British Colonial Empire", as used by Sir Keith Hancock to distinguish the collection of British colonies from the French or Portuguese colonies. In this sense it seems to me permissible but unnecessary: "the colonies" is a simple expressive phrase which does not carry with it the trappings of imperial might—although it is open to the etymological objection that its original meaning has been distorted to cover countries which are not the product of colonization but of annexation, conquest and agreements of various kinds. My reason for suggesting that the term "the British Empire" should now be left out of all but historical discussions is that it creates misunderstandings and prejudices and no longer corresponds to the facts of life in the Commonwealth.

However, this still leaves the question of what overall term should be used to replace "the Empire"; should it be "the Commonwealth of Nations" (shortened to "the Commonwealth") or "the British Commonwealth of Nations"? Here present-day usage is divided. It is still customary in Australia and New Zealand, and to a slight extent in Britain, to use the adjective "British". But this is not the practice of the meetings of Commonwealth Prime Ministers, and has not been since 1946. The Prime Ministers' Conference of that year was the last to be attended by Smuts and Mackenzie King; its communique can fittingly be regarded as the swan-song of the "Statute of Westminister Commonwealth" which they

[1] Sir Keith Hancock, *Colonial Self-Government* (Cust Foundation Lecture, University of Nottingham, 1956), p. 4.

had seemed to personify. In the communique the phrases "British Commonwealth" and "Commonwealth" were used indiscriminately.[1] The next meeting of Prime Ministers, which took place in 1948, was the first to be attended by representatives of the Asian member-nations. The Prime Ministers were welcomed by King George VI, with a reference to "our Commonwealth" without any mention of the word "British".[2] When the final communique appeared it did not contain any mention of a "British" Commonwealth, either.[3] There were protests about this, but they were mostly half-hearted; it was recognized, on the whole, that the Indian independence movement was not likely to wish to stress the fact of its country's membership of a specifically British body. In Canada, Mr. St. Laurent met the objections with the comment, "It doesn't make much difference whether we have the word British or whether we don't".[4] Since then, whether it has made any difference or not, the Prime Ministers have refrained from using the term "British" to describe the Commonwealth. One or two of them have done so individually, but it is settled practice that their collective usage is "the Commonwealth"; and this is now adhered to in all publications of the British government.

It is not only Indian sensitivity that has led to the dropping of the adjective "British". For many years there was opposition to it in Canada, South Africa and the Irish Free State—in fact, in all those Commonwealth countries in which the population was either not predominantly British in origin or not in favour of stressing the imperial connection. Nearly half a century ago Richard Jebb was aware of this difficulty in connection with the term "British" in "British Empire", and wished to replace it with "Britannic": it is doubtful whether those who disliked "British" would have seen the distinction as clearly as Jebb did. Whether nationalists object to "British" on grounds of differences of race or of resentment at the thought that the adjective gives the impression that the Commonwealth belongs to Britain, they object to it; and their objections have now been tacitly met. It seems to me that in present conditions there is no escape (even if one wished to escape) from the view that "Commonwealth" or "Commonwealth of Nations" is the correct term to describe the

[1] The communique is in Mansergh, *op. cit.*, Vol. I, pp. 595–6.
[2] See *The Times*, October 15, 1948.
[3] The communique is in Mansergh, *op. cit.*, Vol. II, pp. 1137–8 and 1210–11.
[4] See *Winnipeg Free Press*, October 29, 1948.

body about which this book is written, and that "British Commonwealth of Nations" has now become an historical term of reference.

Finally, what is the correct generic term for such countries as Britain, Canada, Australia, New Zealand, India, Pakistan, Ceylon and Ghana? "Member of the Commonwealth" is surely the answer. According to context, this can be reduced to "member" or "member-nation" or "member-country". "Member" is preferable to "Dominion", a term which, in any case, was never applied to Britain. While we can say Australia, Canada and New Zealand are still Dominions, India and Pakistan, which were given that status by the Indian Independence Act, relinquished it on becoming republics. The Ceylon Independence Act did not speak of Dominion status, but of "fully responsible status"; the Ghana Independence Act did the same, but added that Ghana would "form part of Her Majesty's dominions"; the Federation of Malaya Independence Act spoke of establishing that country as "an independent sovereign country". In all three cases the words "within the British Commonwealth of Nations" or "within the Commonwealth" were added. Thus, while it would be unwise to suggest that Dominion status is entirely dead (some Rhodesians still aspire to it), it is clearly not a term to use to describe the members of the Commonwealth. They may be subdivided into "realms" (those of which the Queen is Head of State) and "republics"; but even this distinction fails to take account of Malaysia, which is not a republic, but of which the Queen is not Head of State.

To summarize, this book uses "Commonwealth" or "Commonwealth of Nations" in preference to either "British Empire" or "British Commonwealth of Nations", and "member of the Commonwealth", "realm" and "republic" in preference to "Dominion". This usage seems justified in terms of historical development and current practice.

Part I

THE GROWTH OF THE COMMONWEALTH

THE GROWTH OF THE COMMONWEALTH

THE story of the growth of the Commonwealth is the story of the growth of national sentiment in the colonies which were to become member-nations, and of constitutional concessions by Britain which enabled a link to be preserved between the former colonial power and the developing nations, without offending their national self-respect. No one would now suggest that British policy in this regard had always been consistent, or that it had always developed according to plan. But it is possible to say that the most enduring decisions of British policy towards the overseas countries have been those which recognized the inevitability of the development of self-government and the need to avoid the sort of abrupt break that took place with the American colonies at the end of the eighteenth century. Attitudes and theories about colonial policy have varied considerably in Britain in the past century and a half, but British practice has tended to accept the implications of self-government and to direct its energies towards preserving bonds of sympathy and sentiment rather than those of sovereignty. British policy has not run ahead of colonial nationalism, but has been a response to its demands. There has been no clearly connected thread of intention about British policy, but there is discernible a succession of similar responses to colonial pressures.

Just as it is important to recognize the empirical character of British policy in the growth of the Commonwealth of Nations, so it is necessary to recognize that national sentiment did not develop uniformly in the overseas territories, and that, where it did develop, it did so for a variety of reasons. In South Africa the main urge came from Afrikaner self-esteem, and the desire to wipe out the marks of subservience to "British" and "imperial" power which were held to have resulted from British victory in the Boer War. In Canada, nationalism got its driving force largely from French-Canadian sentiment, but also from the fear that unless Canada could speak with a voice of its own, Canadian interests would be subordinated to British in negotiations with the United States. In Australia, nationalism received a particular stimulus from the transfer by Irish immigrants of the anti-imperial feeling they had had in Ireland to their new land; if English dominance was wrong for Ireland, it was wrong for Australia, too. In New

Zealand there was no such racial stimulus to nationalism as was provided by the Afrikaners, French-Canadians and Irish in the other three countries. But national self-esteem grew there also, for a reason which operated strongly in each of the other countries as well: the natural tendency of British migrants to take pride in the country in which they had made a new and better life, and of their children to believe that they had been born into a new, free country which had put behind it the outworn customs of the Old World. This sentiment, the feeling of the "native-born", provided a link between the growing nationalisms of Australia, Canada, South Africa and New Zealand, and still gives people from those countries a common sense of distinction from people born in Britain.

There were, then, solid reasons for the growth of national sentiment in the four "original dominions", countries which got their white populations from Europe, and to a large extent from the British Isles. There were different reasons again for the growth of national sentiment in such countries as India, Pakistan, Ceylon and Ghana. Here the burden of complaint was similar, arising from impatience with tutelage from Britain and a wish to achieve the status of a sovereign state. But this kind of nationalism was exacerbated far more by racial factors. Canadians and Australians who objected to British tutelage were arguing with men of the same colour and religion as themselves, and arguing within an area of discourse bounded by a common culture. Although they might argue with one another, they were all white men and tended to hold similar views about their superiority to coloured men; in fact, the Australians, Canadians, South Africans and New Zealanders tended to be more "racialist", in their resistance to coloured immigration, than the British themselves. But when there were arguments between the British on the one hand and Indians or Africans on the other, these were necessarily of a different kind. Although they might be about the same things—constitutions, the franchise, taxation, citizenship—as the arguments with Australians and Canadians, they were conducted in a different atmosphere. Colonial nationalism of the Indian and African kind has been harsher and more bitter than colonial nationalism of the older, "white" variety, because across it has fallen the shadow of the colour bar.

The disparate character of the colonial nationalism with which

Britain was faced in the nineteenth and twentieth centuries goes a long way towards explaining the empirical character of British constitutional policy. Only a thoroughly empirical policy could cope with such a variety of demands voiced for such different reasons. The remarkable fact about the Commonwealth of Nations as a constitutional entity, as an outcome of what were formerly colonial conditions, is that it has been able to accommodate, at successive stages of its growth, ex-colonies of such a different character.

The development of the Commonwealth can best be seen in three stages: before World War I, between the wars, and since World War II. Each of the wars had a catalytic effect upon the status of what are now member-nations of the Commonwealth. Both wars encouraged national sentiment and created demands for new forms of status. In recent years the sheer momentum of colonial self-government has itself become sufficient reason for the process to continue.

Chapter One

BEFORE WORLD WAR I

THE status of British colonies at the beginning of the twentieth century was largely the outcome of decisions made by the British government between the 1830's and the 1860's. The general tendency of these decisions (except in the West Indies) had been towards colonial self-government. All the bigger colonies, with substantial white settler populations, had been granted internal self-government by means of constitutions which gave power to local ministries responsible to local parliaments. The franchise in these parliaments was often wider than in Britain itself. In the smaller colonies there were some cases of local assemblies; but broadly speaking, it is fair to say that in those dependencies where coloured people were in the majority, government was carried on by officials appointed by the British government and responsible to it. The supreme example of this system was the Empire of India.

The system of responsible government, which obtained in the South African and Australian colonies, in Canada, Newfoundland and New Zealand, took the lines of Lord Durham's prescription for the troubles of Canada in the 1830's. In his view, the colonists should not only make the laws but execute them as well; the actual administration of affairs should be in the hands of colonial politicians, responsible to their own parliaments, instead of in those of administrators appointed from Britain and irremovable by colonial protest. The only matters on which, in Durham's view, the colonists could not be trusted to legislate were "the constitution of the form of government—the regulation of foreign relations, and of trade with the Mother Country, the other British colonies and foreign nations—and the disposal of the public lands". By the end of the century the self-governing colonies had obtained control over their constitutions and their public lands; it was only in the field of foreign relations and foreign trade that they were still dependent on Britain, and in regard to trade they had achieved a considerable degree of autonomy.[1]

[1] Two qualifications to this general statement need to be kept in mind. First, while the self-governing colonies had power to legislate on their domestic affairs their Governors and Governors-General had a reserve power of veto which could be exercised at the will of the British government, to which these officials

In foreign policy, however, they had no initiative and no responsibility. They were not sovereign states; in terms of international law the British Empire was a single state, and treaties and agreements could be made only by the Monarch, on the advice of the British government. In constitutional terms, it was impossible to divide the monarchy, and so impossible to have more than one foreign policy for the Empire as a whole. In any case, the self-governing colonies were not in a position to defend themselves. Some of them had small military forces for which they paid, but it was assumed on all sides that ultimately their defence was the responsibility of the Royal Navy. A single Fleet and a single foreign policy were assumed to go together.

Yet there were cracks in this smooth surface of imperial unity. The biggest related to Canadian relations with the United States. Obviously, the primary responsibility for Canadian defence lay not with Britain but with the United States, simply in terms of its own interest; it could not afford to stand idly by and see its northern neighbour invaded by a European power. This vitiated the common argument that imperial policy rested upon imperial defence. At the same time, Canadians were aware that in a number of matters it was possible to distinguish Canadian from British interests in relations with the United States. In various instances, notably the Washington Treaty of 1871, agreements between Britain and the United States were held by Canadians to have neglected Canadian interests. In response to Canadian pressure, the custom arose of associating colonial representatives with the British negotiating teams in cases where the matters under discussion affected the interests of a particular colony. Also, in matters of trade it became British practice to exclude the self-governing colonies from the effects of treaties made between Britain and a foreign country; the colonies could, if they wished, accede to such treaties by signifying their intention of doing so. By these means the diplomatic unity of the Empire was preserved and the conflicting fiscal interests of the colonies reconciled with those of Britain; this became necessary since the self-governing

were responsible. But this was rarely used. Second, Canada was not, and still is not, in full control of its own constitution, since till 1964 it had been impossible to find a means of changing the Canadian constitution in Canada itself which was acceptable to provincial opinion, notably in Quebec. But this did not mean, any more than it means now, that a British parliament would attempt to change the Canadian constitution against the will of Canada.

colonies were all developing protectionist systems in one form or another, while Britain remained a free-trader.

Thus, in the economic sphere, differences of interest were developing. They developed also in political matters. In the first place the self-governing colonies, scattered over the surface of the globe, were likely to take a different view of movements by European powers near their borders from that taken by Britain, herself a European power. In the last twenty years of the nineteenth century, colonial interests began to show themselves in such matters as Australian perturbation over German colonization in New Guinea and French designs on the New Hebrides; New Zealand anxiety over Samoa; and the concern of British settlers at the Cape, led by Cecil Rhodes, over German penetration into South-West Africa. In all these cases it was a colonial complaint that Britain did not take seriously enough the establishment of foreign power on the doorsteps of the colonies. The colonies had a slight degree of initiative in the matter, in so far as their politicians could make inflammatory speeches and create "incidents", even to the length of themselves attempting to occupy allegedly empty land threatened with foreign settlement, as Queensland did in 1883 when it attempted to annex Papua. But they had no staying power in such matters. If the British government was not prepared to move when they prodded it, nothing which was legal and final could be achieved.

Some colonies were also developing special interests in the field of migration. Wishing to restrict Asian immigration, they found themselves at odds with the British government over the terms of their restrictive legislation. The British government was naturally anxious that this should not prove offensive to its own Asian subjects, particularly in India, and it wished to preserve as much as possible of the semblance of equal citizenship and equality before the law of British subjects. Brash colonial nationalism was not likely to show much sympathy with this imperial desire.

The growing sense of importance of the self-governing colonies was recognized in 1907, when they were officially granted the special name of "Dominions" and were provided with a special means of expression in the Imperial Conference. There had been occasional conferences of the colonies before, but the Imperial Conference was meant to be something more significant. It was laid down that the countries represented must be self-governing, that they should meet every four years to discuss common problems, that the British Prime Minister should preside, and that they should have one vote each, irrespective of their size or population. From the standpoint of the leaders of the Dominions, the Imperial Conference provided a number of advantages. It enabled them to approach the British Cabinet direct without having to find their way through the labyrinths of the Colonial Office; none of them liked the Colonial Office. It offered a public forum where they could advertise the prospects of development of their territories, and could urge on the British government and the British people such policies of imperial preference as suited their own interests. It was also a means of creating bodies for co-operation in such fields as shipping, telecommunications and scientific research. In all these ways it gave the Dominions a sense of extra status, of a unique position shared with no one else. But it did not produce much advance in the two major fields of defence and foreign policy.

In regard to defence, the discussions at Imperial Conferences before 1914 produced a general agreement that each Dominion was primarily responsible for the defence of its own shores, but that the Empire as a whole depended for its protection against foreign attack upon the Royal Navy. The principal question to be decided was how the Dominions were to be associated with the maintenance of the Royal Navy. On the whole, British opinion favoured the view that the Dominions should freely contribute towards the cost of upkeep; there was no question of forcing them to do so, but it would have been appreciated if they had offered to do so. This policy met with sympathy in "loyalist" quarters in the various Dominions—i.e. in those circles which favoured the closest association of the various parts of the Empire, and wished to emphasize British leadership above local aspirations towards autonomy. But the "loyalist" response met with two main difficulties. The first, and more important though less emotionally expressed, was the reluctance of the Dominion populations to tax themselves consistently to pay for continued imperial defence. They could, and did, make sporadic contributions, as during the Boer War and in the years immediately before World War I, when some "emergency contributions" were received by Britain from Dominion budgets. But these were on a different plane from consistent subventions; these the Dominions failed to make because of their pressing needs for expenditure at home. The second difficulty was the presence of truculent radical sentiment in the Dominions, which demanded "Dominion navies" instead of contributions to the Royal Navy. This demand was loudest in Australia and least evident in New Zealand. But in all the Dominions there were influential people who wished to see their countries provided with their own men-o'-war, manned by their own countrymen, paid for by their own exchequers, stationed on their own coasts and perpetually serving as a reminder of their national sentiment. At the outbreak of war in 1914 only Australia had provided herself with such a navy, and it was understood to be under Royal Navy control if war should actually break out. In Canada the question of a local navy had been one of the foremost at issue between the political parties.

Thus in defence policy there was scope for the expression and satisfaction of Dominion national sentiment through the provision of Dominion navies, but there was general recognition that the Royal Navy was the final means of defence against a determined foreign power. In foreign affairs generally there was no counterpart to the Dominion navies, no means of providing the Dominions with even limited status. They were subordinate and dependent. At Imperial Conferences it was customary for the British Foreign Secretary to explain the world situation and invite comments, but there was no question of the Dominions having any independent role in foreign affairs. They might advise and warn, but they could not operate as powers in their own right. In particular, the issue of peace and war could be decided only by the British government. It was thus possible for the Dominions to find themselves automatically at war in circumstances which might prove offensive to substantial sections of their own people and politicians. In legal terms, there was no arguing against this: the British Empire was assumed to be a single state in international law, and no part of it could be at peace when the rest was at war. This was accepted by the Dominion governments. But it was asserted without effective contradiction by Sir Wilfrid Laurier, the Prime Minister of Canada between 1896 and 1910, that while Canada might be at war through some action of Britain's, she was not necessarily obliged to send troops to fight; she could engage in passive belligerency, thereby avoiding the miserable condition of a nation at war while divided internally. Laurier's hypothetical example was not needed in 1914, but might have been if the war had been against a different enemy and with different allies.

It was inevitable that the anomalous position of the Dominions in this period should arouse comment, and that attempts should be made to suggest remedies. The problem was easily stated. In strict terms, the Dominions were subordinate entities for which laws of any kind could be made without their consent by the Parliament at Westminster; they had no sovereignty of their own, and no power of independent movement in international society. Yet at the same time it was clear that they represented communities of great vitality and independence of mind, which could not easily be coerced by Britain and might wish to take their own lines in certain circumstances. Legally they were bound; in fact, they might cause a good deal of trouble if any attempt were made by Britain to bind them. How could they be effectively associated with the making of British policy, so that their acquiescence in some major decision could be by consent and not by force?

As it happened no clear answer was given to this question, and the Dominions entered the war in 1914 by a mixture of legal force and *ex post facto* consent, but with consent plainly uttermost. They were at war whether they liked it or not; but they did like it; so the question of their status in the matter was unimportant. Nevertheless, it is instructive to see what suggestions were made for associating them with British foreign policy during the period 1900 to 1914, when no one clearly envisaged the kind of acceptance of belligerency which the Dominions were, in fact, to show when Britain declared war against Germany. The various suggestions made can be polarized in the arguments of two men, Lionel Curtis and Richard Jebb.

Lionel Curtis spent the years immediately after the Boer War in the work of reconstruction in South Africa, and particularly in providing arguments for a Union of the South African colonies and former republics, such as eventually came into being in 1909. Curtis derived from this experience a philosophy of government which he later attempted to apply to the British Empire as a whole. The core of it was the view that if a number of separate territories wished to operate together for purposes of common defence and common development they must do so on a basis of "organic union"; it was not enough that they should be in alliance or confederation; they must become a practical unity so that sovereignty could be exercised by a single instrument in the service of all. Deriving much instruction from the process of federation in the United States, Curtis insisted that only through imperial federation, with a common imperial parliament responsible for foreign policy and capable of taxing the citizens of the Empire to pay for defence, could the Dominions and Britain act effectively together. Curtis gave great weight to the importance of sovereignty in the situation in which the Empire found itself. Only a sovereign parliament could tax and compel; and only if there were such a sovereign could a common policy be both agreed and acted on. If there were no single sovereign parliament to which each citizen of the Dominions felt committed, his loyalty in times of crisis would naturally go to the local parliament in the electing of which he had taken a hand, and whose authority he recognized in matters of ordinary law. In a crisis loyalty would need to be mobilized by a single authority, if the Empire was to act as a whole. But if there were no such authority, loyalty would be dispersed and common action would prove impossible. Curtis had two main notions in addition to, and complementary with, his ideas on sovereignty. One was that only the creation of organic union through a federation could give the citizens of the Empire the reality of self-government in major matters of peace and war. The other was that "influence is not government", a saying of George Washington's to which he constantly referred, and which he used to emphasize his point that if the Dominions were not joined in active unity with Britain, but tried to rely upon influence and consultation in forming foreign policy, they would have no effective voice in deciding major issues.

Such a viewpoint was not new; imperial federation had been widely advocated in the 1880's. In the 1910's, however, Curtis brought to its advocacy a determined disposition, a great talent for backstairs influence and a constant reminder of the possibility of a war with Germany. Through his "Round Table" groups in Britain and the Dominions he directed a constant stream of suggestions at politicians, though he failed to arouse any sustained interest or enthusiasm among voters. His argument was simple and difficult to refute, given the premises on which it rested: if people wanted the Empire to act as one, should it not have a single directing unit, representative of all the free peoples within it?

Was there any other way of making it a Commonwealth of Nations? [1]

One of Curtis's principal opponents in controversy, though much less influential in his contacts with politicians, was Richard Jebb. Jebb's basic views on imperial organization were formulated during an extensive tour of the self-governing colonies at the turn of the century. The phenomenon which struck him most strongly was that of "colonial nationalism", which he equated with "national self-respect": the pride in their new countries which was felt by the people of the self-governing colonies and their desire to develop in their own way without taking orders from Britain. Jebb was quick to see that this self-respect need not interfere with friendship and even loyalty to Britain—so long as "loyalty" was understood in the context of loyalty to culture, ideals and common institutions and not in that of subservience. Jebb distinguished colonial "nationalism" from colonial "separatism", and protested against the British tendency to mistake the first of these for the second. He argued that the colonies did not wish to break away from Britain, but would do so if any attempt were made to coerce them. What was needed was an arrangement of "alliance" or "partnership" whereby they would be associated with the making of British foreign policy but left free to develop their own defence forces and to satisfy their national aspirations. He rejected federation as impracticable and liable to conflict at every point with legitimate colonial nationalism. Instead, he wished to see the self-governing colonies represented in London by officials of high power who would be constantly in touch with the shaping of British policy; and he seized on the Imperial Conference as an institution capable of development to serve the kind of "Britannic alliance" which he was convinced was the only practicable kind of imperial organization. If each Dominion had its navy, and each was kept constantly in touch with British policy (in making which it had taken a hand), imperial co-operation could proceed without hurting the growing national pride of the Dominions. It would be nourished by a generous system of imperial preference, negotiated freely between Britain and the Dominions. But it would be co-operation of a genuine kind,

[1] The term had been used before in a variety of contexts, but Curtis was the first to popularize it—though he did so in the service of a form of organization much more unified and compact than the Commonwealth was ever in fact to assume.

in which the threat of ultimate sovereignty was never used by Britain.

In Jebb and Curtis we see exemplified not only two views which were constantly at odds before 1914, but also two emphases which have haunted discussions of Commonwealth relations ever since —the one stressing the need for unity, the other stressing diversity and the need to find institutions which could derive unity from diversity and not appear to impose unity where none existed. Both arose directly from the anomalous position of the Dominions before 1914. Either would have provided at least a temporary solution to the problems posed by the existence of the Dominions. But neither was adopted. Curtis's scheme was too elaborate and could arouse no popular enthusiasm. Jebb's was more practical, and indeed came close to the course which events actually took in the 1920's and 1930's; but in earlier decades it was put out of court by the reluctance of the British government to take any step which might seem to force the Dominions, by the lack of agreement in the Dominions themselves, and by the association of his ideas with Tariff Reform and Imperial Preference. Perhaps more than anything else, it was this latter controversy which inhibited the British government from taking any steps towards a tidying-up of imperial relations before World War I. A movement in any direction would bring up the question of preferential trade relations between the Dominions and Britain, their principal market; this immediately brought up Britain's Free Trade policy, to which the Liberal Party adhered tenaciously and over which the Conservative Party became badly split. First a Conservative government and then a Liberal government found the question too dangerous for action, if action could have been agreed on.

As things went in fact, the British decision to go to war in 1914 was taken without any consultation of the Dominions and involved them automatically. None of the Dominion governments seems to have minded this, although there were murmurs from various minority groups. It was everywhere considered that Britain was fighting in a just cause, and the Dominions went to great lengths to help. But it became plain in the course of the war that new arrangements would be necessary when the war was over.

Chapter Two

FROM 1914 TO 1939

DURING World War I the Dominions experienced a number of changes, the effect of which was to speed up their national development and make the question of their common status more obtrusive than it had been before the war. The basic changes were those which took place in their economies and in their organization of military effort. Each participated wholeheartedly in the war, sending troops overseas in numbers which challenged comparison with the efforts of the greatest powers engaged. In economic terms, the war meant the growth of new industries to supply the forces with equipment and to make up for civilian supplies which were not forthcoming from Britain; it also meant, for countries which were great suppliers of foodstuffs to Britain and Europe, the organization by the state of the production and distribution of such products as wheat to an extent unknown before. But troops had not only to be raised and supplied; they had also to be transported to where they were needed, and commanded in the field. Although they were British Empire troops, there was strong opposition in each Dominion to having them merged with troops from Britain itself. In each case national pride demanded that they be kept in separate units, and, wherever possible, under the orders of their own commanders, even though they might be subject in major matters to a British or Allied Commander-in-Chief. Something of this same sentiment had been manifested in regard to the colonial troops in the Boer War, but these were fewer and not occupied in such long and hard fighting as Dominion troops between 1914 and 1918. The general effect was to stimulate national pride in each of the Dominions, and to create an atmosphere of thought in which it was assumed, in each case, that the country deserved recognition for its individual effort, and should not allow the British government to take all the credit and give all the orders simply because Britain possessed legal sovereignty over the Dominions.

The effect of World War I upon the development of the Commonwealth can be estimated if we consider changes at two levels

—the level of direction of the war effort of the British Empire and the level of local politics in each of the Dominions.

The war gave the leading figures of the Dominions opportunities such as they had never had before. For the first time they became significant figures in the British political scene, while some of them became persons of international repute as a result of their appearance at Versailles and their influence on the Peace Treaty. Borden of Canada, Hughes of Australia and Smuts of South Africa all gained reputation and esteem from the gallant efforts of their countries' soldiers, and were all able to play distinctive parts in British politics because of their non-involvement in the intricate and confused relationships of British politicians and parties. Especially from 1917 onwards, the fighting strength of their countries became so formidable that they were admitted to the highest levels of direction of the war. During decisive periods of 1917 and 1918, Dominion representatives were added to the British War Cabinet to form a new body, the Imperial War Cabinet, and one of them (Smuts) remained a member of the British War Cabinet in between these times. Both before and after the establishment of the Imperial War Cabinet they continued to insist, politely but firmly, that their countries' efforts in the war were so considerable that, once the war was over, there could be no return to the former system of foreign policy being entirely in the hands of the British government. And they were supported in this by British leaders like Bonar Law and Milner. But the problem still remained of *how* these overseas Dominions were to be associated with the making of Imperial foreign policy. The Imperial War Cabinet was no real solution. It existed primarily to explain the conduct of the war to Dominion leaders, and to receive suggestions from them about how it might be improved. The word "Cabinet" was a misnomer. The body in question was not responsible to any one parliament, not did it possess any collective responsibility such as cabinets possessed in each of the countries from which these Ministers had come. It was, in fact, simply the Imperial Conference, meeting more often under another name. It could function satisfactorily so long as its members were united in a supreme struggle with a single enemy. But it could hardly hope to do so in the ordinary climate of peacetime diplomacy. And it was subject to a physical handicap which had already shown itself to be awkward in war and would undoubtedly prove even more awkward in peace. This was the fact that the Prime Ministers of the overseas Dominions had to spend long periods away from their own countries if they were to deliberate in London; and while they were away their domestic politics persisted in developing new aspects which threatened the stability of their governments. Thus the authority of the Dominion Prime Ministers to parley in London might be adversely affected by developments at home, over which they could not keep a watching eye.

During the war, political events in each of the Dominions took a roughly similar course. On the one hand, there was an intoxicating upsurge of imperial patriotism among the majority of people of British descent, a sense of solidarity with the Mother Country which gave the "win the war" governments of Botha, Hughes and Borden their driving force and kept them in power. On the other hand, in each Dominion there developed opposition which was to weaken the position of the government once the excitement of war was over. In some cases this opposition was racial; in others it arose from the hardships of the war, and especially from the attempt to impose conscription. In South Africa Botha and Smuts put down a Boer rebellion, thus laying themselves open to the persistent charge by Afrikaner nationalists that they had gone over to the British. In Australia, proposals for conscription for service overseas split the Labour Party, led to the formation of a new political party and a succession of anti-Labour governments, and were narrowly rejected at two national referendums. In Canada there was a split in the Liberal Party over Borden's conscription proposals, and French-Canadian nationalists bitterly opposed the government. Only in New Zealand did conscription have a fairly smooth passage, though there it was opposed by the infant Labour Party. The effect of this opposition in each Dominion was twofold. In the short run it strengthened the government, which was able to label its opponents as disloyal and unpatriotic, and secure electoral gains at their expense. But in the long run it worked against the "win the war" governments by building up long-standing complaints against their administration and by labelling the governments as subservient to British influence.

What is interesting about these wartime struggles in the Dominions is that they led to a strengthening of national feeling on both sides. Among the patriotic supporters of the governments there was increased national pride in the efforts of the Dominion soldiers and a conviction that, while the Dominions must remain "loyal", in the sense of retaining their veneration for the Throne and their support for the unity of the Empire, they must also be given a voice in the making of Imperial policy. Among the governments' opponents there was a strong emphasis upon local patriotism as against imperial patriotism, a tendency to denigrate British leadership and a demand that "loyalty" must be primarily loyalty to the Dominion and not to the Empire. So, no matter how much the governments and their opponents might conflict, each was helping to intensify a form of national feeling. In each country there could be detected two sets of nationalists: the disrespectful ones who put their own country first and Britain second; and the respectful ones, who wished to put neither first but were convinced that the legitimate interests of their own country and Britain were compatible within the ambit of imperial unity.

The momentum of wartime patriotism carried the governments of respectful nationalists into the negotiations at Paris, there to represent their countries, not as fully sovereign states but as constituents of "the British Empire"; and it was in the name of "the British Empire" that British and Dominion signatures were appended to the Treaty. In spite of the efforts of the Dominion soldiers, their countries were still not recognized by the world at large as sovereign states; and any attempt to have them so recognized would, it seemed, imperil the unity of the Empire and the authority of the Crown. Nevertheless, the Dominions (and India) were accepted as members of the League of Nations, the constitution of which did not demand that its members be fully sovereign states. Obviously, by 1920, the Dominions were more considerable as national entities than they had been in 1914. But their constitutional position was still peculiar, and the old question of responsibility for foreign policy was unsolved. The general problem of Commonwealth relations was put by an acute observer in 1920 as follows:[1]

"To make further progress possible we must first define the status of the Dominions (reconciling, if they can be reconciled, equality of nationhood and the formal unity of the Empire), and also the exact

[1] H. Duncan Hall, *The British Commonwealth of Nations* (London, 1920), p. viii.

nature of the relationships of the members of the British Group of States to one another; in the second place we must construct the machinery of co-operation required by the Group to satisfy their common needs and desires; in the third place we must define the relations between the British Group of States and the wider League of Nations."

The story of the next two decades is of the attempt formally to settle these three questions, in circumstances in which some of them retained their importance while others diminished in significance under the pressure of events.

The period began with the respectful nationalists still in the saddle, and with the idea of general control of Imperial policy still apparently an effective one. The combined representation of "the British Empire" which had functioned at Versailles was continued at the Washington Conference of 1921–2. Moreover, it was explicitly stated by the British Prime Minister that "the Dominions since the war have been given equal rights with Great Britain in the control of the foreign policy of the Empire. . . . Joint control means joint responsibility, and when the burden of Empire has become so vast it is well that we should have the shoulders of these young giants under the burden to help us along. It introduces a broader and calmer view into foreign policy."[1] The occasion on which Mr. Lloyd George said this was the presentation of the Irish Treaty to the House of Commons: the new Irish Free State had been offered "the same constitutional status" as Canada, Australia, New Zealand and South Africa, though no attempt was made to define that status other than to say that they possessed it. The Free State was being offered the same right of joint control of British foreign policy as those countries were said to possess. In the further definition of status Irish opinion was to play an important part, as will be seen below; but in the meantime, the question of whether there could in fact be "joint control" of foreign policy was put and settled. Within twelve months of Mr. Lloyd George's ebullient speech, he found neither joint control nor joint responsibility was a reality. The issue in question was that of Chanak. Since this represented a decisive moment in the development of Commonwealth relations on the issue of peace and war, it deserves attention here.

[1] Mr. Lloyd George, speech in the House of Commons, December 14, 1921. Reprinted in A. B. Keith, *Speeches and Documents on the British Dominions, 1918–1931* (London, 1932), pp. 83–97.

The essence of the Chanak situation in September 1922 was that an attempt by the British government, to back Greek ambitions in Asia Minor and to keep Turkish nationalism within the limits imposed by the defeat of Turkey in the war, was being frustrated by the unwillingness of France and the other former Allies to support British policy and by the superiority of Turkish forces over Greek. The actual incident which might have provoked war between Britain and the Turks was a threatened attempt by Turkish forces under Kemal Pasha to enter a neutral zone at Chanak, manned by British troops. Mr. Lloyd George's government was prepared to fight in support of its policy. It cabled to the Dominion Prime Ministers, asking for military help; in the case of Australia and New Zealand there were good reasons to think that this would be forthcoming, since to both these countries the area of the Dardanelles was one of reverent memory of the deeds performed by their soldiers in 1915. In fact, both these countries cabled their assent, though this was a little more guarded in the case of Australia than of New Zealand. But both Canada and South Africa declined to send immediate help on the ground that this would be an act of war and that war was a matter which should be decided by their parliaments. In addition, there were complaints that the British action had presented the Dominions with a *fait accompli* (not for the last time, some of their governments learnt first about the British action from the newspapers, not from official cables), and that no attempt had been made to formulate a joint policy. In the event, the British and Turkish troops on the spot managed to come to an accommodation, and the only casualty was Mr. Lloyd George's government, which fell soon after from a variety of causes of which Chanak was only one.

The importance of Chanak was twofold. In the first place, it showed that international affairs were likely to be too complicated and swift in action to permit lengthy consultation with the Dominions before British policy was determined; and that, even if foreign policy was narrowed down to the issue of "peace or war", the Dominions would not kindly accept a situation in which they were asked to answer this question without having been consulted on the questions of detailed negotiation which preceded it. Thus it illustrated the shortsightedness of the view that the kind of consultation which had taken place in the Imperial War Cabinet would be adequate for the making of important policy in peacetime, when the objectives of policy were so much less a matter of simple common agreement than they had been in 1917 and 1918. In the second place, Chanak showed that the era of the respectful nationalists in the Dominions was coming to a close. While these still remained in command in Australia and New Zealand, their influence had waned elsewhere. Smuts was still in charge in South Africa, but precariously; in 1924 he was to be succeeded by the Nationalist Hertzog, who would be Prime Minister for fifteen years. In Canada the government in office was that of Mackenzie King, who had come to power through his welding together of elements of public opinion opposed to the actions of the Borden government. It was Mackenzie King who formulated most explicitly the contention that for Canada the issue of peace or war could be decided only by Canadians.

Just as Chanak showed the unreality of joint control in foreign policy, and the rise to power and influence of the disrespectful nationalists, so the coming decade was to see a clearer statement of the status of the Dominions, in response to the disrespectful demands of those nationalists in Ireland, Canada and South Africa. The changes which occurred between 1926 and 1931 have been often described, and there is no need to do more than enumerate them here. In 1926 the Imperial Conference was under strong pressure from the three countries in question. It produced the classic statement of the position of the Dominions, in the Balfour Report of the Inter-Imperial Relations Committee. This said that nothing would be gained from trying to lay down a constitution for the British Empire, since it defied classification in its character as a collection of parts at different stages of evolution. But the "group of self-governing communities composed of Great Britain and the Dominions" had now "reached its full development" and their "position and mutual relation" could be readily defined. They were

> ". . . autonomous communities within the British Empire, equal in status, in no way subordinate one to another in any aspect of their domestic or external affairs, though united by a common allegiance to the Crown, and freely associated as members of the British Commonwealth of Nations."

The Report added that "though every Dominion is now, and must always remain, the sole judge of the nature and extent of its co-operation, no common cause will, in our opinion, be imperilled"; and it concluded with various practical suggestions about how the remnants of formal British control over Dominion legislation might be disposed of.[1] The Report was adopted by the Imperial Conference, added to by the next conference in 1930, and given legal effect by the British parliament in the Statute of Westminster in 1931. The Statute referred to the "common allegiance" and "free association" of the members of the British Commonwealth of Nations; admitted the Dominions to responsibility for the succession to the Throne; gave the Dominions power to make laws with extra-territorial effect; and promised that in future the British parliament would make no laws affecting them without their consent. The Statute was (and remains) a self-denying ordinance on the part of the British parliament, designed to assure the Dominions that whatever legal sovereignty it might possess over them would not be used unless they specifically asked for it to be used, and that their own legal sovereignty could be used in whatever manner was stated in their constitutions. It was now legally possible for them to be regarded as sovereign states.

But the problem of how they were to *act* as sovereign states in the field of international politics remained a difficult one. After Chanak the notion of "joint control" of foreign policy had been decently buried by the Imperial Conference of 1923, which decided that each part of the Empire was free to negotiate its own treaties with foreign states (so long as it informed other interested Dominions of what it proposed to do), and that no treaty was to be regarded as committing the Dominions unless they had signed it individually. This freed Britain to make her own policy, and also freed Canada from the previous obligation to conduct negotiations with the United States through a formal British intermediary. The Locarno Treaty of 1925 was the first major example of the new arrangement. It was negotiated by Britain without Dominion assistance; and Article 9 specifically exempted the Dominions and India from its provisions unless they gave their assent to it. None did. Yet the position of the Dominions in regard to foreign policy was by no means settled; and that was still the case after the Statute of Westminster was passed in 1931.

[1] The Report is to be found in Keith, *op. cit.*, together with the Statute of Westminster and a number of useful subsidiary documents and extracts from parliamentary debates.

The essence of the difficulty was that, although the Dominions might pride themselves on their defined status and the assurance that they were sovereign states, they were in fact small, weak nations, which were heavily dependent upon Britain for defence, capital, population and markets. This position applied much less to Canada than to Australia, New Zealand and South Africa; yet even Canada found that, once the United States was drawn into the economic maelstrom of the 1930's, Britain was a necessary market. The Dominions were white communities with high standards of living, set down in parts of the world which might prove eminently desirable to foreign nations, and with economies built to take goods and capital from Britain and send other goods in return. Their territories were large and might prove difficult to defend. They were members of the League of Nations, but made little impact there. They had defence forces, but were unwilling to tax themselves sufficiently to provide adequate quantities of arms and men; in any case, there was considerable argument about how they could best be defended, given their vulnerable geographical position and their sparse populations. Again, Canada was something of an exception; but even there considerable bewilderment reigned as to how an independent Canada ought to act.

The individual policies developed by the Dominions to deal with the problems of the 1930's showed some degree of diplomatic initiative; but each remained essentially in the British camp, showing little stomach for alliance with other nations (except Canada with the United States) or for neutrality on the Swiss pattern. Each wanted a quiet life and hoped that war would not occur. Each hoped that if war did occur it would be able to stay out of trouble or that the British side would win. None went very far with independent diplomatic representation, although the opportunity for this existed from the 1920's onwards: Canada and South Africa were represented in a few capitals where they had special interests or racial ties, but in neither case was representation adequate for the conduct of an independent foreign policy. Thus the Dominions developed as sovereign states which continued to ask favours and help from Britain. More important, they developed something of a veto over British policy.

It is important to be clear about what is meant by this. The idea of "joint control" had been dropped, as we have seen; but, although the idea of independent Dominion policies in minor fields had become generally accepted, there was still doubt about whether the British Commonwealth of Nations was a single unit for purposes of war and peace. The question whether the King could be at war in one part of his Dominions and at peace in another had still to be answered. All that the Statute of Westminster said on the mater was that the Dominions owed a "common allegiance" to the Crown: it left unanswered the question whether the Crown itself could be divided into a separate Crown for each Dominion. Some people said that it could, others that it could not. There was no accepted doctrine. The upshot was that no British government could disregard Dominion opinion on a major matter of foreign policy, since there was a widely held presumption that the Dominions were involved in some way in any British decision that might lead to war. At the same time no Dominion government could entirely ignore British foreign policy, since it might find itself dragged into a state of belligerency on the coat-tails of Britain, whether it wanted to be or not. The conventional way of describing the relations between Britain and the Dominions was that they were in "consultation" over foreign policy. This was an ambiguous word which fitted an ambiguous situation. Did it mean that Britain would take no decisive step without securing the consent of the Dominions, or that she would take no such step without informing them of what she proposed to do? What details of policy was Britain obliged to disclose to the Dominions? At what point in the development of a particular policy should they be consulted? And if they took up independent diplomatic lines of their own, to what extent could this be said to involve the others? These questions had all been answered in 1923 in regard to treaties, but they were still unanswered in regard to the ordinary processes of diplomacy.

The situation was made even more unrealistic and ambiguous by the fact that, after the Statute of Westminster, neither Britain nor the majority of the Dominions found the nature of consultation an easy matter to raise. The British government was apparently reluctant to ask Dominion opinions on matters of policy, except at an Imperial Conference. It saw its role as that of providing information which the Dominions could consult about if they wished.[1] Of the Dominions, on the other hand, Australia was the

[1] Paul Hasluck, *The Government and the People, 1939–1941* (Canberra, 1952) p. 59.

only one which, in the 1930's, attempted to make consultation a process even approaching joint discussion of policy. At the 1937 Imperial Conference, Australia was the only country to call for close general examination of foreign policy; the other Dominions wanted discussion to be private and bilateral between themselves and Britain, not multilateral among all the Commonwealth countries.[1] The general effect was bad. The Dominions were in a position of power without responsibility. They had no formal responsibility for British policy, yet any British government which wished to preserve "the unity of the Empire" (a phrase still much in use, with powerful emotional overtones) would hesitate before following a policy which even a single Dominion would not support. Yet no Dominion government wished to be known as having taken the responsibility for pushing the British government in any particular direction; and no British government could afford to say that it had allowed Dominion governments to exercise a veto over its policies. The situation had all the elements of secrecy, confusion and misunderstanding. The Dominions very rarely had anything positive to offer in the way of suggestions; but they all (except New Zealand) had governments in the 1930's which were even more cautious and conciliatory about Germany and Japan than the government of the United Kingdom.

The position may be illustrated by reference to the Munich decisions of 1938. It has been pointed out by Professor Nicholas Mansergh that there is no reference to Dominion pressure on the British government in either Professor Namier's *Diplomatic Prelude* or Sir Winston Churchill's *The Gathering Storm*.[2] But it is now one of the stock arguments in favour of the Chamberlain policy of the time, that it was made necessary by the reluctance of the Dominions to support any other. Lord Templewood takes this view;[3] and in a brief Conservative history the attitude of the Dominions is taken to have been the decisive influence on British policy:[4]

[1] Paul Hasluck, *The Government and the People, 1939–1941* (Canberra, 1952), p. 56.

[2] Nicholas Mansergh, *Survey of British Commonwealth Affairs, Problems of External Policy, 1931–1939* (London, 1952), p. 438.

[3] Viscount Templewood, *Nine Troubled Years* (London, 1954), p. 326.

[4] Angus Maude and Enoch Powell, *Biography of a Nation* (London, 1955), p. 199.

"By 1938 Germany was ready to make big advances. She annexed Austria in the spring and later demanded from France's ally, Czecho-Slovakia, under threat of force, the cession of the German-speaking parts of her territory. France would not intervene without being sure of the United Kingdom, and the United Kingdom felt no certainty that if a European war resulted the rest of the Empire would participate. If it did not, the old conflict of unity and self-government would be forced to breaking-point. The structure itself could not survive a situation in which the King would be at war in respect of some parts of his dominions and at peace in respect of others. . . . Accordingly, Czecho-Slovakia was dismembered without war.

Whether this is a complete explanation of the British policy or not is a matter which need not be gone into here. Most people would say that when the Australian, South African, Canadian and Irish governments urged appeasement on Mr. Chamberlain, they were pushing at an open door. The important things for our purposes are that there was, in fact, Dominion pressure upon the British government; that this was regarded as a matter of considerable seriousness by the British government at the time;[1] that the attitude of the Dominions was used in negotiations with the French as a reason why Britain should not commit herself about Czecho-Slovakia;[2] and, above all, that practically no reference to Dominion attitudes should have been made in the House of Commons and in other places where British policy was being debated. The British government was under pressure which it could not, or would not, admit. The Dominion governments were endeavouring to influence a policy over which they had no effective control and about which they knew very little. This is what "consultation" amounted to. In the absence of clear-cut Dominion opinion about what was happening in Europe, it could amount to little more.

By the time Britain declared war on Germany on September 3, 1939, Dominion opinion had become much more settled. Only in South Africa and in Eire was there opposition to joining Britain. Australia, Canada and New Zealand all entered the war willingly; they differed in their manner of doing so, but their agreement with British policy was plain. The events of 1939 also settled the question of whether the Crown was divisible. Not only did Eire

[1] See Duff Cooper, *Old Men Forget* (London, 1954), pp. 239–40 for the reactions of the British Cabinet.

[2] Mansergh, *op. cit.*

remain neutral; Canada declared war after Britain, allowing herself a few days of aloofness from the war in which her own declaration of hostilities could be prepared. The stage was set for the growth of Dominion foreign policies on a scale previously unknown.

If we refer back to the problem of Commonwealth relations as seen by Duncan Hall in 1920 (above, p. 34) we can assess what changes took place in those relations between the wars. The three aspects of the problem, as Hall had stated them, were dealt with as follows:

First, the status of the Dominions was defined in words in 1926 and 1931 and in deeds in 1939: they were clearly sovereign states, sharing a common Crown which could be divided for purposes of foreign policy, even to the length of the King being at war in one part of his Dominions and at peace in another.

Second, no "machinery of co-operation" had been devised to satisfy the "common needs and desires" of the Dominions: they had failed to make "joint control" of foreign policy a reality, and "consultation" had proved to be little more than a means of putting pressure upon the British government when there was any likelihood of that government adopting a policy which a particular Dominion did not like. Although from time to time there were suggestions that an Empire or Commonwealth secretariat should be established to co-ordinate policy among the Dominions, nothing ever came of this, because of the strong objections of Canada, South Africa and the Irish Free State. Even the institution of Imperial Preference at the Ottawa Conference of 1932 involved no *general* system of control or co-ordination of economic policy throughout the Empire. There was no central plan, no attempt to apportion resources; the Ottawa Conference amounted to little more than a series of bilateral negotiations between Britain on the one hand and individual Dominions on the other. In fact, the conference showed the British Commonwealth of Nations to be much less a unity than a congeries of individual states, each with special interests of its own. No common interest was discovered, except that of raising tariff walls against foreign goods and thus giving more space in the shrinking imperial markets of the day to goods from within the Empire. In sum, then, "machinery of co-operation" was not fashioned for either political or economic purposes. When the Dominions (except Eire) eventually acted together in 1939, it was because of "ties of common funk" (an earlier phrase of Kipling's) rather than "common needs and desires", as Duncan Hall had envisaged these.

Third, events had shown that there was no need to define relations between the British Commonwealth of Nations and the League of Nations. For a while, theorists of the Commonwealth thought that the League might prove either a hindrance to Commonwealth relations or a means of putting those relations on a workable basis; [1] but after the Abyssinian débâcle most Dominions were convinced that the League offered no means of ensuring peace. They then gave up even the token reliance they had placed on it. League commitments, such as they were, proved to be no obstacle to joint action in the Commonwealth. The two kinds of association were different in character and did not clash: one (the Commonwealth) was a natural historical growth; the other (the League) a transient fabrication.

[1] L. S. Amery was continually of the opinion that the League diverted the attention of the Dominions from their common concerns. For the opposite view, that the League was a means of preserving the unity of the British Commonwealth, see Alfred Zimmern, *The Third British Empire* (London, 1926), Ch. II.

Chapter Three

FROM 1939 TO 1964

THE main effects of World War II upon the Commonwealth were to bring the existing Dominions closer to international maturity, and to accelerate, in the British dependencies, the movements towards self-government which were already present there. The first effect showed itself in the increasing participation of the Dominions in diplomacy, the second in the granting of Dominion status to new countries soon after the war was over. The two together have created the kind of Commonwealth which exists now. It will be convenient here to indicate the course of the two effects, and then, in the following chapter, to describe the special features of the Commonwealth today, as these have resulted from the impact of recent developments upon the structure of Commonwealth relations which was visible in 1939.

South Africa was affected by the war in a different way from the other Dominions. South Africa had entered the war with a divided parliament and a divided nation, and ended it in a similar condition, although it seemed for the moment, as in 1919, that Smuts had secured massive support for a "win the war" government, whose opponents could be stigmatized as disloyal. South Africa's own territory was not in danger, and the country's participation in actual fighting was small. It made no new friends of any consequence; its diplomatic activity did not markedly increase. The effect of the war was almost entirely domestic. It showed that the white people of South Africa were still divided into two potentially antagonistic groups, and that the conceptions of the Commonwealth which these held were what mattered in any discussion of Commonwealth relations, not the kind of association which South Africa might have with other members of the Commonwealth. South Africans were still concerned with the Boer–British conflict of the past, reflected in arguments about the meaning of the Statute of Westminster, and about flags and national anthems.

For the other three Dominions the war was a more serious affair, involving greater contact than before with foreign powers. Canada was already in virtual alliance with the United States when the war began, and strengthened its joint defence arrangements as the war went on. Australia and New Zealand were exposed for the first time to the possibility of direct invasion. Moreover, both found themselves bereft of the British naval protection which had been a constant overriding factor in their defence plans. Both were consequently brought into sudden alliance with the United States, an alliance which produced not only joint fighting commands and joint schemes for supplying troops, but also joint consultation at the highest levels of Allied strategy. For all three countries the war presented a challenge: they were called upon to provide diplomatic capacity in a hurry, to operate in fields of negotiation where their experience was small. At times their responses were awkward and unhandy. But their general sense of national self-respect was enhanced by their acceptance as allies by the United States and their experience of independent negotiation. In addition to rapid growth in the field of diplomacy, all three experienced less division at home than in World War I. Conscription was not the menace to national unity that it had been before; parties did not split; only one Dominion Prime Minister returned from a visit to London to find his government falling to pieces through domestic differences, and this event (in Australia in 1941) caused no persistent loss of effective leadership. Thus, in contrast with South Africa, the other three countries preserved their unity and achieved greater diplomatic maturity.

The most significant difference from the previous war was that the attention of the Dominions (as of all nations fighting on the Allied side) was not centred in London or Paris, but, after 1941, in Washington. The Dominions were not willing to accept British leadership in all cases. While they approved of Mr. Churchill in those instances where his policy chimed with theirs, they could not afford to have him as their sole representative in negotiations with President Roosevelt. This is why, in early 1942, the Australian and New Zealand governments demanded a Pacific War Council in Washington as well as one in London; they wanted to be sure that their views on strategy and supplies were transmitted independently to the American government, and were not filtered through a mesh of British interests. In desperate times, a break with the past seemed justified and inevitable. Australia and New Zealand made their demands, not because of any altered view of Commonwealth relations as such, but because they felt that their national security was at stake. The reality of power lay in Washington;

they must have direct access to it in a situation where there was not enough war material to go round, and their own requests for guns, troops and aircraft might prove to be in direct competition with Britain's.

This is the main reason why there was so much less talk about imperial co-operation in the Second World War than in the First. The significant councils were those of the Allies, not of the Empire. But there are two important reservations to be made to this generalization. The first is that, before the United States entered the war, the Dominions wished to have full knowledge of British strategy and schemes for supply, and to this end sent their Prime Ministers to London to sit for periods with the War Cabinet. Not all of them did this to the same degree: Australia and New Zealand were the most active. Again, once the dangers of the Pacific War had lessened and victory seemed in sight in Europe, the Dominions showed more interest in the British connection and in the possibility of devising and using Commonwealth forms to serve their postwar ends. Here, once more, the initiative was taken by Australia. In 1943 and 1944, the Australian Prime Minister, Mr. Curtin, voiced proposals for an Empire Council which would co-ordinate foreign policy and defence policy for the Commonwealth as a whole, so that important decisions might be made with adequate consultation and not on a snap judgment. Again, in 1943 and 1944, Australia made various suggestions for a system of Commonwealth co-operation whereby each Dominion could assume responsibility for representing the Commonwealth as a whole in the particular region of the world in which it was situated. Such a policy was, indeed, put into operation, at Australia's insistence, in the appointment of single Commonwealth representatives on the Japanese War Crimes Commission and the Advisory Council in Tokyo during the Allied occupation of Japan. But Australian proposals (supported by New Zealand) for permanent forms of co-operation received little support from South Africa, and none from Canada. Each was clearly devised to suit the interests of the Dominions concerned and looked different from another angle; each excited Mackenzie King's long-standing distrust of anything which saddled Canada with responsibility for other countries' affairs. Similarly, a proposal by Smuts that Dominions should assume some responsibility for British colonies in their vicinity made little appeal to the British government; it was so obviously intended to advance South Africa's interest in preventing the emergence of a more liberal native policy than her own in British colonies in Southern Africa. Britain herself had little reason to fly kites about postwar imperial co-operation. It was known that President Roosevelt and majority American opinion looked with suspicion on any "ganging up" by the Commonwealth countries; and, in any case, British attention, in imperial matters, was focused upon getting back the colonies in Asia and the Pacific that had fallen to the Japanese and upon settling the future status of India.[1]

The effect of these wartime happenings was seen in 1946, when the first postwar meeting of Commonwealth Prime Ministers took place. The Australian and New Zealand representatives came, it seemed, with ambitious plans for defence co-operation on a regional basis. Something of this kind had the support of the British Chiefs of Staff and of Conservative newspapers in Britain, which were looking for anything which might make "the Empire" an effective counterweight to the United States on the one hand and the Soviet Union on the other. The scheme had some support also in the British Labour government, where the idea of a "third force" led by Britain was strong; as an additional attraction, the Australian and New Zealand governments, which proposed closer co-operation, were Labour too. But the scheme withered when submitted to the attention of Smuts and Mackenzie King. Neither considered that his country could stomach a full-blooded system of imperial co-operation. Their influence was plainly visible in the statement issued at the end of the Prime Ministers' meeting: it bears all the marks of the political circumstances which moulded the declaration of 1926 and the Statute of Westminster, and may, indeed, be regarded as the last words of the "Statute of Westminster Commonwealth" of which Smuts and Mackenzie King had been such typical figures. Neither was to attend a Prime Ministers' meeting again. The 1946 statement said:[2]

> "The existing methods of consultation have proved their worth. They include a continuous exchange of information and comment between the different members of the Commonwealth. They are flexible and can be used to meet a variety of situations and needs, both those

[1] For further details of wartime statements on imperial co-operation, see Heather J. Harvey, *Consultation and Co-operation in the Commonwealth* (London, 1952), pp. 94–107, and Nicholas Mansergh, *Documents and Speeches on British Commonwealth Affairs, 1931–1952* (London, 1953), Vol. I, pp. 528–96.

[2] Nicholas Mansergh, *op. cit.*, Vol. I, p. 596.

where the responsibility is on one member alone and where the responsibility may have to be shared. They are peculiarly appropriate to the character of the British Commonwealth, with its independent members, who have shown by their sacrifices in the common cause their devotion to kindred ideals and their community of outlook. While all are willing to consider and adopt practical proposals for developing the existing system, it is agreed that the methods now practised are preferable to any rigid centralised machinery. In their view such centralised machinery would not facilitate, and might even hamper, the combination of autonomy and unity which is characteristic of the British Commonwealth and is one of their joint achievements."

The 1946 Prime Ministers' meeting thus came to no conclusion about constituting the Commonwealth a Third Force in world affairs, in spite of the reminder by *The Times* that "by planning their strategy in concert they can, by virtue of their unique geographical advantages, still wield an authority not inferior to that of either of the more populous great Powers with which they are associated".[1] The reason was not far to seek. In so far as there were demands for more unity and co-operation, these arose not so much from a sense of common purpose and determination as from a desire to use the Commonwealth relationship to further national ends—in Britain's case a continued prominence in world affairs, in Australia's and New Zealand's a position of importance and security in the Pacific, in South Africa's the solution of complicated racial difficulties. Britain and the Dominions had just concluded a war in which each had had a separate role to play. Whereas in 1914–18 it had been usual to find British and Dominion troops concentrated in the one area of operations, in 1939–45 each had carried on its operations in different places. It is true that some of the most notable experiences of Australian and New Zealand troops had been in Greece, North Africa and Italy, alongside British troops, and that Canadians had been prominent in the invasion of Occupied France. Nevertheless, the fact of two distinct wars, one European and one Pacific, and of conflicts of policy in the allocation to these of troops, supplies and shipping, created divisions of purpose which had not existed in World War I. And, above all, the superior power of the United States made Britain less of a magnet than she had been in 1914–18. It was not a matter of

[1] Editorial in *The Times*, April 23, 1946.

"loyalty" having diminished, in the sense of loyalty to the Crown; it was much more a matter of the discovery of separate national interests which demanded separate policies. Nor was it a matter of these interests being entirely new; they had been latent in the situation of Britain and the Dominions in past years, but required the catalyst of war to make them apparent.

It is not surprising, therefore, that when the war ended there should have been confusion about the position of the Dominions and the Commonwealth as an institution. It was not a matter of the Dominions' status. As indicated above, this was now settled beyond any reasonable doubt. But there was understandable confusion about the future relations of Britain to the Dominions and of them to one another. It was typical of the time that Australia, the Dominion with the most pushful external policy, should have been advocating closer "Empire" co-operation, and, at the same time, urging at the San Francisco conference and in the early meetings of the United Nations a foreign policy sometimes at variance with Britain's. The general inclination of the Dominions was to seek co-operation where it seemed to further their interests but to assume no responsibilities which might interfere with the development of their national policies. In many ways their attitude was similar to that which had characterized them in the 1930's; but now they felt stronger and more capable of defending themselves, either alone or with the help of powerful outside allies, and they did not seek such direct protection from Britain.

When the next Prime Ministers' meeting assembled in 1948, a quite new situation presented itself. Three new Dominions had been created, in India, Pakistan and Ceylon; and a fourth, Burma, had appeared for a moment and then disappeared from membership of the Commonwealth. The Commonwealth was no longer an association in which the effective populations were white men; now it was an association of both white and coloured nations. Furthermore, the new members had backgrounds and aspirations different from those of the old. Their histories and cultures were different; so were their significant recollections of the immediate past. The Asian Dominions' memory was of triumphant national independence, gained from the British. The war had been to them, not a crusade against German and Japanese aggression but a liberating agent which had weakened the grip on Asia of Britain, France and Holland. Whereas the older Dominions looked on Europe as the source not only of their culture and religion but also of their economic strength, the Asian Dominions saw Europe as the source of domination—even though it had also been the source of the culture which had proved congenial to many of the Asian leaders. Was it possible that the Commonwealth could contain these new elements, so different from the old, and still satisfy the old? What was even more to the point, could the Commonwealth contain elements which were actually in dispute with one another? For India and Pakistan were already in dispute about Kashmir, and both had taken up an old quarrel with South Africa.

These questions were answered for the moment by the success of the conference. The final communique welcomed the new members in the name of the older ones by saying that "these new representatives of sovereign nations brought to the deliberations of their colleagues from the other free countries of the Commonwealth the wisdom of their ancient civilizations vivified by the dynamism of the modern age".[1] Two factors in particular seem to have made such a happy outcome possible. The first is that the Commonwealth had become, by now, a sufficiently loose organization to satisfy even such " anti-colonialists" as the Prime Ministers of the Asian Dominions. There was no talk of returning to the Imperial Conference; it had sunk without trace in 1937, although no one had been aware of the fact at the time. The meetings of Prime Ministers were in future not even to be given officially the name of "conference". When King George VI asked the Prime Ministers to dinner he did not refer to the "British" Commonwealth, but simply to "our Commonwealth" and "our brotherhood of nations"; and the final communique referred simply to the "Commonwealth" without any adjective. No legislation or even agreement was needed to make these changes. The Commonwealth was already sufficiently loose and flexible for them to occur without overt discussion. Also, it was already crystal-clear that membership involved no special responsibilities, and that the Asian Dominions were committing themselves to nothing more than informal and unspecified consultation with Britain and the other Dominions.

The second factor, however, was more important. The fact that the Commonwealth was loose in structure and could accommodate the Asian Dominions, if they wished, was only significant so long

[1] Nicholas Mansergh, *op. cit.*, Vol. II, pp. 1210–11.

as the Asian Dominions did wish to be part of it. What made them wish to be so was their discovery of their concrete interests in the world as it was. In the short period since gaining independence, the Prime Ministers of the Asian Dominions had begun to see what a complicated place the world of sovereign states could be. At the United Nations and elsewhere they had discovered how valuable it was to have friends and supporters, and how intricate might be the negotiations if a particular objective was to be secured. They had also discovered that Asia's connections with Europe could not be summarized as simply those of exploited and exploiter, and that, once formal independence was achieved, the need for economic and cultural links remained. They had become aware of some of the connections between the Great Powers, and of the fact that their own geographical situation gave them particular weight in world politics. Above all, perhaps, they had discovered that the economic connections between their countries and Britain were beneficial to both sides, and deserved to be fostered. In the fields of trade, investment and technology, and in services such as shipping and banking, it had become clear to them that solid advantages were to be derived from continuing some connection with Britain. And membership of the Sterling Area, although it was not the same as membership of the Commonwealth, was something which their economists and financiers prized as a means of making more effective their countries' slender resources in foreign trade. The Sterling Area was essentially a British creation and might, in itself, be sufficient justification for remaining in the Commonwealth; for there was no body to decide policy for the Sterling Area as a whole, except the occasional meetings of Commonwealth Prime Ministers.

It seems likely that all these considerations prevailed with the Asian Prime Ministers, but more especially the economic ones. The 1948 meeting of Prime Ministers did in fact take up economic questions in considerable detail; and for the next ten years the meetings of Prime Ministers were to consider much the same questions—the need for more capital in the overseas Commonwealth, the special needs of the under-developed countries in Asia, the necessity of keeping national economies stable so that the Sterling Area's gold and dollar reserve might remain healthy, and the desirability of a relaxation of American restrictions on imports. These matters were to be discussed in detail at conferences of

Commonwealth Finance Ministers in 1949, 1952, 1954 and 1957, and were given their most thorough treatment at a Commonwealth Economic Conference in the last months of 1952; but they were first raised at the 1948 meeting of Prime Ministers. We may sum up the situation by saying that once the Asian Dominions had achieved independence they found that they had urgent economic problems on their hands; that dealing with these problems demanded close association with other Commonwealth members, and especially with Britain; and that the other Commonwealth members were happy to have the Asian members with them, since they considered that they also derived advantages from such a comprehensive association of sovereign states as the Commonwealth had come to be. This in itself is sufficient to explain why the "old" and "new" Dominions found it easy to belong to the same body, in spite of their divergent backgrounds and the disputes which had developed between some of them.

Both the loose character of the Commonwealth relationship and the importance placed on it by the member-countries were demonstrated in 1949, when the Prime Ministers decided that it would be possible for India to become a republic and still remain in the Commonwealth. Again, no legislation or treaty was called for. The preamble to the Statute of Westminster said that the nations of the Commonwealth were united by "common allegiance to the Crown", and also that the Crown was "the symbol of the free association" between them; the Prime Ministers interpreted this to mean that only one of the two conditions mentioned—i.e. allegiance, and recognition of a symbol—was necessary to Commonwealth membership. India intended to recognize the King as the symbol of the free association of members of the Commonwealth; so there was no need for her to show him allegiance as King. She could become a republic, and this need disturb no one. Such an interpretation would have seemed outrageous to most of the theorists of the Commonwealth at the time when the Statute was actually passed. But the changed conditions of the 1940's caused almost everyone to hail the Prime Ministers' interpretation as a piece of statesmanship, an achievement which enabled each party to have his cake and eat it too. The fact of Indian adhesion to the Commonwealth had become more significant than the notion of loyalty to the Crown. In any case, it was evident that the divisibility of the Crown could be carried only so far, and that, since there was the possibility that India might take sharply different international action from other Commonwealth members, it might be better in the long run if the King were released from even token responsibility for Indian laws and policy. As symbol of the free association of the members of the Commonwealth, the King was safe from awkward choices.

The recognition that a country could become a republic and remain a Commonwealth member was the last major change in the constitutional form of the Commonwealth relationship, although some people might consider that a more recent example, that of Malaya, was even more bizarre; that a country might achieve independence, have a head of state who was royal and yet not the monarch recognized by the realms of the Commonwealth, and at the same time be within the Commonwealth, was a possibility not considered before. However, it was the Indian example that put the Commonwealth relationship on its present footing. The assumption of republican status by Pakistan, and the decision of Ghana and Malaya to remain within the Commonwealth, followed naturally from Indian membership of the Commonwealth as a republic. Neither demanded new constitutional doctrine, and each was easily absorbed into the existing stream of Commonwealth arrangements.

The most notable features of the growth of the Commonwealth from 1939 onwards were the absence of arguments about status (except in South Africa), and the acceptance of the Commonwealth relationship as one involving no commitments and no obligation to achieve unity of policy among the members. It became possible to vary the structure of the Commonwealth without exciting more than an occasional protest from people who regretted that past assumptions about "loyalty" were no longer accepted. At the same time it proved something of a relief to most Commonwealth leaders to find that there was less necessity than before the war to pretend to a unity of purpose which did not exist. To a considerable extent, the advent of "non-British" member-states can be held responsible for this state of affairs: it was difficult to sustain the view that countries like India, Ceylon and Ghana should feel obliged to make common cause with Britain in the same way as "British" countries like Australia and New Zealand might feel obliged. This particular difficulty had been present with the French-Canadians in Canada and the Afrikaners in South Africa, but it was possible for ardent proponents of "unity" to disregard these either as minorities or as fundamentally "disloyal". Now that the greater part of the Commonwealth's population was of non-British stock, anyone who wished the Commonwealth well as an institution had to come to terms, willy-nilly, with the fact that British ancestry was not, of itself, a sufficient condition to explain the persistence of the Commonwealth or to ensure its future.

By 1964, the "non-British" aspect of the Commonwealth had become its dominant characteristic as a political entity. The communiques of its Prime Ministers' meetings were largely concerned with the problems of economic development for backward countries, and with delicate issues of racism and anti-colonialism, such as those involving South Africa and Southern Rhodesia. South Africa's departure in 1961, under pressure from the Afro-Asian members, was a clear indication that the Commonwealth had long ceased to be a "white man's club".

However, this negative understanding—that the Commonwealth is not simply a matter of "loyalty" and British blood—does not help much if we wish to understand the kind of thing the Commonwealth is now, and what it means to its various members. Accordingly, after the next chapter in which the present structure of Commonwealth relationships is described in institutional terms, we shall first discuss the interests and policies of the member-nations as they affect the Commonwealth, and then examine the Commonwealth in action as an international entity.

Chapter Four

CONTEMPORARY INSTITUTIONS

THE Commonwealth does not have a written constitution, but it does have institutions which are the outward sign of its existence. Which of these should be regarded as essential to its continuance would be difficult to say, when one bears in mind the flexibility of its institutions during the past two decades. The Commonwealth is an entity which remains in being, not because of particular laws or institutions but because its members wish it to: the institutions are subordinate to the effective wishes of the members. At any rate, that is the lesson of the past two decades; but at no time in that period has there been a head-on clash between two members of the Commonwealth, in which one demanded the retention of a particular institution for the whole of the Commonwealth while the other demanded its removal. If such a clash occurred, it would be difficult to imagine the Commonwealth remaining in existence in anything like its present form. The essence of Commonwealth institutions, which are described below, is that they have a very high permissive quality and almost no obligation about them. In so far as obligation does exist, it is the obligation of convention and not of binding law.

The institutions of the Commonwealth as they stood in 1964 are divided here into four kinds: the Crown; the rights of members to enter and leave the Commonwealth; means of consultation between the members; and institutions shared between members in order either to enrich the Commonwealth association or to further the joint and several interests of the members.

The Crown

The Queen has two distinct functions in the Commonwealth. The first is to be the symbol of the free association between the members, whether those members have monarchical systems or not; in performing this function the Queen is known as Head of the Commonwealth. The office (if it can be called such) has no powers or activities attached to it; nor does the Queen, as Head of the Commonwealth, have any Ministers to advise her. She is a symbol which depends for its effectiveness upon the continuance of free association between the member-nations. There is no question of sovereignty in this symbolic existence: neither Queen nor member-nations exercise any, and sovereignty cannot be associated with the relationship between a symbol and the thing which the symbol stands for. Nevertheless, although the Queen, as Head of the Commonwealth, has nothing to do but be, the fact of her being in this capacity has some relevance in the world of sovereign states. It is the Queen's Headship of the Commonwealth that enables the Commonwealth countries to persuade the rest of the world that they form something more than a shifting and fortuitous collection of sovereign states. The point is put thus by a former Secretary of State for Commonwealth Relations:[1]

> "Other countries recognise that, since the Members of the Commonwealth together form a political entity, they can confer benefits on each other that need not be extended under most-favoured nation treaties and the like to foreign countries. This is an aspect of the recognition of the Queen as Head of the Commonwealth that is often overlooked—it is the mark by which foreign countries recognise that the Members of the Commonwealth form a close association that has a certain status as such in the comity of nations."

Such an arrangement has its advantages, apart from those of persuading foreign nations that the Commonwealth is an entity. It also assures monarchists in various parts of the Commonwealth that the Commonwealth as a whole is monarchical. While this is true, in a special sense, it is important to be clear that when the Queen is photographed with "her Prime Ministers" she stands in the relation of Queen only to those Prime Ministers who represent realms; for the Prime Ministers of the republics she is simply a living symbol, with whom they can have no directly political relationship.

It is the role of the Queen in the realms of the Commonwealth (such as Australia, Canada, the United Kingdom, New Zealand, Jamaica and Ceylon) that forms the second function of the Crown in the Commonwealth. Here the Queen is a constitutional sovereign. She reigns but does not rule; she is advised in all that she does by the Ministers of the country concerned. The situation is best described as the union of a number of crowns in a single

[1] P. C. Gordon Walker, "Policy for the Commonwealth", in T. E. M. McKitterick and Kenneth Younger (eds.), *Fabian International Essays* (London, 1957), p. 163.

person. But it is only in the United Kingdom that the Queen personally signs documents and commissions Prime Ministers and performs the numerous other duties of a constitutional monarch. In the other realms she is represented by a Governor-General, appointed by her on the advice of the Ministers in the country concerned, and responsible ultimately to her though subject to the ordinary limitations of a constitutional monarch in relation to Ministers. Her Ministers in the United Kingdom have no power of appointment or advice in regard to these Governors-General.

Such a set of arrangements for monarchy is unique in human history; but they have all followed decorously from the implications of responsible government as a system applied first to the United Kingdom and then to the nations of the Commonwealth as those have come into being. If the Queen had any responsibility for the policies pursued by her several sets of Ministers, it might prove impossible for the system to continue. But since each realm faithfully carries out the practice of responsible government, in which Ministers bear the onus of decisions made in the name of the Queen, it is possible to detach the Monarchy from policies which differ from one realm to another. If the Monarch were personally of a different character—either pushful about delicate matters or distasteful to large numbers of people in any of the realms—the system would be much more difficult to work, since divergences might develop over whether the Monarch was a suitable head of state. But, given the present exemplary character of the Royal family, such a situation is not likely.

A final point of importance is that the Queen has a separate Style and Title in each of her realms, each of these representing the special characteristics which the realm in question wishes to emphasize as possessed by its head of state. But each realm retains its right to decide any variation in the succession to the Throne: a change in the succession, it seems, cannot be made unilaterally on the advice of British Ministers, but must have parliamentary sanction in Britain itself and in each of the other realms.

Rights of Members

It is much easier to say how a member leaves the Commonwealth than to say how one enters it. Secession has been shown, by the example of Eire in 1949, to be simply a matter of action by the country which wishes to secede. In this instance it was clearly

SEPARATE TABLES

(*Copyright, Low and "Evening Standard"*)

stated by the British government that the legislation passed at Westminster afterwards was simply a tidying-up affair, a question of regulating the relations between the United Kingdom and Eire and essentially a consequence of the Irish action. If a member wishes to secede from the Commonwealth, it states the fact in an Act of its own parliament. The other members of the Commonwealth may need, for their own purposes, to pass consequential laws, but so far as the law of the member in question is concerned there is no need for concurrence by other member-nations. The form of the legislation which the seceding nation passes will vary in accordance with its own needs. But there is no question of its right and competence to pass such legislation. Nor is there any question of the right and competence of the remaining Commonwealth members to deal with the situation as seems best to them. For example, they might follow the lead of Britain in 1949, in the case of the Republic of Ireland, and decide that, while they recognized the secession of the country concerned from the Commonwealth, they did not propose to treat it as a foreign country.

Entry into the Commonwealth has so far followed upon the achievement of self-government by British dependencies. As each former dependency has achieved independence, it has been accepted into the circle of Commonwealth members. But this does not mean that the achievement of independence is the same thing as membership of the Commonwealth. The achievement of independence is a matter entirely within the competence of the United Kingdom. Whether it keeps control of its dependencies or lets them go free is constitutionally entirely its own concern—although, of course, in practice there is always negotiation with the representatives of the dependency in question. The point is, however, that the decision has constitutionally nothing to do with the other members of the Commonwealth, any more than the New Zealand decision to give independence to its Samoan dependency was anything to do with Britain. The achievement of independence is thus a question between Britain and the dependency concerned.

Whether that dependency then becomes a member of the Commonwealth would seem, on the face of it, to be a matter for all the existing members of the Commonwealth, including Britain. To take an extreme case, it is possible to imagine a situation in which Britain gave full independence to a dependency which some of the other members of the Commonwealth did not wish to have included in their company. It is unlikely that Britain would grant independence under such conditions; but it is possible, especially in an instance such as that of Palestine or undivided India, where the alternative would be civil war which Britain was in no position to quell. If such a case did arise, the status of the new nation would be a matter for considerable debate. According to the Prime Ministers' declaration of 1949, which explained the circumstances in which India might become a republic and yet remain with the Commonwealth, it was stated that *existing* members might continue their membership so long as they fulfilled one of two conditions, allegiance to the Crown and recognition of the King as the symbol of the free association of the members of the Commonwealth. Suppose the new nation stated that it recognized the Monarch in both these capacities: it was a realm, and it recognized the Queen as Head of the Commonwealth. Could the existing members refuse to accept it into their company at a Prime Ministers' meeting? If they did, by making a specific statement of their refusal, could this prevent the new nation from being recognized as part of the Commonwealth by the rest of the world and by itself? And could the United Kingdom remain a member of a Commonwealth in which its former dependency was cold-shouldered in such a manner?

Such questions may seem fanciful; but they had some relevance in 1956, when there were various suggestions that South Africa might attempt to veto the appearance of an independent Gold Coast at the Commonwealth Prime Ministers' meetings. In the event, South Africa did nothing of the kind. Presumably one of the reasons was that the South African government realized that it would be raising more problems than it could solve, and that the domestic advantages of such a move would be outweighed by the disadvantages it would cause in South Africa's relations with the other members of the Commonwealth. It now seems unlikely that an existing Commonwealth member will oppose the entry into the Prime Ministers' meetings of a former British dependency which has been granted independence. But the troubled character of intra-Commonwealth racial relations makes an attempt at a veto still a possibility. It was clear in 1964, for example, that if the British government had granted independence to Southern Rhodesia under its existing white-dominated government, and had then attempted to obtain Commonwealth membership for the new state, the proposal would have been opposed by the other African and the Asian members. In this instance Southern Rhodesia was not even invited to the Prime Ministers' meeting, in spite of the long record of attendance by Southern Rhodesia and the Federation of Rhodesia and Nyasaland in former years. In formal terms, that attendance had always previously been by courtesy of the full members; the courtesy was now withdrawn. It is likely that the British government would not sponsor Commonwealth membership for any ex-colony which it thought to be unacceptable to existing Commonwealth members; as in the case of Southern Rhodesia, independence would probably not be granted if the regime in the colony in question were repugnant to other Commonwealth members.

A further question is whether a member of the Commonwealth can be expelled. No case has occurred to date. The departure of South Africa in 1961 was a case of withdrawal, not of expulsion, although the withdrawal was made under pressure.[1] The circumstances in this case were that South Africa had stated that steps were being taken to turn the country into a republic, and that it wished to remain in the Commonwealth with its changed status. After a discussion of *apartheid* to which the Prime Minister of South Africa, Dr. Verwoerd, consented, South Africa withdrew its request for continued membership of the Commonwealth. So much for the constitutional niceties. The political fact of the matter was that a number of other Commonwealth states had announced that they would not stay in the Commonwealth if South Africa remained without modifying its *apartheid* policy, and the leader of at least one colony about to become independent (Tanganyika) announced that he would not recommend an application for membership if South Africa were still in the Commonwealth. It is clear that if Dr. Verwoerd had persisted with his application, it would have either been rejected by the other Prime Ministers (which would, in effect, have constituted expulsion) or precipitated a number of resignations by other members (which would have radically changed the character of the Commonwealth, and perhaps destroyed it).

The conclusion we may draw from this example is that the

[1] I have dealt with South Africa's departure at some length in an article in *Journal of Commonwealth Political Studies*, Vol. I, No. 1, November 1961.

requirement that a country submit an application for continued membership on becoming a republic constitutes an opportunity for the other members to review its membership and, if they wish, expel it. If they wanted to expel a member which was not going through the republicanizing process, they would have to invent new machinery altogether. It is certain that a member would need to have made itself highly repugnant to most of the others for this to happen. Its international behaviour might be a cause of this. *Apartheid* was an abnormal domestic question, in the sense that no other domestic policy practised by another Commonwealth member seems likely to arouse such indignation among the other members. But we should not leave out of consideration the possibility that some other issue will arise to encourage Commonwealth members to expel one of their fellows, or see that it is eased out. In such cases, the Commonwealth makes its own rules.

Means of Consultation

By "means of consultation" is understood in this context the network of arrangements which the members of the Commonwealth have made for themselves in order the better to know one another's point of view. Before describing these, however, it is necessary to examine the notion of "consultation" in itself. It is almost as ambiguous now as it was in the 1930's, though its ambiguity operates in different conditions. In those days it was understood in the context of an undefined general responsibility for British foreign policy—at any rate, to the extent that no British government wished to embark on a policy which did not have the approval of the oversea Dominions. Now the Commonwealth countries are no longer dependent primarily upon the United Kingdom for their defence, and they have active foreign policies of their own. But there is a general assumption that they ought to consult with one another about their policies. The question is how far this consultation ought to go and what effects it ought to have. What we might call the orthodox view of Commonwealth consultation is put thus by the Commonwealth Relations Office:[1]

> "There is a general understanding, affirmed at past Imperial Conferences and given formal expression in the External Affairs Agreement with Ceylon of the 11th November 1947, that Membership of

[1] *The Commonwealth Relations Office List* (H.M.S.O., London, 1957), p. 65.

the Commonwealth carries with it an obligation to inform or consult, as may be appropriate, all the other Members on any projected action which might affect their interests, especially in relation to foreign affairs, and thus to give them the opportunity of expressing their own individual views."

The same view was expressed in more homely terms by the Prime Minister of Australia, Mr. (now Sir Robert) Menzies:[1]

"I am no carping critic; but I would courteously suggest that one text might be boldly printed in every Department in London, New Delhi, Canberra, and the other Seats of Government—'Will any decision I am today contemplating affect some other nation of the Commonwealth? If so, have I informed or consulted it?' "

Both these statements were made before the British action in Egypt in October and November 1956. Up to that time there was a general impression that even where Commonwealth members disagreed they did habitually inform one another of what they proposed to do, taking each other into their confidence. There was uncertainty about how far this consultation went between, say, India and South Africa; but it was confidently believed by most students of Commonwealth relations that the British government considered itself bound to inform other members of its policy, even though it did not feel bound to accept any advice they might give it in return. A statement by Mr. Attlee, when Prime Minister, was given considerable weight:[2]

"It is our practice and duty as members of the British Commonwealth to keep other Members of the Commonwealth fully and continuously informed of all matters which we are called upon to decide, that may affect Commonwealth interests. The object is to give them the opportunity of expressing their views if they so desire. These views are taken fully into account but the decision must be ours, and other Governments are not asked, and would not wish, to share the responsibility for it. Dominion governments follow the same practice."

Certainly no Conservative Prime Minister had repudiated this view of consultation. Yet once the British action at Suez had been taken it became evident, and was admitted on all sides, that there had been no consultation beforehand with any Commonwealth member. The British action had been entirely unilateral. Some of

[1] R. G. Menzies, "The Ever Changing Commonwealth—Need for New Forms of Consultation", in *The Times*, June 12, 1956.
[2] *H. of C. Debates*, May 24, 1946, Vol. 423, Cols. 789–90.

the other Commonwealth Prime Ministers—from both "old" and "new" member countries—regretted this; others—notably Mr. Menzies of Australia—were not concerned about it. The position was stated by Mr. Lester Pearson, the Canadian Secretary of State for External Affairs: [1]

> "There was no consultation . . . with other members of the Commonwealth, and no advance information that this very important action, for better or for worse, was about to be taken. In that sense consultation had broken down between London and Paris on the one hand, the Commonwealth capitals and—even more important, possibly—Washington on the other."

Objections to the British lack of consultation [2] met little response from the British government, except in terms of practical difficulties relating to time; Sir Anthony Eden put it thus: "Our friends inside the Commonwealth, and outside, could not in the very nature of things be consulted in time. You just cannot have immediate action and extensive consultation as well." [3] More representative of Conservative opinion, perhaps, was the argument of the *Sunday Times*: [4]

> "If the charge is that the Government addressed its ultimatum to Egypt and Israel without previously informing other Commonwealth members, there can be no plea but guilty. Whether the delay involved would have been too costly cannot be debated without fuller knowledge than the public possesses. But that there was a lapse at least of tact cannot be gainsaid. It has, however, little to do with consultation.
>
> "There was certainly no time for consultation in the sense of obtaining and pondering the reactions of seven Cabinets to a proposed British course of action. That would have occupied days when minutes were precious. And to what end? No one suggests that prior persuasion would have reversed the hostility of any of the Asian countries; nor was Canada's critical attitude likely to be altered by consultation. What the critics are really saying is that Britain ought not to take any action which does not commend itself to all, or at the very least the majority, of her fellows in the Commonwealth. This is

[1] Speech in Canadian House of Commons, November 27, 1956; taken from *Statements and Speeches*, Information Division, Dept. of External Affairs, Ottawa, 56/35.

[2] Notably by Professor Nicholas Mansergh, in a letter to *The Times*, November 15, 1956.

[3] Sir Anthony Eden, "The Government's Policy in the Middle East", in *The Listener*, November 8, 1956.

[4] Editorial, "Knowing our Friends", *Sunday Times*, December 9, 1956.

an absurdity. It has never been part of the doctrine or practice of Commonwealth relations, before the war or since.

"If it were so it would have to be reciprocal, so that India could no more decide anything without 'consultation' of that kind with Britain, than Britain could without consulting India. A rule of unanimity, or even of majority consent, in a group so diverse, would stultify action almost everywhere, and reduce every member of the Commonwealth to the impotence of the United Nations."

I have gone into such detail about the issue of consultation as it arose in 1956, because the incident illustrates the dependence of a member-nation's interpretation of the concept upon its own view of its national interests. So long as the British government considered that its interests were broadly in harmony with those of the other members of the Commonwealth, it was prepared to inform them about what it proposed to do, although it was not prepared to give them a veto over its action; Mr. Attlee's statement shows that. When an issue arose in which the British government considered that its interests would conflict with those of other Commonwealth members—even though their interests were directly bound up in the issue—it refused to allow its chances of successful action to be prejudiced by the delay, and the possible leakage of information which informing them would involve. In this particular instance, a Commonwealth member, India, had been in close contact with Egypt, the country against which the British government proposed to take action; and the government seems to have decided that omitting to inform India of its intentions could be extended to omitting to inform all the other member-nations. It did not regard its Commonwealth membership as entailing either an "obligation" (the Commonwealth Relations Office's term) or a "duty" (Mr. Attlee's term) to inform the other members. Evidently it considered that informing them was something which it ought to do so long as its own interests were not endangered in the process; but where there was any possibility of their being imperilled, no duty to inform remained.

This seems a fair description of how any member of the Commonwealth would view the situation if it considered that its vital interests were in danger. The attitude of Sir Robert Menzies is to the point here. Before the Suez affair began he was the apostle of greater consultation, as the quotation above indicates; his references to the Commonwealth always included some reference to the need for improved methods of consultation. But in November 1956 his attitude was that Britain had been under no obligation to consult, and that Britain was right in going ahead without informing the other members. The inconsistency here is explained by the fact that Sir Robert's conception of Australian national interests was one in which a successful British and French action against Egypt would increase Australia's security. He was convinced that such an action would need to be swift and silent, and so he excused the lack of consultation in the face of the greater advantage which seemed likely to arise from it. His political opponent, Dr. Evatt, took a different view of Australia's interests in the matter, and if he had been in office he would presumably have upbraided the British government for its lack of consultation. The important point is not that the British government was right or wrong in not consulting, but that the whole notion of informing or consulting fellow-members rested, and rests still, on a prior assumption that the interests of the member in question must not be subordinated to any supposed obligation to consult.

We may summarize the practice of "consultation" since Suez by saying that members of the Commonwealth habitually inform one another of their policies, unless they consider that they will be inconvenienced by doing so. They do not recognize any right of veto over one another's policies, and they put their own conception of national interest before any supposed Commonwealth interest. At the same time, they may consider that their own long-term national interest in the preservation of the Commonwealth outweighs some short-term national interest. Consultation means information, when and how the informer pleases.

We may now proceed to examine the arrangements by which information is exchanged. Among these the most important are the meetings of Prime Ministers and the system of High Commissioners. Meetings of Prime Ministers are the lineal descendants of the Imperial Conference, though they do not have the same tradition of either regular occurrence or power to make decisions. They take place when it seems desirable to the Prime Ministers. The British government evidently took the initiative in inviting the Prime Ministers to meetings, in 1946, 1948, 1949, 1951, 1953, 1955, 1956, 1957, 1960, 1961, 1962 and 1964. This means that they have been more frequent than Imperial Conferences; and recent experience suggests that the Prime Ministers expect them to take place every year or every two years. To some extent this greater frequency is due to the ease of air travel; to an even greater extent it is due to the pressure of economic and political events in the world at large and to the strong desire of the British government to maintain close contacts with the Commonwealth countries. Frequent meetings mean that the fact of the Commonwealth's existence is kept continually before the world, and also that the Prime Ministers (who also include Presidents) show, by their continued attendance, that they value them.

Whereas the Imperial Conference had something approaching a constitution (in the resolutions of the conference of 1907, which laid down rules about eligibility, periodicity, chairmanship and voting), and was continually being exhorted to create for itself a secretariat to serve it between meetings, the meetings of Commonwealth Prime Ministers studiously avoid any suggestion that they are other than *ad hoc* responses to common needs. They are not called "conferences" but "meetings"; they issue no reports, only uninformative communiques; they hardly make decisions; it is understood that nothing is done which will commit members. So far they have all been held in London, though it has been understood for some years that they could be held elsewhere. In fact, meetings of other Commonwealth Ministers—e.g. Finance and Foreign Ministers—have been held in other Commonwealth capitals. But London is convenient to the Prime Ministers, not only because officialdom there is accustomed to handling distinguished visitors with dignity and dispatch, but also because London contains so many of the people whom Commonwealth Prime Ministers wish to see outside their formal meetings: bankers, industrialists, soldiers, scientists and others whose money or advice is desired by countries which consider themselves underdeveloped.

The meetings are made up of the Prime Ministers of the independent nations of the Commonwealth, but did include a standing anomaly in the person of the Prime Minister of the Federation of Rhodesia and Nyasaland, which never attained independent status. The reason for this was that Sir Godfrey Huggins (now Lord Malvern) did habitually attend meetings of Prime Ministers as Prime Minister of Southern Rhodesia before the Federation was established; and he was invited to the 1955 meeting after assuming the Prime Ministership of the Federation, not as an indication that the Federation had become independent (it had not), but as an act of personal courtesy. On this precedent, it should be possible for any British colony on the verge of independence to be invited to a Prime Ministers' meeting. But it seems to be the intention of the Prime Ministers that the Federation of Rhodesia and Nyasaland will be the one exception to the rule that only sovereign states can attend. There was a partial exception in the case of the Commonwealth Economic Conference of 1952, which included representatives from Malaya, Nigeria and Jamaica. This conference does not rank as a Prime Ministers' meeting in the opinion of the Commonwealth Relations Office, though it apparently had the authority to issue a statement about the Queen's Style and Titles.

In general, however, it is attendance at the Prime Ministers' meetings that indicates that a country is a member of the Commonwealth; and in so far as the Commonwealth has any sort of directorate or policy-making body, the Prime Ministers constitute it. They issue statements of joint purpose in international affairs and economic intercourse; they decided whether it would be possible for India, Pakistan and Ceylon, on becoming republics, to remain within the Commonwealth; they have even gone so far as to express their hope for an early establishment of such a contentious body as the European Defence Community (at the meeting of 1953). During the dollar shortage, the meetings of Prime Ministers were the only occasions on which it was possible to get direct discussion between leading politicians of the Sterling Area. But the general public has no means of knowing exactly what is discussed at the meetings, or what form the discussion takes. From hints dropped now and then it is fairly plain that the Prime Ministers put before the meetings the views of their governments upon the main issues of the day, but that nothing is discussed in formal session if any individual Prime Minister objects to its being discussed. To what extent this objection occurs before the meetings begin, and to what extent it takes place in the meetings themselves we do not know; there is even dispute over whether the Prime Ministers have an agenda or not. In this regard the key question has been that of Kashmir, which threatened to disrupt altogether the conference of 1951.[1] It seems that at no stage have the Prime Ministers discussed Kashmir in their official sessions, but that

[1] The details are given in J. D. B. Miller, "Commonwealth Conferences 1945–1955", *Year Book of World Affairs*, 10 (London, 1956), pp. 158–60.

various informal attempts have been made to bring together India and Pakistan under the general auspices of the other Prime Ministers. The Prime Ministers thus confine themselves to matters where no members' vital interests are likely to be endangered by any other member, and to those regarded as non-domestic.

In these circumstances it may be asked what the Prime Ministers find to talk about, since so many questions are likely to offend the susceptibilities of at least some of them. The answer is that in their discussions (in so far as these are reflected in their communiques) they have found that their interests coincide in a number of fields. In the economic field they have all wished to see the Sterling Area remain stable, and to prevent a flight from the pound. They have also wished to encourage a flow of capital into their economies, both from the United Kingdom and the United States. And they have all been of one mind in urging the United States to lower its tariff barriers and behave more generously to countries which wish to sell to it. In the field of international politics the Prime Ministers have found themselves united in wishing to see the restoration of prosperity in Western Europe and the maintenance of peace in Asia. In particular, they have all been convinced that nothing but harm could come from a war between the United States and China. In the face of such considerable agreement, it is not surprising that the Prime Ministers have found something to talk about.

The future of the meetings of Prime Ministers is the future of the Commonwealth itself. There is nothing institutional about the meetings which would enable them to continue in the absence of a general wish to keep the Commonwealth in being. Already they have acquired a flexibility which corresponds to the flexibility of the whole Commonwealth relationship: for example, it is now customary for those members which consider that they have common defence problems to discuss these in separate session, while the neutralist members absent themselves. But this does not mean that the members which discuss defence are regarded as superior to those which do not; it is simply an arrangement of convenience. One of the advantages of the system is that members which have common interests in some field can discuss these separately without disturbing the general sessions of the meetings. Indeed, it is possible to imagine a situation in which, while world events were quiescent and so did not force the members of the Commonwealth into a sense of common danger and common interest, each member found enough in common with *some* of the others on such matters as trade, currency and defence to warrant Prime Ministers' meetings which had few full sessions but split up into a series of changing groups to discuss problems common to sections of the membership. Such a prospect might be shocking to anyone whose main interest was the "unity" of the Commonwealth; but it would be a logical development from the habits of recent years.[1] As we have seen, consultation means information, not agreement; and meetings may well take any form which facilitates the giving of information in fields and to fellow-members that are thought appropriate.

The meetings of Prime Ministers constitute the highest level of Commonwealth consultation, and have their counterparts between one meeting and another in the cables and letters which pass between the Prime Ministers, who have full constitutional authority to consult with one another on any subject. In addition, there is a constant flow of messages between the Commonwealth Relations Office in London (representing the British government) and departments of the Commonwealth governments in their capitals. However, the distinctive diplomatic agents who carry on the process of consultation are the High Commissioners.

In all but name, the High Commissioners are Ambassadors from one Commonwealth member to another. They have had ambassadorial precedence since 1948 and full diplomatic immunity since 1952. The growth of the office had been slow, corresponding to the definition of status of the overseas members of the Commonwealth. The term "High Commissioner" has traditionally been used in British practice to describe a high official who is on mission to some other country or area but does not fit into the ordinary diplomatic categories. About the beginning of this century the oversea Dominions adopted it to describe their representatives in London, whose task was to represent their views to the British government and also to arrange contracts and in other ways act as agents for them. The duties were broadly those still performed by the Agents-General in London for the Australian States and Canadian Provinces. Britain did not send High Commissioners to the oversea Dominions, since it was considered that the Governor-

[1] Cf. R. G. Menzies, *op. cit.*: "There will always be scope for a general conference, like that of Prime Ministers. But on specific matters I believe that more functional conferences, political or official, will need to be the practice. Indeed there may well be some problems in which limited or regional conferences between selected British countries will need to occur."

General of a Dominion was not only the representative of the Monarch but also of the British government—that he was ultimately subject to the advice of British ministers and acted as their representative in the country in question. However, the redefinition of status which took place at the 1926 Imperial Conference included a decision that Governors-General would in future be subject to the advice of their ministers and not to that of the British government; accordingly, it became necessary for the British government to find some other means of representation in the Dominions. The appointment of High Commissioners was the solution. They were appointed first to Canada in 1928, to South Africa in 1931, to Australia in 1936, to New Zealand in 1939, and have been appointed to each of the newer Commonwealth members as those became independent.

There are British High Commissioners in all the Commonwealth capitals, and High Commissioners from all the member-nations in London, but not all overseas members are represented in each other's capitals. Sometimes the reason is antipathy (as between India and South Africa), but more often it is lack of business for the High Commissioners to do: New Zealand and Ghana, for example, find that their paths cross only seldom, and they do not consider the expense of High Commissioners to be justified. It is in London that there is the heaviest concentration of High Commissioners, who have frequent contact with the Secretary of State for Commonwealth Relations, and, through their staffs, with the various departments of the British government. It is also customary for the Secretary of State to meet the assembled High Commissioners regularly. Since it is relations with Britain, rather than with one another, that make up "Commonwealth relations" for most of the member-nations, they attach considerable importance to the post of High Commissioner in London and treat it differently from their other diplomatic posts. The Australian practice, while not universal, illustrates the position: whereas High Commissioners and Ambassadors from Australia are generally subject to the Department of External Affairs, the Australian High Commissioner in London is directly responsible to the Australian Prime Minister, and is always his personal choice—usually an ex-Minister and colleague of long standing, whom the Prime Minister trusts to put his personal views before the British government.

There is Commonwealth consultation elsewhere at the diplomatic level. In Washington, according to a former British Ambassador there:[1]

> "Every fortnight, except in the summer, the eight Ambassadors of the Commonwealth met in our Embassy to exchange views and consult informally together. We discussed everything: the movement of affairs in the world, the latest phase of American policy—and the opinions of our different countries about them. We did not mince words. Even difficulties between individual members, like Kashmir, were regularly talked over by all of us, including India and Pakistan, with conviction but without heat. Further, the discussions took place between like-minded people who shared a common political tradition. No one had to insist on the freedom of his country because nobody ever questioned it. We had a common approach. We accepted common standards. We had forbearance, which is essential between members of a continuing club when they differ."

It is understood that at the United Nations, too, the members of the Commonwealth habitually discuss beforehand the lines which they propose to take, not so much in order to reach agreement as to make each other aware of any differences which may arise.

The system of consultation between Commonwealth members may be summed up as one in which certain sovereign states are accustomed to discuss policy more often and more informally than groups of sovereign states usually do. It has no fixed rules, and may be changed either by agreement or by some member simply failing to observe what has been regarded as accepted practice. In so far as it has formal institutions, these are to be found in the meetings of Prime Ministers, the constant cabling of information, and the private discussions of High Commissioners and Ambassadors; but in all these, as already noted, the permissive element is great and the obligatory element small. If any obligation exists, it is the sort which arises from prudence, custom and good manners, not from binding law.

Common Institutions

Under this heading we consider Commonwealth arrangements which are less a matter of consultation than of common effort. The borderline between the two is a matter of dispute, and it is possible that some things considered here would be better regarded as aspects of consultation. In addition, not all the arrangements

[1] Sir Oliver Franks, "A Fellowship of Free Nations", in *The Listener*, November 18, 1954.

discussed here are common to all members of the Commonwealth; but they are included if they had their genesis in an attempt to provide something on a Commonwealth-wide scale.

The question of *nationality* need not take up much space. In essence, the position is that while Britain grants the common status of British subject to all citizens of Commonwealth countries, and until 1962 gave them free entry, this practice is not followed by any other member of the Commonwealth. Each has its own separate nationality. Most give special status or consideration to citizens of other Commonwealth countries, but all have immigration laws and special qualifications for nationality. There is no such thing as reciprocal citizenship over the whole of the Commonwealth. The origins of the differences in citizenship and nationality laws lie less in national self-assertion by Commonwealth members than in the desire of the "old" Commonwealth countries to protect themselves against coloured immigration. This has been a feature of their policies since the latter part of the nineteenth century.

The system of *judicial appeal* provides a common institution for some members. In 1963 the only overseas members retaining the appeal to the Judicial Committee of the Privy Council were Australia, New Zealand, Ceylon, Malaya, Nigeria, Sierra Leone, Jamaica, Trinidad and Tobago, and Uganda. Legal precedent and decision remain important elements in maintaining a sense of common practice among the Commonwealth countries. Bodies of lawyers are in close communion, the decisions of courts in one member-nation are quoted in those of another, and the common law tradition remains a bond.

In *transport and communications* there is a good deal of common effort. The Commonwealth Shipping Committee, the Commonwealth Air Transport Council and the Commonwealth Telecommunications Boards are advisory bodies with headquarters in London, the function of which is to co-ordinate the demands and interests of the various member-nations and recommend joint arrangements which may harmonize these. None of the three has executive power, but they work closely with the national bodies which do have it.

In *scientific research* a similar situation exists, though in this case the nature of the enterprise makes it possible and economical to have certain common efforts financed by the various Commonwealth governments. There is a British Commonwealth Scientific

Conference with a Standing Committee; there are joint Scientific Liaison Offices in London for the various Commonwealth countries; there is an extensive network of Commonwealth Agricultural Bureaux, operating in places where their particular kinds of research can be most profitably carried on.

In regard to *economic policy* the position is not easy to state, since much depends upon informal links, and there is relatively little that can be regarded as directly institutional or deciding policy. It may be best to start with some consideration of the history and operation of the Sterling Area, quoting from an official British publication:[1]

> "As a result of the United Kingdom's leading position in international trade, and as a centre of finance, during the 19th century, many countries tended to use sterling as the most convenient medium for international transactions and to maintain central currency reserves in London. In some cases they also used British currency for their domestic needs. When the United Kingdom abandoned the gold standard in 1931, the members of the sterling Commonwealth, plus certain other countries which were already operating a sterling exchange standard, did likewise and maintained unchanged the relationship between the exchange rate for their own currency and the pound sterling; these countries became known as the 'sterling bloc'. In 1939, with the outbreak of war, the pound sterling was no longer freely convertible into other currencies, and the group, now somewhat contracted in numbers, became legally defined for exchange control purposes as 'the sterling area'. Within this area the United Kingdom imposed virtually no restrictions on payments for current or capital transactions.
>
> "All the Commonwealth countries (except Canada) and their dependencies, together with Burma, Iceland, the Irish Republic, Jordan, Kuwait, Libya, South Africa and South-West Africa, and Western Samoa, comprise the present membership of the sterling area. These countries contain one-quarter of the world's population and do one-quarter of the world's trade. The bulk of their overseas trade is financed in sterling; they keep their foreign currency reserves largely in sterling; and they maintain a fixed value for their currencies against sterling. Because their external banking is in sterling, any margin of foreign currency that accrues to them is turned into sterling, or any margin that they may need is purchased with sterling; much of the gold produced within the sterling area is

[1] Reference Division, Central Office of Information, *Consultation and Co-operation in the Commonwealth* (London, 1963), pp. 16–17.

also sold in the London market for sterling. The transactions of the sterling area with the rest of the world are thus cleared through London, and the Exchange Equalisation Account, which holds the British reserves, buys and sells exchange in the market as appropriate.

"In addition to the free use of sterling by the sterling area countries, other countries earning sterling use it freely in multilateral trade; over a third of total world trade is estimated to be financed in sterling. Sterling was made freely transferable as between residents of all non-sterling area countries, except dollar countries, in 1954; in 1958 this was extended to include dollar countries, also. Capital can move freely from Britain to other countries in the sterling area, although most of the main sterling area countries apply exchange control against sterling.

"These currency arrangements derive essentially from the close trade and financial links between Britain and Commonwealth countries. They continue because they best suit the convenience of the traders and countries concerned. They do not depend on any legal or formal agreements."

We are confronted here with a system which is delicate, informal and abstruse. It depends for its success upon general confidence in sterling, upon the capacity of the Sterling Area as a whole to balance its books, and upon the continued conviction of the member-countries that it is better to remain part of a multilateral trading and payments system than to conduct their trade on a bilateral, semi-barter basis. Britain's capacity to maintain itself as a trading and capital-exporting country is the foundation of the system.

During the 1950's, when the dollar shortage was still widespread, it was possible to speak of "control" of the Sterling Area (as the first edition of this book did) in a way that is not possible in 1964. The wiping out of the wartime sterling balances, the growth of multilateral trade, the revival of British investment abroad, the use of American funds to assist the balance of payments of countries such as India, have all combined with general prosperity to make the Sterling Area a largely uncontrolled affair. As indicated in the quotation above, members do not now maintain the exclusive quality of their sterling transactions as those were carried on in the period after the war: "the bulk" of their trade takes place in sterling; they keep their currency reserves "largely" in it; "much" of the gold they produce is sold for sterling. The diversification of their trade has meant that they are not so dependent upon their economic links with Britain as they were before. Nevertheless they still find it convenient to keep the bulk of their reserves in sterling, and retain an interest in the economic well-being of the Area as a whole.

To the extent that the Sterling Area can be said to be managed, it is by the Central Banks and Treasuries of the member-countries, working in close touch with the Bank of England and the British Treasury, which are central to the system. Contact between these bodies is maintained largely on a personal basis. The number of people involved is not large, and they all know each other. They meet at various international conferences; some have helped to train the others; all tend to share a common frame of reference, although all are concerned with their individual countries' special interests. At a more formal level, Commonwealth economic matters, including the continued health of the Sterling Area system, are discussed at meetings of the Commonwealth Economic Consultative Council, a body which arose out of the Commonwealth Trade and Economic Conference at Montreal in 1958, and incorporates a number of arrangements previously in existence. This body meets regularly in London at the official level, and each year or so at the Ministerial level. It has no fixed agenda, but considers whatever problems of economic policy and development are placed before it. It is also the progenitor of the Special Commonwealth African Assistance Plan, launched in 1960 as a kind of modest African counterpart of the Colombo Plan. In the 1960's the emphasis of the Council has been laid very much upon questions of economic development and expanded world trade (especially when it seemed likely that Britain would become a member of the European Economic Community), rather than upon the management of currency matters.

It should not be thought that either the arrangements of the Sterling Area or the efforts to promote Commonwealth economic development constitute a closed economic system; for example, there are no general Commonwealth institutions in the field of trade. The Ottawa agreements of 1932, which instituted the system of Imperial Preference, provided for no policy-making bodies for the system as a whole. In any event, each agreement was bilateral, worked out between particular members of the Commonwealth in regard to particular aspects of their trade; and while each might be negotiated again after a period of time, it was fixed in its operation and did not require the sort of constant surveillance which might be demanded by a monetary body with such changing fortunes as those of the Sterling Area.

Similarly, there is no general Commonwealth institution in the field of investment. From time to time there are suggestions that some sort of Commonwealth Investment Fund might be established, but these have met with little success: Britain is the only Commonwealth country with large funds to invest (apart from Canada, which is a special case), and it is difficult to imagine the British money market responding to demands that it should invest heavily in the Commonwealth simply because it was the Commonwealth. The nearest approaches have been the establishment in 1953, by the Bank of England and certain firms in manufacturing, shipping, mining and banking, of the Commonwealth Development Finance Company Ltd., and the conversion in 1963 of the Colonial Development Corporation to the Commonwealth Corporation; both were solely British efforts.

However, the Colombo Plan should be mentioned in the context of investment, although it is not simply a matter of capital investment, nor is it now confined to Commonwealth members. It began as a result of a meeting of Commonwealth Foreign Ministers at Colombo in 1950, and the element of Commonwealth influence and joint endeavour has remained a strong one. The Consultative Committee, which is the managing body, has held all its meetings in Commonwealth capitals. The scheme was proposed in the first place by Australia, and Australia and New Zealand have continued to play a leading part in it, as have Britain and Canada. The donor countries now include the United States and Japan, and the recipients have grown in number beyond the Commonwealth countries in South and South-east Asia. But it is fair to say that the Colombo Plan represents the most practical means of mutual help developed by the Commonwealth, especially as regards its newer Asian members.

In matters of *defence* one can easily become deeply enmeshed in discussions of what Commonwealth arrangements were in the past and what they ought to be now. Put briefly, the facts are that whereas before the war it was assumed throughout the Commonwealth that there was a single defence problem, the assumption now is that each member has its own problem, necessitating arrangements with foreign countries as well as with those in the Commonwealth. Individual defence policies have grown with individual foreign policies. It is impossible to think seriously of a single defence problem for the Commonwealth, at a time when international alignments and modern weapons conspire to make the idea an absurdity. Translated into practical terms, this means that each Commonwealth country now makes its own arrangements, if it wishes, for alliance with the United Kingdom and with such other powers as it considers to be suitable. But there is a considerable area of agreement and co-operation which falls short of alliance. Britain, as the most experienced and developed Commonwealth member, in warfare as in other fields, is able to provide training facilities, scientific knowledge and discussions of strategy which Commonwealth members would find difficult to obtain elsewhere. So it comes about that even India, which is not a party to any of the alliances which link other members, sends representatives to discussions of Commonwealth Chiefs of Staff and sends her naval ships to exercise with those of other Commonwealth navies. At the professional level, then, there is considerable co-operation and joint action by the member-nations.

A *Commonwealth secretariat* was a dream of early supporters of the idea of Commonwealth unity; it is ironic that it should have had to wait for concrete proposals until 1964, when "unity" was a thing of the past. The formation of a basis for a secretariat to exchange information and prepare for Commonwealth meetings was a task given to officials after the Prime Ministers' meeting of that year.

It would be inappropriate to end this chapter without some mention of *unofficial joint action* in the Commonwealth. By this is meant the existence of professional, scientific, educational, charitable, religious, economic and recreational associations which link together activities of similar kinds in the various Commonwealth countries and provide for a vast number of unofficial contacts. Some of these began as "Empire" bodies; others are of recent growth. They range from semi-public bodies like the Commonwealth Parliamentary Association and the Association of Universities of the British Commonwealth to the organizations concerned with sports and pastimes. Some are concerned with only a few Commonwealth countries, while others embrace them all. Taken together, their work has a good deal to do with the climate of opinion in which members approach questions of Commonwealth relations.

Part II

INTERESTS AND POLICIES OF COMMONWEALTH MEMBERS

Chapter Five

THE RELATIONSHIP OF INTERESTS AND POLICY

To discuss the relations of the sovereign states of the Commonwealth, and to estimate the influence of the Commonwealth as an institution upon them, it is necessary to examine their interests and policies as these have emerged in the post-war world. But I think it desirable first to examine what is meant by "interests" and "policies", and to sketch in broad strokes the kind of world to which Commonwealth members have had to develop their distinctive approaches.

When one discusses national interests it is necessary always to attempt to be realistic and not to be enslaved by terms. Such phrases as "vital national interests" or simply "the national interest" have about them a sense of command: they call upon the citizen to support something which he is obliged to adhere to as he might adhere to the religion of his fathers or the national anthem. These phrases assume implicitly that the national interest is something given, something which remains constant and does not call for questioning—something, in fact, which it would be disloyal to question. Not only is it assumed that something called the national interest exists; it is also assumed that this is to a considerable extent external to the ordinary processes of politics, and so fundamental as to be remote from attack. This is the ordinary tone in which national interest is spoken of by those who invoke it. As we shall see, it is a half- or perhaps a quarter-truth, and in so far as it contains elements of truth they are potent elements which the student will neglect at his peril; but to treat it as a whole truth is to invite misunderstanding and false conclusions.

Along with the frequent assumption that the national interest is static and not to be questioned goes another assumption (not always by the same people) that national interest is invariably material, in the sense that it is bound up with trade, investment, colonization, conquest and war. These are seen as elements of international life which bring concrete advantage of disadvantage to countries, and which can be shown to have immediate influence upon the condition of life of given peoples. Any attempt to formulate national interest in other terms is dismissed as abstract or sentimental. In fact, this materialist assumption goes easily with the former assumption about the static character of interests, because it transfers attention from the arena of political argument to what are so often called the "cold facts" of geography and strategy and trade. These are assumed to have a remote, external quality, and a permanence which forbid critical examination of their effective influence; it is assumed that they exercise a direct control over the possibilities of foreign policy to the extent that interests are definable only in their terms. This, too, is a half- or quarter-truth.

The two assumptions about national interest which I have described may not often be put so bluntly, but they certainly affect discussions of foreign policy in all the Commonwealth countries. They have an extra relevance in that they have often been used to postulate interests for the Commonwealth *as a whole* in much the same way as for an individual state. In this usage the Commonwealth is taken to be an actual or potential super-state, the limits of whose interests are set by geography, trade and strategy, and whose ultimate interest is postulated in terms of a destiny which demands that "unity" be sought for the whole Commonwealth, in spite of objections made from time to time by some of its citizens. Both assumptions have been widely accepted in the fields of Commonwealth trade and investment: it was very much part of run-of-the-mill Conservative opinion in Britain that the Commonwealth has a general interest in becoming a unity, and that this can be attained by confining trade and investment as much as possible within it. Such a state of affairs is taken to be the higher interest of the Commonwealth as a whole, one to which conceptions of national interest for the individual members must defer. The higher interest is seen as destined, but it is to be secured by strictly material means, each of which is seen to be itself a concrete Commonwealth interest.

Both assumptions lead to rigidity of thought about national interests. They allow for neither change nor criticism. They need to be supplemented and corrected by at least three qualifications, as follows:

National interests cannot be separated from the minds of the men who formulate them. For example, it is true that Britain is an island, or a series of islands; but what is important is not the fact itself but the view which is taken of it by those in charge of policy. They may decide that Britain's being an island means that her policy ought to be insular and that she should shun contact with the nearest land-mass—i.e. with Europe. Here the national interest is interpreted as being the preservation of insularity, by whatever means seem appropriate. Alternatively, those in charge of policy may decide that it is being an island off the coast of Europe that matters for Britain, and that, as an island with resources which can be complemented by those of different parts of Europe, the national interest lies in the extension of contacts and ties with Europe. Both estimates of national interest will be based upon the facts of geography. Each has plausibility. Each will appeal to a different kind of mind; each will chime with a different sort of estimate of the advantages to be gained from policy. Each is a conception of national interest, to be advanced, discussed, and, if found acceptable, to be turned into policy. It cannot be said that in a case like this the national interest is something which is external and imposed; it is rather something which is thought out, from particular standpoints, on the evidence available. In other words, when we speak of national interest we should always ask whose formulation of it is in question, and whether there are other formulations in the field which may issue their challenges. There will still be room for argument as to which formulation accords best with the facts of international life, and whether there are facts of national existence which have not been taken into account; but this does not affect the main point, that national interest has reality only as someone's conception of it.

Ideas of national interest have a grounding in the facts of geography and economics, but these facts are subject to change. Just as generals are said to have a tendency to fight the last war over again, so it is often assumed that, once significant facts of geography and economics have been established, their significance remains the same. But this is not true. Facts about the distance between spots on the earth's surface and their location in relation to one another have significance only in terms of the means of communication and transport. As those means change, so do the significances of distance, separation by sea, separation by high mountains and connection by rivers. Not only means of communication and transport, but other aspects of scientific discovery, transform the "facts" of geography: the elimination of malarial mosquitoes or the cultivation of frost-resistant plants may have a similar effect. They become further facts of geography which must be taken into account if the total position is to be truly assessed. Similarly, the facts of trade and investment may change. The fact that a country like Canada or Australia gets its economic impetus as a result of gold discoveries or the production of wheat or wool does not mean that it will continue to be mainly dependent for its economic progress upon this kind of activity. The fact that a producer of, say, sugar looks for a protected market at one time may not continue to reproduce itself, as it were: changed conditions elsewhere may cause the producer to seek wider markets and to sacrifice his protection in quest of a bigger income. There are certain facts of geography and economics which retain a fairly constant force, but this does not mean that all of them do. The point is that a conception of national interest which is said to be based upon the "cold facts" of trade or strategy needs to be scrutinized to see if the facts in question have ceased to operate or have been overborne by new facts.

Ultimately, ideas of national interest depend upon the ideas which men have of the place which they would like their country to occupy in the world; and these ideas change in time, apart from never being unanimous within a country at a given time. The most potent single factor in determining national interest is the image which policy-makers have of their country as a force in the world at large. Nationalism as a sentiment is overwhelmingly a sense of self-importance, cultivated either as a result of external domination or in consequence of a national past which is viewed with self-esteem. Even those who reject Hegelian and Idealist interpretations of national self-consciousness will agree that there is considerable accuracy in Hegel's description of the view which men take of their country:[1]

> "Thus is it with the Spirit of a people: it is a Spirit having strictly defined characteristics, which erects itself into an objective world, that exists and persists in a particular religious form of worship, customs, constitution, and political laws—in the whole complex of its institutions—in the events and transactions which make up its history. That is its work—that is what this particular Nation *is*. Nations are what their deeds are. Every Englishman will say: We

[1] G. W. F. Hegel, *Lectures on the Philosophy of History*, trans. J. Sibree (London, 1914), p. 77.

are the men who navigate the ocean, and have the commerce of the world; to whom the East Indies belong and their riches; who have a parliament, juries, &c.—The relation of the individual to that Spirit is that he appropriates to himself this substantial existence; that it becomes his character and capability, enabling him to have a definite place in the world—to be *something*. For he finds the being of the people to which he belongs an already established, firm world—objectively present to him—with which he has to incorporate himself. In this its work, therefore—its world—the Spirit of the people enjoys its existence and finds its satisfaction.—A Nation is moral—virtuous—vigorous—while it is engaged in realising its grand objects, and defends its work against external violence during the process of giving to its purposes an objective existence."

Obviously it would be foolish to suggest that all men take this view of their country; and in any case I should personally contest the argument that this is the view they *ought* to take. But that most people *do* take this idealizing view of their country in relation to others I have little doubt. It is at times of crisis that they indulge in such sentiments; and the ideas of national interest are inseparably connected with critical times in the past or future. However, the point I wish to stress is not that this kind of view is typical of national sentiment in most countries, but that, within such a general state of mind, there is room for quite acute difference of opinion over the way in which the national Spirit may be best expressed. In the example which Hegel gave his students in Berlin in the 1820's, there is ample illustration of this point. He said that Englishmen thought of themselves as the men "who navigate the ocean, and have the commerce of the world; to whom the East Indies belong and their riches; who have a parliament, juries, etc." This was true. But within such an image of themselves, Englishmen had room for divergent interpretations. They could take either of what Sir Harold Nicolson has called the "warrior or heroic", and the "mercantile or shopkeeper" view of their national interests.[1] The one would stress conquest, imperial power and law and order; the other would stress peaceful commerce, representative institutions and non-intervention. The two could come into acute conflict, as they did when they were typified by Palmerston and Cobden. But both would proceed from much the same image of what, by virtue of its deeds, the British nation

[1] Harold Nicolson, *Diplomacy* (London, 1939), pp. 52–4.

was. The emphasis would vary as between one kind of deed and another. Thus there is room for divergence about national interests at any given time, even though a national image may stay steady. But there is also room for change in the national image itself over periods of time. New facts may emerge, new limitations on power, which force a change. "Romantic Ireland's dead and gone; it's with O'Leary in the grave." One may contest the judgment in particular cases, but that there can be a shift of national awareness is hardly in doubt. In sum, two points may be stressed when we are attempting to understand the significance of the national image: the first is that the ideas which men have about the part they would like their country to play on the world's stage have immense power and influence, and obviously affect any judgment of national interest; the second is that national images can be the subject of acute controversy when an attempt is being made to decide the national interest.

The effect of these three qualifications upon the two assumptions described above is to remove their rigidity and reveal their limitations. It is true that there is an enduring element in ideas of national interest; but it is the enduring element of historical memory and geographical location, both of which are subject to alteration and divergent interpretation over any period of time. It is true that there are brute facts of geography and economics which policy-makers must always take into account when trying to enunciate national interests; but these have no final deterministic quality and their significance can be hotly contested. If we wish to be realistic about the nature of national interests we must recognize that they are not cut and dried, but must be interpreted afresh in each generation, and are likely to be subject to acute controversy. To suggest that they are final and immutable is to invite denial from the facts of everyday life.

Essentially, national interest is what the person, or the party, or the government enunciating it would like to advance and protect in the name of the nation. It is a concept influenced mainly by the national image, as that is seen by the person stating the interest. The national image depends upon historical memory and upon one's estimation of power and resources, as these are decided by the facts of strategy, geography and economics. We cannot lay down a country's interests in advance of its own formulation of those interests; all we can say is that its lines of action in the world will be restricted by its size, its wealth, its associations with other nations, and the kind of vision which its people possess of their future and past. We cannot say, with any accuracy, that these factors will *determine* its interests; the only sensible thing we can say is that they will *influence* the choices which its people make in formulating their interests. These factors will limit the area of argument. They will not finally determine either policy or the goals at which policy aims. However, while it is true that we cannot speak of national interests except in terms of these being actually formulated by someone, there is a sense in which interests can be said to be latent before they become apparent, can be seen in embryo before anyone states them. Anyone looking at the situation of Australia and New Zealand in the 1890's, for example, might have said that it would one day be in the national interest of these two countries to cultivate the friendship of independent Asian nations if those should appear. It was not said by the politicians of the time; when they talked about Asia they talked about the exclusion of Asian immigrants from Australia and New Zealand. In doing so they were stating what was widely felt to be a national interest of both countries: it was clear, there was widespread agreement about it. Anyone who voiced the view that eventually Australia and New Zealand would have to come to terms with Asian countries on a friendly basis would probably have been told that this contention was far-fetched or academic. Nevertheless, he could have replied that this was a latent interest for the two countries, one which they could neither see nor act upon at the time but which they would eventually recognize.

The notion of latent national interest is of considerable relevance to our discussion of the growth of national policies in the Commonwealth. Each Commonwealth country, except Britain, has had to develop its own national image in a relatively short time. Whereas Canada has had a century in which to do this, Ghana and Malaysia, India and Pakistan have had almost no time at all. With them (and, to a lesser extent, with the "old Dominions" too), the process has been one of quickly developing an idealized national image as a reaction against British domination: it has been built up, not in terms of the strategic and economic needs of the country but in terms of patriotic resistance to European rule. Once that rule has been removed, a national interest has obviously in some sense been realized, simply by the act of creation of a new nation;

but it soon becomes plain that the new nation has other interests to discover, interests which arise not from its having been subject to imperial exploitation but from its position on the earth's surface, its economic life, its religious complexion, the degree of unity among its people, and the ambitions of its politicians. In such a situation, the national image which was constructed as a simple reaction against imperial control becomes modified; it takes on a more individual shape. Whereas it was previously a stereotyped "anti-colonialist" image, it is now adapted to the circumstances and strivings of the nation to which it is intended to apply. Latent national interests come to the surface. This does not mean that they are so clear and unarguable that everyone agrees about them; as indicated above, the whole notion of national interest is so tricky as to stimulate controversy even in the face of the most durable facts of geography and economics. But the new nation is impelled, by outside pressure and by the release of divergent indigenous political forces, to formulate interests which correspond to its place in the world and the political ambitions of its people. A seer might have discerned them in advance; what he could not have discerned would be the emphasis to be given them, the precedence among them, the practical possibilities of achieving them.

Obviously there is always a close connection between national interest and foreign policy. We assume that a government has formulated certain ideas of national interest, and we expect its foreign policy to exemplify those ideas, or at any rate to be capable of being related to them. If not, we have on our hands a case of national schizophrenia. Some rough correspondence between the formulation of national interests and the execution of foreign policy is to be expected. Foreign policy is taken here to be the things which a government does in its relations with the governments of other countries: it embraces alliances, treaties, diplomatic conversations, trade pacts, and the implications of membership of international organizations such as the United Nations or the ILO. But it would be a mistake to assume that foreign policy is simply the carrying into effect of a formulation of national interest. Ideally one might expect a country's government to sit down solemnly and work out its national interests and then seek to pursue them; but this can rarely be the case. One reason is that no country has absolute power; each must take into account the policies of other countries, and modify its own accordingly. This restriction has been particularly evident in the experience of the Commonwealth countries as sovereign states. In spite of a growing sense of national self-importance and a sharper formulation of national interests, they have found it difficult to play independent, self-determined roles on the world stage. They have been forced into associations which, ideally, they might not have welcomed; they have been coerced by events into actions which often they, or important elements of opinion within them, have deplored. This has been true of Britain, as it has of the newer sovereign states of the Commonwealth.

But there is another reason why the Commonwealth countries have often not been able to formulate their national interests and then apply them in policy. It is that interests could not be discerned until the need to have a policy arose. In international life today, a new nation is immediately called upon to display policy. It is given no breathing-space in which to decide its interests and develop its public opinion about world affairs; as soon as it achieves independence it becomes a member of the UN, with the immediate obligation of declaring itself on major issues, and must soon make plain its position in the cold war. It has to make up its policy as it goes along, using for a basis not any cut-and-dried formulation of national interest, but a sort of instinct in its diplomats and politicians that, if national interest were formulated, it would be of a particular kind as exemplified in the policies which they pursue. This sort of process, the process of discovering latent national interests by trial and error in the execution of foreign policy, has been particularly characteristic of the "new" Commonwealth members in Asia and Africa. But it is also true, to a greater extent than they might be prepared to admit, of "old" members such as Canada and Australia. Since 1945 the diplomats of these countries have been confronted with a vast number of international decisions, to which the rather vague formulation of national interests by their politicians has offered only the most tenuous clue. They (and their Ministers of External Affairs) have achieved their sense of national interests in the cut and thrust of diplomacy. Above all, they have become painfully aware of the factor of *possibility* in foreign policy, which has already been referred to: whatever their wishes, they have often found that the facts of international life denied these and demanded other courses which seemed second best.

The relationship between interests and policy is thus a mutual one; the difficulties of policy have a good deal to do with the modifications of ideas about interest. The two influence one another. In what follows, it will be seen that frequently the formulation of national interests by Commonwealth countries has gone along with the need to make policy, often to an extent which makes the two inseparable. But before seeing what interests and policies have emerged in each member-nation in recent years, we must see what sort of world has confronted Britain and the other Commonwealth countries.

Chapter Six

THE WORLD OF STATES SINCE 1945

SINCE 1945 many of the changes in the Commonwealth, both in membership and institutions, have been responses to thrusts of the major forces in world politics. Those forces have been the eclipse of Europe, the rise of new nations, the irruption of Russia and China, the intervention of the United States, the power of new weapons, and the pressure of prosperity.

The eclipse of Europe is used here to describe the removal of Western Europe from the centre of gravity of Great Power politics. For the first time since the contraction of the Ottoman Empire, the decisions made outside Western Europe matter more than those made within it. Russia, China and the United States have replaced the traditional European Powers as preponderant factors in diplomacy. Britain, France, Germany and Italy matter still, both politically and economically; but they cannot parade the force which made them great before World War II. The eclipse of Europe can be seen from three aspects. The first is the shrinkage of colonial empires, whether by consent, as with the British, or under protest from the colonial power, as with the French and Dutch. In both Asia and Africa this is the most marked effect of Europe's decline. The second is dependence in foreign relations: Western Europe is dependent upon the United States, and Eastern Europe upon the Soviet Union, in very different ways but to an extent which precludes the rise of Great Powers in either area in the foreseeable future. The third is the various efforts at mutual aid which have characterized European diplomacy since 1945; this aspect is perhaps the most significant of all. Nothing but a sense of decline and eclipse could force the former Great Powers into such attempts at co-operation as the European Defence Community and the European Economic Community. As we shall see, Britain is in a rather different position from her European neighbours, in relation to these attempts to "faire l'Europe"; but the fact that these attempts are given serious consideration in Britain is itself an admission of decline, by the standards of the past.

The rise of new nations in Asia, the Middle East and Africa is a familiar theme, but it needs to be constantly reiterated when one is considering the present position of the Commonwealth. The effect of this rise has been to put whole areas of the world out of control, compared with their pre-war position—if by control we mean control by Europeans. Whereas it was possible before the war to think of the Middle East, South and South-east Asia and the whole of Africa as susceptible to European power, it is now quite impossible. The fact that sovereign states have risen in these formerly colonial areas does not mean, however, that these states are lacking in dependence and can call their own tunes. All of them are weak in military force; all have low standards of living which their governments wish passionately to raise. Most are thoroughly enmeshed in the demands of the developed countries for raw materials such as oil, food and fibres. In consequence, their newly won independence provides them with the trappings of sovereignty—ambassadors, parliaments, presidents, membership of the United Nations—but does not free them from the need to seek the friendship and help of bigger and wealthier countries. At the same time, their significance on the world stage is not measured simply by their lack of economic and military power. It is measured also by their capacity for protest against the decisions of greater powers, their opportunities to sabotage world trade by cutting pipe-lines and closing canals, their nuisance value as pressure-groups at the United Nations, and, ultimately, their appeal to the consciences of the more developed countries. Hungry, poor and disorganized in comparison with their former masters, they constitute a continual embarrassment. In addition they provide both encouragement and warning to existing colonial territories in which the sense of nationalism is either stirring or already impatient: their existence quickens the pace of independence and weakens the power of the colonialists to determine the course which independence will take.

The irruption of Russia and China into world politics is often treated as the spread of an ideology. There is force in this; for undoubtedly the extension of Russian and Chinese power means the extension of Marxist–Leninism as a conditioning force in men's minds. But in point of fact the doctrine has followed the power, not preceded it: the Russians and Chinese are now important in world affairs, not because more people became convinced of the truth of Communism, but because territory was seized by Communist arms. Again, the irruption of Russia and China is often treated as a warning that Communism makes its strongest

(Copyright, Low and "Evening Standard")

appeal to under-developed countries in which poverty causes resentment against the old order. There is force in this too; for the actual extension of Communist power has occurred, on the whole, in the less-developed countries. But it has occurred, not because the masses had become convinced of the futility of the old order, but because a relatively small number of Communist organizers, mainly from the middle classes, have been given the opportunity to rule by Russian bayonets or by the incompetence or military defeat of the former ruling forces—as in China and Vietnam. While Communism should be regarded as the driving force behind the power of Russia and China, it must also be kept in mind that Communist successes have been gained by arms and not by peaceful conversion—and that the rulers of Russia and China are fully aware of this, having come to power by force and kept their power by force. In consequence, the leaders of other countries must treat Russia and China as powers with a dual approach, both aspects of which must be kept in play. In the first place they are Great Powers of a brutality and determination fit to rank with those of the most cynical European despots of the past; they will play power politics to the limit and will not hesitate to start wars, as in Finland and Korea, if they think they can win them or at any rate improve their positions as a result of them. In the second place they are countries whose adherents throughout the world are not to be discovered by the test of blood, the test which was previously used to discover the supporters of a Great Power such as Germany, Italy or France; their adherents are the Communists of the world at large, recruited by admiration of Russia or China or by dissatisfaction with their own regimes, but thereafter likely to follow the policies laid down in the headquarters of Communist activity. The combination of power and doctrine is thus not only potent; it is also unfamiliar to other states, which hardly know how to handle it. This is particularly true of the new nations of Asia and the Middle East, in which the regimes usually recognize the domestic danger of the local Communists, but wish to have either the favour or the benevolent neutrality of those Communists' masters in Moscow and Peking.

The intervention of the United States in world affairs has particularly affected the Commonwealth. In 1964 Britain, Canada, Australia, New Zealand and Pakistan were all accustomed to a situation of direct alliance with the United States; and all member-nations have benefited from American economic aid in one form or another. But, as we shall see, no Commonwealth member has found American help entirely welcome. For Britain it has been an embarrassment as indicating Britain's own reduced position in world affairs. For the traditionally "British" members like Australia and New Zealand it has sometimes been hard to reconcile with continued adherence to the British connection. To Canada it has entailed the special problems of propinquity and economic dependence. For the Asian members it has implied commitment to one side in the cold war, and with it an association with "colonialism". Such reactions from Commonwealth countries can be paralleled by the reactions of other countries which have found American aid a mixed blessing. But it is not only American association with themselves that has created problems for non-Communist countries like those of the Commonwealth. American intervention in the postwar world has been essentially intervention against Communism. While this intervention in Europe has been broadly approved by the Commonwealth countries, which have considered themselves either directly benefited or not involved, American intervention in Asia, with its threatened possibility of a war with China, has been one of the preoccupations of Commonwealth leaders. They were agreed about the undesirability of American intervention over Formosa, divided over American policy in Korea, fearful about the possibilities of American policy in Indo-China, again divided over SEATO. Their inability to agree, and their inability to remain detached from the issues which American policy has raised, have been increased by the general uncertainty of American policy in Asia and the difficulty of knowing which American voice, at any given time, has been the most likely to prevail. In this, again, Commonwealth leaders have been typical of general non-Communist reaction to American involvement in the affairs of other nations. No country has been able to disregard American intervention; some have welcomed it wholeheartedly; others have been qualified in their approval; some have disliked it from the start. None has been able to ignore it. And it has provided a focus for the policies of Russia and China, which have been consistently anti-American, whatever other changes have occurred in these two countries' attitudes.

The power of new weapons is the most difficult to assess of all the major forces of world politics. It is plain that nuclear weapons and rocket projectiles have revolutionized all-out warfare, and that the realization of this has tempered the attitudes of the Great Powers towards one another. But beyond this it is hard to go. The Suez operation upset the balance of world forces for the time being, though it was not carried out with modern weapons; at the same time there have been suggestions that it came to a stop because the Russians threatened to use rockets. For the nations which possess them, nuclear weapons offer the possibility of inflicting destruction upon one another, with no clear indication of how the conflict would end; for those which do not possess them, or which, while possessing them, are of such small size as to be defenceless against nuclear retaliation, the prospect is one of little wars with out-of-date weapons or of destruction by superior force in the hands of the Great Powers. In general, the effect of the latest developments seems to have been to increase the significance of diplomacy as a means of settling disputes between Great Powers, since the alternative is mutual destruction, and to increase the importance of little wars carried on with conventional weapons. Countries like Indonesia, which have the power to wage such wars in their immediate vicinity, thus acquire more importance than if the Great Powers possessed effective means of disciplining them; Great Power discipline with out-of-date weapons is risky, since it may turn into conflict with another Great Power at the nuclear level. In addition, the more devastating the new weapons become, the harder it is to calculate the advantage of a particular alliance. For example, it was much easier for Britain and France to calculate the advantages of NATO when its operations were likely to be with conventional weapons than now, when the effect of the new weapons in Europe is an enigma. For countries contemplating new alliances, the problem is whether it is worthwhile to ally oneself with any other than one of the Greatest Powers, and whether to do so will invite nuclear retaliation by that Greatest Power's greatest rival.

The pressure of prosperity is used here to describe that condition of inflation and high employment which most countries have experienced since 1945, a condition in which prices have been above the pre-war level, demand for capital and consumer goods has risen, investment has been heavy, and taxation higher than before the war but equably borne because of continually rising incomes. The contrast with the 1930's is obvious, but its consequences have been insufficiently marked. The 1930's were characterized by dwindling international investment, low prices for raw materials and food, restrictive and protectionist policies on an international scale, and determined attempts at self-sufficiency by countries which had the means to make them. The late 1940's and 1950's were characterized by growing international investment, mainly by the United States, but increasingly by European countries such as Britain and Western Germany, and by smaller but rich countries of which Canada was the most notable. Domestic expansion produced for these countries savings which could be invested abroad. But the investment was largely confined to areas in which high or stable profits could be assured, such as countries with deposits of oil and metals, and high-standard countries like Canada and Australia. Many countries with low living standards, poor resources but boundless ambition failed to attract capital. Similarly, the period was characterized by fairly stable prices for raw materials and food, but this did not satisfy the countries which provided these commodities. They were anxious to diversify their economies, on the ground that specialization in the production of a narrow range of raw materials put them at the mercy of the buyers, and that only countries with manufacturing industries had managed to raise their standard of living with any rapidity. This led them to protectionist policies in order to shelter their infant manufactures, and to policies of economic control in order to husband the scarce capital resources available to equip them. Whereas the 1930's saw restrictionist policies applied vigorously at both the domestic and international levels, the world since the war has seen a vigorous attack on them at the international level. This has been a reflex of the expansionist character of the developed economies, which have not needed so much protection as in depression times. The United States and Britain have both displayed examples of this tendency to seek a free-trading world. But the same has not been true of the under-developed countries, which have increased domestic protection in order to nurse their infant industries.

In sum, the effect of the pressure of postwar prosperity has been to make life easier for the developed economies (incidentally enabling them to bear with equanimity the heavy burden of armaments which they have felt obliged to shoulder), and to encourage them in greater international trade and investment. But, while it has also made life easier in some ways for the under-developed economies of Asia and Africa (notably by the long period of high prices for their primary products), it has created in them a hunger for higher standards which has proved difficult to satisfy—because of the inadequacy of their own savings and the fact that the surpluses of the developed economies have been insufficient to finance the demands made upon them. In such a situation it is natural that from the under-developed countries eyes should turn to the Soviet Union and China, economies in which it has been possible to achieve forced savings and to apply them to the expansion of productive capacity. The eyes have been those of planners, public servants and politicians rather than of the plain people, for whom the Five Year Plan pattern means, if anything, tighter belts. It is understandable, though, that the most democratically minded of African planners should contemplate in despair his own country's poverty of capital and ask if the Soviet methods would produce a more effective result. This is not the same as the acceptance of Communism; it is simply the recognition that planning, under absolute power, can produce results which seem impossible where capital is scarce and is free to dispose itself at its owners' whims decide.

At least six major forces, then, have been at work in the postwar world. It has been impossible for nations to be unaffected by them or to ignore them—impossible, that is, for their governments to ignore them. But governments do not always understand what is going on around them, and they are hampered in their adjustment of national interests to policy by a variety of forces. Even where there is no direct opposition from other powers, even where a government seems in a position internationally to do as it wishes, its pursuit of national interests will be affected by the changing character of the circumstances in which it is operating, and the persistence of a national image which may not be appropriate to the new conditions. Broadly speaking, the Commonwealth countries outside Britain began their experience of the postwar world with three kinds of national image. That which had characterized South Africa and Canada was predominantly of a nation securing its own free status peaceably, and preparing to cut a dash in the world of states; that of Australia and New Zealand was of countries still predominantly British, though troubled by wartime difficulties which had made unaccustomed associations necessary; and that of

India and Pakistan was of a totally new world, made fresh and clean by the withdrawal of British power, and capable of any result which the will might seek to bring about. All three of these broad attitudes have suffered from the impact of major international forces, as we shall see. In the late 1950's they were joined by a fourth kind of image, that of the emerging African countries. In its most extreme form, as displayed by Ghana, this was an image not simply of national self-assertion, but also of the need to free the whole of Africa from European and white settler control. This image too has suffered some change, but, as the most recent and politically the most active, it has retained much of its early condition.

Britain has been intimately concerned with the development of national images by the other Commonwealth countries; it is appropriate that we should now examine the impact of postwar forces upon the interests and policies of Britain itself.

Chapter Seven

BRITAIN

THERE are three traditional British interests: the Empire, trade, and the inviolability of British shores. It is possible to find a fourth in the encouragement of free governments abroad, although this has not been pursued so consistently as the other three.

Historically, the three traditional interests were served by British naval and military power. New territories were either acquired by arms or defended by garrisons or units of the British fleet; the Navy provided a world-wide threat to any European power which might make war on Britain at home, try to steal British possessions or menace the trade routes; the Indian Army provided a reservoir of power for use in Asia, the Middle East and even Africa. The management of forces overseas required considerable skill, which was not always forthcoming. Nevertheless, in the days of surface transport the system of a big fleet and small strategically-placed garrisons was sufficient to satisfy the first two British interests—so long as the third, the preservation of Britain's own shores, could also be satisfied. The method used was that of alliances with the principal friendly powers in Europe. It is not necessary to show that British governments were either very ingenious or very devious in the operation of the balance of power, in order to suggest that British safety demanded a friendly coalition on the Continent. And it would be taking too ideological a view of European politics to suggest that this coalition was always found among "free" countries. Yet it is a fact that in both the wars of the twentieth century, Britain was allied with more democracies than despotisms, and opposed to more despotisms than democracies. In so far as the fourth interest was pursued, it provided a reinforcement to the third; it was sometimes argued that it provided a reinforcement to all three.[1]

But today all these conceptions must be seen differently, in the light of the forces already discussed. The whole notion of the Empire and its preservation must be put in different terms, in the light of the disintegration of a unified imperial foreign policy, and the appearance of Commonwealth member-nations with inter-

[1] This was the contention of Eyre Crowe's famous memorandum of 1907.

ests and policies of their own. In addition, the anticipated further disintegration of "the Empire", as more dependencies become independent, means that British interests in this field must obviously change. The protection and expansion of trade remains a solid British interest, but its content must change as protectionist measures, invention, currency difficulties and strategic embargoes combine to complicate the simple nineteenth-century pattern of an industrial Britain processing the raw materials which are all that other countries can produce. The inviolability of British shores is something which any government must strive for; but developments in warfare which relegate navies to guard duties and make it possible to render the whole of Britain uninhabitable, demand quite new relationships. Of the four interests mentioned, it is the fourth and least consistent which has been most strengthened by recent events. Alliance with a Communist state would now be difficult for a British government to contemplate, unless that state was in full opposition to the main centres of Communist power. Communism as a political system is Oriental despotism rendered technically efficient; on the face of it, one of the principal tests to be made before choosing an ally is whether that ally has what nineteenth-century British opinion would have called a "free" or "liberal" system, or is likely to develop one. If not, it will hardly be regarded as trustworthy.

Given that traditional British interests have been modified under the stress of contemporary forces, what effects have these forces had upon the behaviour of British governments in the international field? In the first place, British ideas about Empire have obviously been modified considerably by the realization that far-flung territories with rebellious peoples are no longer either governable or defensible. The movement for self-government of the colonies has not had to rely entirely upon such reasoning—it has always had a good head of moral steam to give it pressure—but there is no doubt that the acceptance of self-government for the African and Asian colonies has been greatly eased by the recognition that the rise of new nations and the development of modern weapons make such colonies expensive luxuries. Until the international agreements of 1959, the demand for self-government in Cyprus received little consideration. The reason was the belief that Cyprus, unlike colonies in Africa and Asia, was in fact essential to defence. It had been retained in the face of pressure because successive British governments considered that Britain could still afford a Middle East policy as part of her general defence of her interests, and that Cyprus was necessary for this. But no such arguments have been used about colonies farther afield, with the doubtful exception of Aden. The ring of outer British defence bases is closing in, under the pressure of British incapacity to provide the massive armaments which would be needed to equip a ring with a circumference farther flung.

Another result has been to make postwar British governments increasingly reluctant to take much hand in Asian affairs, in spite of their determination still to intervene in Middle East affairs. A century ago, British intervention in China and other parts of Asia was regarded as normal. This assumption persisted in some degree until the 1930's, when British inability to check Japanese attacks on British interests, and to contain Japanese interference in China, showed that British power could no longer be extended so far. The postwar years have seen the further development of this incapacity. Defeat by Japanese arms, wiped out only by American counter-effort, was followed for British Asian policy by the rise of new nations in former colonial territories, and then by the sudden appearance of a Chinese regime capable for the first time of not only defending China against foreigners but also extending Chinese influence by force. The lesson of these developments has been read and absorbed by most influential sections of British opinion. A war with China has been seen to be suicidal; not only "the wrong war in the wrong place against the wrong enemy", but also a war in which Britain could do little but gesture, and might lose much. A good deal of Britain's postwar anxiety about the preservation of the Commonwealth can be understood only in terms of the government's wish to have friends among the new nations of Asia, and not to be involved in such agonizing struggles as those of the French in Indo-China and the Dutch in Indonesia, or a war with China which might develop into one with the Soviet Union. Trade has played only a small part in this reasoning, in spite of American suspicions that Britain has recognized Communist China in order to enhance British trade and keep Hong Kong. From the British point of view, Asia in the 1950's was a place where not much could be done except harm. British policy could not decisively change Asian relationships; but it could be exerted to hinder American efforts to change the existing position in China. A forward American policy in the 1950's would not have been able effectively to disrupt the Communist control in China, but would almost certainly have linked potentially friendly Asian countries with China. British membership of SEATO is thus to be interpreted, not as an attempt to liberate China from the Communists but as a wish to preserve the present position in Asia—freezing not only Communist gains but also Britain's own right to decide the future of her present dependencies. At the same time Britain has shown a wish to give military aid to other Commonwealth countries under threat, such as Malaysia and India.

Britain has begun to contract out of Asia. But in Europe she is still contracting in. All postwar governments in Britain have been convinced that Britain ought to be in the closest possible alliance with France, the Low Countries, the Scandinavian countries, and, if possible, Germany; and also that American intervention in Europe is essential. A similar conviction has been manifest among the European governments. But there have been important differences of emphasis which have involved British governments in continual fruitless negotiations with European countries. British demands were fairly well satisfied by NATO, an alliance to which the United States was committed, which contained in addition to Britain another Commonwealth member (Canada), and which provided for the co-ordinated defence of Western Europe against Russian attack. The only liabilities which Britain incurred were those of having to consult with other countries in Western Europe, and having American forces stationed on British soil. Neither was felt to be a discomfort; and in return Britain secured defence in depth across the European continent. Also, the United States was committed to European defence more thoroughly than anyone familiar with pre-war conditions would have considered possible. But the other countries of Western Europe were not satisfied with this situation—nor was the United States. Predominant European opinion was in favour of a closer political and economic relationship between Britain and the several states of Western Europe, in order to secure some of the benefits of large-scale economic organization and to even up living standards. In American eyes, this amounted to the sort of common-sense arrangement which the American States had arrived at in the eighteenth century; and it looked like a means of strengthening democratic forces generally. From the British point of view it had several drawbacks. One was directly related to the Commonwealth: it was that British colonial policy and British relations with her former dependencies might both receive nothing but harm from a closer political association with such notorious "colonialists" as the French, Dutch and Belgians. A policy of full political union with Europe would, in any case, leave no room for continuance of the Commonwealth on anything like its present basis. There were also doubts about the effect on Britain's economic relations with the Commonwealth of any closer association with Europe. The particular matter seized on was Imperial Preference; but there were others less obvious, which might cause a weakening of Commonwealth relations. Among these were the possibilities of British investment finding Europe a more satisfying field than the Commonwealth, and European firms undercutting British firms in formerly protected areas.

The most solid British objections to closer union with Europe, however, have arisen from the problematical effects upon domestic standards of life in Britain—the possibility of an influx of foreign migrants, the difficulties of affording protection to British agriculture, the problem of retaining control over basic industries, the undermining of peculiar standards set by British trade union custom. These have reinforced the conviction of a great many British people that they are not Europeans—that in spite of geography they have more in common with Australians, Canadians and even Americans than with Frenchmen and Germans. In consequence, the story of British negotiations with Europe since the war has been one of elegant British equivocation. Britain has been ready, indeed eager, to offer military help, but reluctant to contemplate political union or to sign any economic treaties which reduced British control over the British economy. Yet at the same time there have been obvious advantages in belonging to such bodies as the European Payments Union, and in making sterling an acceptable currency to as many European countries as possible. And British economists have shown that closer connections with European markets, both to buy and sell, entail "natural" economies for Britain. To be of Europe, yet not in it, has been the British desire; against this, quite understandably, President de Gaulle has strongly emphasized that Britain cannot hope to get all the advantages of being European while evading all the disadvantages. British interests in this regard are confused, and not all realizable together. Yet it is plain that they are quite different interests from those which British politicians envisaged before the war.

In regard to the United States, there is a significant gap between what is accepted as the vital interest of continued American friendship, and any general British willingness to accept American leadership. Suspicion of American actions is still to be found in British politics. On the extreme Left and the extreme Right it is endemic. In both cases it must be attributed to envy and indignation: on the extreme Left, envy of American prosperity, and indignation that the foremost capitalist country has been able to settle its social problems without recourse to socialist measures; on the extreme Right, envy of American pre-eminence in the non-Communist world, and indignation that the leadership which is rightfully Britain's should be usurped by brash, uncivilized, indiscreet and greedy Americans. The joint effects of these groups at opposite ends of the political spectrum have occasionally made it seem that a British government might some day repudiate the American alliance. But this is impossible. One cannot envisage a British government in which the majority of members were opposed to co-operation with the United States. It is recognized that dreams of either British isolation or British leadership of a group of socialist states are only dreams; the facts of international life continually belie them. British strength is simply not enough to meet the challenge of a possible enemy; willy-nilly Britain depends upon American military help, and must play second fiddle to the United States.

Such a conclusion has plainly been arrived at by all postwar British governments. But it still leaves the problem of what to do in particular cases, and of the circumstances in which Britain would be justified in refusing to take the American lead and attempting a policy of her own. On the whole, British governments have taken the view that independent action is desirable so long as it does not strain the alliance too much. The development of the hydrogen bomb by Britain was justified on grounds of the need to preserve some independence of the United States; if Britain had the bomb, the American deterrent would not be the only one to which the Soviet Union might respond. On Asian questions, as indicated above, Britain has fairly consistently attempted to modify American policy: such issues as the Korean truce, the cease-fire in Indo-China, and the position of Formosa, have seen the two countries adopting different policies. Throughout British opinion there is a widespread fear that American foreign policy may exhibit haste, crudity, irresponsibility and weakness in the face of electoral pressure; in such circumstances, it is felt, the United States should welcome the restraining hand of a wiser Britain. But it is noticeable that on certain issues, such as disarmament and the unification of Germany, the two countries have worked harmoniously together in spite of the lead having been taken by the United States. The relationship between Britain and the United States is thus an ambivalent one. Where British *amour propre* is not outraged, and where the issues do not seem to involve vital British interests, Britain has been prepared to take second place. Where American policy seems either wrong-headed, as in China, or to cut directly across British interests, as in the Middle East, there is widespread resentment against it.

The Middle East is the area in which postwar British policy has had to face its biggest problems of deploying power and revising conceptions of the national interest. When World War II ended Britain was the most significant force in the Middle East, having defeated the Germans and Italians in North Africa, retained control of Egypt, built up the prosperity of the Sudan, continued to keep Arabs and Jews in play in Palestine, erected client states in Iraq and Transjordan, and retained primacy in the Persian Gulf. To this was added soon afterwards the virtual expulsion of the French from Syria and Lebanon. It is not surprising, in the face of this state of affairs, that British people should have continued to assume that Britain could make and unmake the Middle East at will, and have suffered dismay when events contradicted this view. Nor is it surprising that they should have expected the United States to underwrite British claims, and that the United States should not have done so. The change from the supine Egypt of 1945 to an Egypt which in 1956 could negotiate the withdrawal of British troops and then successfully command a majority of Security Council votes against Britain and France, represented an advance of nationalism which Britain alone could not prevent. The British inability to settle the Palestine question peaceably was a symptom of declining British power. The defiance of British policies by Persia, Jordan and Saudi Arabia could not be quelled; and Britain had no means of preventing Russian influence becoming manifest in Syria and Egypt. In all these instances it was easy for British opinion to turn to the United States for help in safeguarding what were felt to be vital British interests. When that help was not forthcoming it was easy, and perhaps natural too, for some British opinion to consider that American policy was made in deference to New York Jews and American oil companies and not with reference to major issues.

Here there was for long a gap between American and British conceptions of the general anti-Communist interest. It seemed obvious to much highly vocal British opinion that the preservation of British power in the Middle East was the best guarantee that a "vacuum" would not develop, to be filled by the Russians. In the event of superior British power not being available (which has in fact been the case), Britons often assumed that the United States should step in to preserve British interests, or, alternatively, to take over these interests itself—though there was some difficulty in formulating this alternative, because in some cases, notably Palestine and the general question of oil, the British argument had usually assumed that separate American and British interests were already in opposition. At all events, the United States refused to follow this reasoning, for its own assessment of the situation had begun with the view that the Middle East was an area in which "colonialism" must disappear before the Western countries would have a chance of establishing friendly relations with the local regimes, and buttressing them against Russian interference. Policies about oil and Zionism were both subsidiary to this general approach, which was the view of Mr. John Foster Dulles and explains the strong American opposition to the Suez adventure of late 1956. In the American view the Suez thrust was a throwback to a past era, an attempt to re-establish relationships which were impossible to sustain. British opinion in the matter was deeply divided; but the reasoning behind the government's decision to intervene was that Britain should still play a policeman's part in the Middle East. Although Britain might no longer police the China coast or Southern Asia, she could still call the Middle East to order.

Whether a British government would take such a view again is yet to be seen; but it seems likely that the inglorious stop to which the Suez campaign came, and the loss of British prestige, which it involved, will have a profound effect upon the future of British engagement outside Europe. Since Suez, Britain has been a fairly quiet power in the Middle East, concentrating upon South Arabia and Aden (where attempts to apply solutions successful in other colonial areas have not done much good). However, this does not represent a total withdrawal from distant commitments: as each colony has achieved independence in the 1950's and 60's, Britain has usually sought a defence agreement. Only in Malaysia has it been necessary to honour the agreement in fighting terms; elsewhere it has either lapsed or been a matter of peaceful assistance.

The stress of contemporary forces upon Britain has thus made her abandon some areas in which she was previously interested, and concentrate more upon her immediate surroundings. Her greater interest in Europe is itself an aspect of the eclipse of Europe which we have seen to be one of the great happenings of the postwar period. Her dependence upon the United States, her lack of ability to deal on equal terms with the Soviet Union, her inability to subdue nationalist eruptions in the Middle East, suggest that she may be finished as a major power—that her destiny is now to become a sort of Sweden or Switzerland. But this conclusion is strongly opposed by most sections of opinion in Britain. And if one looks at the general position of Britain it is seen to be a difficult conclusion to draw, one which may in fact be incorrect. For one thing, neither Sweden nor Switzerland has the extensive colonial responsibilities which Britain has. If Britain is to finish the stated course of leading these colonies to self-government, and if she is to be responsible for their safety in the meantime, she must play a major part among the colonial powers—and in negotiation with the anti-colonialist powers. Similarly, the British economic position is dependent upon not only world-wide trade but also a world-wide financial network which is ultimately supported by the credit of the British government and its ability to keep British prestige high. Again, Britain is too big a country in terms of population, and too exposed geographically, to leave the conduct of the anti-Communist alliance to the United States simply because the United States possesses decisive military strength. Britain is indefensible against all-out nuclear attack. In consequence, it is essential for British safety that the government should be able to influence American policy in ways which do not encourage Russian or Chinese aggression, which do not alienate the United States from foreign commitments and force it back into isolationism, and which minimize the possibility of Americans in authority setting off a war by immoderate action in some particular area. Folded hands will not produce the results which Britain wants.

Yet, clearly, military strength will not produce them either, because Britain has not enough of it. Deployed alone, it might lead to more Suez fiascos. What else can Britain bring to bear to achieve the results desired? It is here, perhaps, that we can find the principal significance of the Commonwealth as an element in British foreign policy. Being "the centre of a great Commonwealth" (a phrase much used by British politicians, the legal overtones of which are incorrect, though the common sense of the words is reliable enough), Britain is able to give the impression that she carries more weight in world affairs than her military strength alone might warrant. Since the Commonwealth contains groups of both white and coloured nations, and exists by virtue of the consent of its members and not by any sort of coercion, Britain can claim that, since she is the only major power involved in such a grouping of states, she can interpret one group to another and so provide an effective link between the white and coloured non-Communist worlds. Again, since the Commonwealth contains North American, European, African and Asian members, each of them with other associations in its immediate vicinity, it can be said to act as a meeting-place for opinions and policies which otherwise would not be found in one another's company.

It has already been pointed out—and is, indeed, often reiterated by British politicians—that the Commonwealth is an association of sovereign states, and that, although all the other members are former dependencies of Britain, Britain now exercises no control over them. It is this fact which gives the Commonwealth its unique quality. Nevertheless, the association retains a strong British tinge. The meetings of Prime Ministers have all, up to 1964, taken place in London. The British Prime Minister has always been host. The Queen, while she is constitutionally Queen of each of the realms and Head of the Commonwealth, is manifestly Queen of the United Kingdom; there she has her home, and there the greater part of her time is spent—only there does she perform personally all the functions of a constitutional monarch. The members all have English as an official language, and all have important financial and trade ties with Britain. If any British government should wish to give the impression that the combined weight of the members, or even of only some of them, lies behind British policy, it is not for the United States or other foreign countries to question the statement. They would soon become so enmeshed in constitutional detail as to make the effort of doubt not worth while.

I have deliberately overdrawn the possibility of the Commonwealth being considered a reinforcement to British foreign policy because it is fairly clear that it has suited both Britain and the members so to overdraw it at certain times. When a French newspaper headed its story on the 1953 Prime Ministers' meeting, *Le Commonwealth Derrière Sir Winston*,[1] it paid tribute to an effect which the British government had been most anxious to achieve. In the arguments with the United States over the Korean cease-fire and Indo-China, it is fairly certain that Sir Anthony Eden "pulled a Nehru" on Mr. Dulles—i.e. that he was able to show that Britain spoke not only for herself but for the Asian Commonwealth countries too. One of the most puzzling aspects of the Eden government's Suez intervention was its departure from what had previously been general policy—the co-ordination of British policy with Indian and Canadian views so that, if there was to be a divergence from American policy, Britain would be able to quote her Commonwealth partners in support of what she was doing. Given that the Suez policy would almost certainly have been rejected in advance by India and Canada, it is still surprising, in view of the importance which British governments have attached to a benevolent Commonwealth, that the Eden government proceeded with its intervention.

The Suez example shows that Commonwealth support is not regarded as the most vital of British interests, just as it showed that consultation was not an invariable British practice. Nevertheless, it is still true that the preservation of the Commonwealth as a body of states generally amicable towards Britain is regarded as an important British interest. There are two reasons for this, one relating to British foreign policy in general and the other to British colonial policy. The first is that to have the support or acquiescence of the majority of Commonwealth members gives Britain considerable bargaining power: she has greater manoeuvrability

[1] *Le Monde*, June 10, 1953.

in diplomatic negotiations if she can "pull a Nehru" on those with whom she is discussing policy. The Commonwealth countries are important enough in their own right, in terms of wealth, population and strategy, to make them worth-while partners. But even more important is the vague sense of increased power which Britain derives from the existence of the Commonwealth. The Commonwealth is such a mystery to other countries that British governments can often imply more unity of policy between themselves and other members than exists in fact. At the same time, the fact that the Commonwealth has members in all the continents except South America means that Britain can hope to use the services of other members as go-betweens in delicate negotiations. The use of India for former access to Communist China is the most notable instance; but Pakistan has served the same purpose in negotiations with the Arab states, and Canada and Australia have done so at times when British relations with the United States were strained. The fact that the Commonwealth can be termed "multi-racial" enables Britain to defend herself against charges of seeking white supremacy. And the vague feeling that, in the long run, the interests of Commonwealth countries are identical with Britain's, is evidently a comfort to British politicians and publicists when they consider the possibilities of foreign policy. In general terms, then, the preservation of the Commonwealth as a collection of friendly states is a major British interest.

It is also a major British interest in the field of colonial policy. Not only does the existence of the Commonwealth enable Britain to assert an effortless superiority over other European countries which have, or have had, colonial empires and have been unable to come to terms with their ex-colonies. In addition, the fact that the Commonwealth exists and is continually reinforced by new members, such as Ghana and Malaya, has made the process of self-government easier in the remaining British dependencies. It meant that the African and Asian colonies had a definite goal to aim at. Just as it was possible in 1921 to promise Ireland a status like Canada's, so later it was possible to promise Nigeria a status like India's or Ghana's. No other colonial power has such a device at its hand. It has even been used in connection with the "fortress territories"—areas held for their strategic importance alone, such as Cyprus, Malta and Gibraltar—where the Commonwealth pattern, as elsewhere, provides the road to independence; it supplies the key to peaceful autonomy, provided that agreement can be achieved between communal groups within the territory concerned.

Obviously, then, the existence of the Commonwealth is a matter of great moment for British policy. Most British politicians would agree that they ought to go to considerable lengths to preserve harmony within the Commonwealth, and prevent the association deteriorating or falling to pieces through the secession of any substantial number of members. They regard the Commonwealth relationship as a fortunate dispensation, sent to smooth Britain's path through the world, and to be retained at most—if not all—costs. Most of them are well aware of the change from Empire to Commonwealth, and of the fact that only by treating Commonwealth members as sovereign states, on a basis of strict equality with Britain, will cordiality be preserved. But in this regard there has been a wider gap than usual between the politicians' appreciation of a situation and the public's. The tone of some British newspapers, and of a good deal of popular discussion, seems to suggest that many British people are still Hegelians at heart, in the sense of the quotation in a previous chapter: they are the men to whom the East Indies belong, and their riches. There is a *proprietorial* tone about much popular discussion which suggests that the public at large has not caught up with the march of events and the politicians' appreciation of it; and that, on the whole, the politicians prefer this state of affairs. It would obviously be more difficult to explain to the public that the Commonwealth is simply a loose association, an assembly of convenience, than to maintain or (more usually) to imply that it is somehow dependent upon British wisdom and direction, even though it stands on a basis of autonomy. But in the long run it is probably more in British interests to present the Commonwealth frankly to opinion at home and abroad as what it is rather than what emotion might wish it to be. This does at least forestall public indignation at un-British practices in Ghana and incipient neutralism in Ceylon; and it can make the British position less embarrassing internationally at times when Britain finds herself without substantial Commonwealth support.

It is possible now to see how the traditional British interests have been transformed by the pressure of events in our time, and especially by the growth of the Commonwealth as an association of sovereign states. "The Empire" exists now only in so far as there are still territories dependent upon Britain. The idea of retaining these indefinitely operates only in regard to some fortress territories and a few St. Helenas and Falkland Islands, for which no means of independence has yet been devised. For the rest, British interest now lies in turning as many colonies as possible into Commonwealth members as quickly as possible, thereby short-circuiting the effects of colonial nationalism, and retaining such ties, economic, cultural, and the like, as will be of mutual benefit to Britain and the colonies in question. "The Commonwealth" has now replaced "the Empire" as a basic British interest. This does not mean that Britain's interest lies in making Commonwealth countries obey her. She has neither the power nor the inclination for this, although now and then there are stirrings of opinion which suggest that some British people would like to discipline Commonwealth countries which show too great a concern either for neutralism or for American friendship. Britain's interest lies rather in showing such understanding and generosity towards the members of the Commonwealth as will cause them to stay in the association and spontaneously to range themselves alongside Britain on major issues, or at any rate not to oppose her with violence. It lies in the Commonwealth growing as a unique grouping of a former colonial power with its ex-dependencies; not as an alliance, a customs union or an association of mutual guarantee, but as a body showing marked British characteristics, and providing prestige for Britain while not detracting from the sovereignty of the other members. Britain's policy towards the Commonwealth has been one of losing her life to save it, of relinquishing control and responsibility in order to secure support or friendly neutrality.

Trade remains a solid British interest, but it must now be seen as involving currency arrangements, investment and the confidence of Sterling Area members in Britain. On the political side, the safeguarding of Britain's external economic position takes in much the same sort of interest as the preservation of the Commonwealth. Trade can be neither safeguarded nor instituted by military force, as it could be in the nineteenth century. Mutual confidence and diplomatic bargaining are the means which must be used to expand opportunities for British trade—aside altogether from the inventiveness and productivity which are necessary in strictly economic terms. The Commonwealth association helps, even where no formal contract such as the Ottawa agreements is involved. The Sterling Area's close correspondence with the Commonwealth enables sterling to be the principal currency actively at work in international trade, and British dollar purchases to be financed sometimes by other countries' dollar earnings. As between Europe and the Commonwealth, the British interest is to choose neither to the exclusion of the other, but to keep both as markets and sources of supply while reserving most of her surplus capital for Commonwealth investment. In such a situation it is an advantage that the Commonwealth is not a customs unit or any other sort of economic unit.

The inviolability of British shores has now to be seen as part of a larger need for the inviolability of Western Europe, and perhaps of a need larger again for the preservation of the earth from nuclear destruction. Certainly the immediate British interest has been expanded into the preservation of the "Atlantic Community"—i.e. West European military unity with American and Canadian backing. In this regard the Commonwealth is no embarrassment to Britain, since she is under no general contractual obligation to defend other member-nations, and need not do so, except where special treaties have been signed. Her direct defence obligations extend only to the colonies, and are liquidated as each colony attains independence; whether new obligations are assumed is a matter for British calculation, and for discussion between the ex-colony and Britain. Britain has been freed from the imponderable pre-war obligation to provide naval defence for the whole of the Commonwealth.

The fourth, but intermittent, traditional British interest, which was defined as the encouragement of free governments abroad, remains effectively in being, but with two distinct aspects. One is direct alliance with anti-Communist states which show their determination to preserve their independence. The other, which may overlap with this, is the active creation of new states with democratic regimes—not necessarily anti-Communist, but certainly non-Communist at their inception, and able to choose the kind of regime they will have in future. The enlargement of the Commonwealth is the second of these aspects. From the British point of view it has the advantage of extending the area of friendship among new sovereign states, at a time when many new sovereign states which are created by different processes (such as

Tunisia, Cambodia and Indonesia) tend to be generally unfriendly towards the European powers, of which Britain, in this context, must necessarily be counted as one.

Given fairly general agreement among politicians and students about the changes that have taken placc in British interests, it is still possible to envisage widely divergent interpretations of those interests, and policies which diverge accordingly. Sir Harold Nicolson's distinction between the "warrior or heroic" and "mercantile or shopkeeper" views of British foreign policy remains as relevant as ever. The Commonwealth can be seen in either of these lights; so can the association with the United States; so can the association with Europe; so can British interests in the Middle East and Asia. The big difference in interpretation of interests in Britain is between those who accept the country's diminished stature in the world and wish to plan accordingly in terms of diminished responsibility, and those who see this diminished stature as a temporary thing, a challenge which calls for policies of daring activity in order to regain world leadership. The distinction cuts across party lines, although, broadly speaking, there is more heroic talk in the Conservative than in the Labour Party. In the community at large I think there is more support for the heroic view than for its opposite, so long as action is confined to symbolic gestures and does not extend to quarrels with major powers. Among politicians, civil servants and academics there is probably more support for the shopkeeper view. The clash between these two kinds of interpretation might decide, at any given time, which line of action was taken by the British government. A strong element of uncertainty remains.

Chapter Eight

CANADA

In attempting to trace British national interests, we are concerned with a country which has built up its particular sense of national consciousness over a long period of time, and which has long been skilled in the management of foreign affairs. Neither of these characteristics applies to the other member-nations of the Commonwealth. Canada has had longest to develop its national self-respect, and has had a longer continuous experience of diplomacy than the others; even so, Canada is a newcomer in the world of states, compared with Britain. In considering the search for interests in policies on the part of the various Commonwealth members, we must bear in mind both their incomplete development of self-consciousness and their diplomatic immaturity. As I have already suggested they have had to work out, first, by trial and error, what being a nation involves for them; and then they have had to improvise policies to reconcile this understanding with the course of events. It is worth remembering, as we proceed, that for each of them the Commonwealth has performed the function of providing both a nursery for nationalism and a sphere in which to practise diplomacy. This is an advantage which their leaders might hesitate to proclaim, since it emphasizes their immaturity as nation-states; nevertheless, it is a very real advantage to young countries.

Canada has been, in many ways, the pioneer among Commonwealth members. It is often said that the present concept of Commonwealth owes more to Canadian thinking and Canadian pressure than to any other influence. Canada led the demands for a clear statement of Dominion status in 1926, and has been prominent in deciding the internal constitutional position of the Commonwealth; Canada appointed the first High Commissioner in London; Canada was the first Dominion to take part (with Britain) in international consultations leading to treaties with foreign countries. There was talk of "Canadian interests" being sacrificed to British well before interests were being formulated in the other parts of the Empire. The reason for this pioneering, so far as it related to external matters, is plain: Canada was the only one of the original Dominions to be forced by geography into continual intercourse with a Great Power outside the Empire. The existence of the United States has been from the beginning a challenge to Canadians. Politically, it has offered the example of an alternative system of democracy and a different tradition of how self-government might be acquired. Economically, it has offered both opportunities and dangers. Geographically, it has been, and is still, impossible for Canadians to ignore the United States; but geography provides few clues to the particular interests which Canadian policy ought to pursue. For a hundred years, the main problem for Canadians in working out their national interests has been that of deciding the terms on which they should associate with the United States. It is often said that the North Atlantic Triangle, with Canada, the United States and Britain as its three points, is the basis on which Canadian policy must be constructed. But it has never been an equilateral triangle: the British point was always farther away from Canada than the American, and the effect of economics and strategy today is to increase the distance between Canada and Britain and narrow the side of the triangle joining Canada with the United States. This effect provides no obvious solution to the Canadian problem. All it does is to make more urgent the quest for Canadian national unity, and for clear-cut national interests, which Canadian politicians have been pursuing since confederation in 1867.

Three main elements enter into the Canadian quest for national interests in relation to the United States. They are respectively economic, strategic and patriotic.

Economically, there are forces which draw Canada to the United States and forces which repel her. She is heavily dependent upon American investment for the development of the great twentieth-century Canadian industries, such as oil and iron ore. Although she consistently buys more from the United States than she sells to it, the difference in her balance of payments has been consistently made up, since the war, by capital imports from the United States. At the same time a good deal of Canadian money has been invested in profitable American concerns, and the easy exchange between the Canadian dollar and the American dollar enables Canadians to enjoy the best which the United States has to offer—so long as the flow of American capital into Canada continues. Apart from investment, much Canadian trade and intercourse has developed on a north–south basis and would be impossible to carry on under any other conditions. Without the insatiable demands of Americans for big newspapers, for example, the Canadian newsprint industry would be in a sorry state. The flow of population between the two countries, turning this way and that in accordance with their comparative prosperity, has also been an economic bond of considerable importance.

But there are economic conflicts between the two countries as well as economic bonds. Some arise directly from the bonds, such as the Canadian awareness that to be dependent upon a constant flow of American capital is to have one's prosperity interwoven with a neighbour's. However, the main economic conflicts arise not from dependence but from competition. In agricultural products—mainly wheat—Canada is a direct competitor with the United States in foreign markets, and is adversely affected by improvements in American efficiency or by U.S. government policies which subsidize the export of American wheat and other competing products. In manufactures, ever since the decision was made to protect Canadian industry and not to have reciprocity between Canada and the United States, there has been continual Canadian concern that the tariff should provide a safeguard against cheap American products—though this has meant, also, conflicts at times within Canada herself when the western provinces, beggared by low food prices, have clamoured for cheaper manufactures. The general picture of economic relations between Canada and the United States is of increasing prosperity for both, so long as prosperity holds in the United States and American investors are ready to put their money into unexploited Canadian resources. But the drawbacks are implicit in the increasing prosperity: if American prosperity should falter, American markets would become tighter, American investment might decline, and Canadian prosperity might prove extremely hard to re-finance at a lower level, given the probability of massive unsaleable stocks of Canadian-grown food. It is too late now to integrate the two economies; and the association between them must inevitably be far more of a problem to the smaller partner than to the bigger. A definition of Canadian national interests will always, therefore, provide scope for controversy at the level of economics.

Strategically, there is rather less room for debate. Canadians know that, whichever of the United States' allies is expendable,

Canada is not. Whether the prospective enemy were Russia, China or some revitalized West European power, Canada would be essential to American strategy. So long as the prospective enemy is Russia, Canada's northern wastes will be the location of the various radar warning systems which are meant to give notice to the United States of a Soviet air attack. This is a new and perplexing situation for Canadians. It makes them indispensable to the United States; but it also makes them a more obvious target for attack than if they were not providing defence in depth for that country. It enables Canadian diplomats to be franker and less complimentary towards American policy than other allies can afford to be; but it commits them irrevocably to American military action in the North American continent. In former times, when a possible attack on the continent had to be naval in character, Canadian defence could be seen as simply a matter of either sheltering behind the American fleet or adding to it some marginal naval contribution. The wars in which Canada did participate took place far from her shores and were undertaken from sentiment and prudence, not for survival. This is not likely to be the case in the future: any major war in which Canada takes part will almost certainly be a war for survival, in which the whole North American continent is involved. This strategic probability has been one of the reasons why Canada has carried on such a vigorous foreign policy since the war. Its object has been to avoid a general conflagration between the Great Powers, and, in particular, to exercise a restraining influence upon the policy of the United States. It is obvious that general war could prove fatal to Canada's centres of population; and in consequence Canada has used every means in her power to see that general war should not occur. In this regard her interest as a neighbour of the United States merges imperceptibly into her interest as a member, not only of the Commonwealth, but of the general community of nations.

However, it has been in what I have called the patriotic field that the main problem of defining Canadian interests in relation to the United States has been evident throughout Canadian history. The United States, established as it was and developing as it has developed, has been a perpetual challenge to Canadians to distinguish for themselves the kind of people they are and the kind of nation to which they belong. Very little is heard now in Canada about possible integration with the United States, either with consent or by force: Canada's nationhood is now beyond dispute. But, up to World War I, it was still an active question whether Canadians had sufficient national unity and sufficient strength of purpose to withstand the pressure of the United States. In this sense the problem of relations with the United States has been a major facet of the problem of Canadian national unity. That problem has had other facets too; and it is no accident that both Canadian historians and Canadian politicians have made it their major theme.

First, there has been the physical problem of a vast area unevenly covered with people, and continually in the process of advancing its frontiers of development. In this regard the problem of unity of Canada has been rather like that of the United States: a problem of old-established settlements in the east, of the extension of settlement by way of the great rivers, of a vast hinterland only gradually mastered and put to use, and of an extension of settlement to the Pacific at a time when the intervening areas were hardly opened up. But for Canada this process has imposed greater difficulties in constructing a viable nation. Canada covers something like the same area as the United States but has only a tenth of the population; if people have been spread sparsely over the United States, they have been far more sparsely spread over Canada. To this problem of sheer communication between the settlements (in their political form as provinces) has been added the constant southward pull of the United States. In British Columbia, the pull has been towards Oregon and Washington; in the prairie provinces, towards the similar wheatlands of the Middle West; in Ontario, towards Michigan; in Quebec, towards Maine, Vermont and upper New York. In all these cases the American attractions of closeness and similar economic conditions have often meant more to Canadians than the preservation of their own tenuous connection. To be effective, Canadian national sentiment must stretch from east to west and back; it has been the constant challenge of geography that movement of men and ideas has been easier from north to south. Well over half the Canadian population lives within a hundred miles of the United States border.

The fact that movement has been easier on a north–south axis than an east–west one has proved a further problem for Canada because of the differences in ethnic origins of her people. French Canadians from Quebec have not diffused themselves over Canada;

they have either stayed put or drifted into contiguous American territory. The predominantly British stock of the Maritime Provinces and Newfoundland has not moved to Quebec or the Prairies; the German and Scandinavian settlers of the Prairies have often had more in common with similar ethnic groups across the American border than with their formal compatriots in Canada. Communalism in Canada, created by differential immigration (differential not only in ethnic terms but also in time), has been fostered by geography and sometimes by inclination and religion. Simply by looking at the map and noting the ethnic origins of Canadians, we can see that the creation of Canadian unity would be a hard task.

Historically, various solutions have been proposed. One was that advocated by Goldwin Smith and some other Canadians in the nineteenth century, that Canada should be merged in the greater unity of the United States. This had a superficial plausibility; but it foundered on the arrogance of Americans, and the determination of Canadians of various origins to retain the religious, political and economic advantages which the Canadian federal constitution offered them. Even when Canadians disagreed violently with one another, they tended to disagree more with Americans. However, it was those internal disagreements which rendered impossible the second solution offered for the problem of Canadian nationality, that of assimilation of Canadians generally to the British pattern of culture, economic advancement and political loyalty. This solution, propounded in the Durham Report and wistfully reverted to by British-minded Canadians in times of national and international crisis, was nullified from the beginning by the intransigence of Quebec, expressing the determination of French Canadians to preserve their language, religion, laws and customs. Later on, with heavy immigration into Canada from Germany, Scandinavia and other parts of Europe, it became even less effective.

If Canada was not to be swamped in the United States or anchored to the traditional symbols of British unity, only one solution remained: to make a Canadian nation. Some internal policies could obviously help in this, such as Sir John Macdonald's schemes for national protection and for railway communication between east and west. So long as these were not cut across by divisions over religion, language and culture—and they often were—it was possible to imagine a Canadian nation emerging slowly from the tightening of economic bonds and the growth of a common concern to preserve Canadian institutions from Americanization. Both these influences have been powerful in building Canadian unity. But in themselves they were not enough. To be effective, Canadian national unity needed the symbols of national status. And it is here that the Commonwealth, as a form of political association, has been of crucial importance in Canadian development. So long as Canada remained a subordinate part of the British Empire, Canadian pretensions to national status could be derided in the United States; there would always be a ready audience in Canada for suggestions that Canadian interests were being subordinated to British; and there would remain, among Canadians of non-British stock, a continual suspicion that the unsuccessful Durham policy of assimilating them into the stream of British culture would some day be pursued again. So long as Canada remained subordinate, there would be opportunities for British-minded Canadians to assert that their fellow-citizens who were lukewarm about loyalty to Britain were bad citizens of Canada. On the other hand, if there was any attempt to sever Canada's connection with Britain altogether, this would alienate those same British-minded Canadians; and it would bring closer, for all Canadians, the unwelcome prospect of absorption into the United States. Dominion status provided a solution which enabled Canadian national sentiment to develop unfettered, but preserved links with Britain which many Canadians held dear. This is why Canadian historians attach such importance to the development of Dominion status, and why one of them can assert of his country: "For generations, against all kinds of opposition both positive and negative, Canada had pursued this goal. To a very large extent, the principle of Dominion status was her own creation—her main contribution to the science of world politics."[1] Once Dominion status was gained, Canadian national sentiment could develop, and with it the symbols and policies of a nation-state.

However, the opportunity to develop a Canadian national consciousness and a sense of unity was not in itself enough to establish those sentiments. They could very easily be affronted and dispelled. In World War I the apparent unity with which Canada had entered the conflict was shattered by the Borden government's

[1] D. G. Creighton, *Dominion of the North* (Boston, 1944), p. 479.

proposal to introduce conscription, which drove a wedge between English- and French-speaking Canadians and poisoned understanding between them. Thus, when Canada did eventually achieve, in the 1920's, the opportunity to develop her own foreign policy, the principal aim of that policy had to be the avoidance of situations in which the fissiparous tendencies of Canadian society might get another chance to work. In particular, Canadian statesmen between the wars were alarmed at the possibility that Canada might be drawn again into a European quarrel. Canada showed a cautious attitude towards the League of Nations from the beginning of her membership; in the Italo-Abyssinian crisis the Canadian government went so far as to disown its representative at Geneva because he seemed to be supporting League action against Italy; and as late as March 1939, the Canadian Prime Minister, Mr. Mackenzie King, had this to say about the factors underlying foreign policy:[1]

> "The first factor is the one that is present and dominant in the policy of every other country, from Britain and Sweden to Argentina and the United States. I mean the existence of a national feeling and the assumption that first place will be given to the interests, immediate or long-range, of the country itself. The growth of national feeling in Canada has been inevitable at a time when nationalism has come to dominate every quarter of the world. . . . A strong and dominant national feeling is not a luxury in Canada, it is a necessity. Without it the country could not exist. . . .
>
> "In many, but certainly not in all cases, this growth of national feelings has strengthened the desire for a policy which its defenders call minding one's own business and which its critics call isolationism. Assuming, it is urged, that Canadians like other people will put their own interests first, what do our interests demand, what amount of knight errantry abroad do our resources permit? . . . We have tremendous tasks to do at home . . . we must, to a greater or less extent, choose between keeping our own house in order, and trying to save Europe and Asia. The idea that every twenty years this country should automatically and as a matter of course take part in a war overseas for democracy or self-determination of small nations, that a country which has all it can do to run itself should feel called upon to save, periodically, a continent that cannot run itself, and to these ends risk the lives of its people, risk bankruptcy and political disunion, seems to many a nightmare and sheer madness."

[1] Quoted in Frank H. Underhill, *The British Commonwealth* (Durham, N.C., 1956), p. 62.

There are several things to note here. First, King did not commit himself to the condemnation of Europe which he voiced; he quoted others, though with implied approval. Second, he did not adopt a policy of isolationism, but made it clear that he regarded it as a policy which might prove necessary if Canada was to have the strong and dominant national feeling which he considered a necessity. Third, what he said was challenged by some of his political opponents, who argued for a more definite Canadian position in world affairs. In the light of these considerations it is worth stressing, at the risk of repetition, that what King had most in mind was the effect upon his citizens of European and American extraction of ill-considered intervention in the affairs of Europe. He feared a divided country. When he was sure that intervention would bring unity and not division, he was quite happy to recommend intervention; less than six months after the speech just quoted he led Canada successfully into World War II, and justified his former stand as follows: [1]

> "I have made it the supreme endeavour of my leadership of my party, and my leadership of the government of this country, to let no hasty or premature threat or pronouncement create mistrust and divisions between the different elements that compose the population of our vast dominion, so that when the moment of decision came all should so see the issue itself that our national effort might be marked by unity of purpose, of heart, and of endeavour."

King's opponents would not have dissented strongly from this, though they might have urged on him a different time-table of declaration; they too, in the years between the wars, recognized the great need for policies which would strengthen or at least not weaken Canadian unity. On the whole, these were policies of a quiet life, of wait and see, of saying little and doing less—except in relation to the United States, the country with which it was necessary to have continuous contact. So far as the rest of the world was concerned Canada's policy might have been described, in one of the clichés of Australian political language, as a necklace of negatives. A more dignified Canadian way of putting the same point is to say that the three dogmas of Canadian policy were "imprecision, no commitments and a reluctance even to consult

[1] Quoted in Nicholas Mansergh, *Survey of British Commonwealth Affairs: Problems of External Policy, 1931–1939* (London, 1952), p. 111.

with other nations on the major issues which could threaten the peace".[1]

Canada today is plainly a different sort of country in its approach to international affairs. It is prominent in NATO; it has taken on a number of thankless tasks from the United Nations, such as service on the Indo-China truce committee and participation in the international force to patrol the Sinai desert; and its spokesmen at the United Nations are among the most vocal there. Moreover, it has expanded its diplomatic staff and the range of its international contacts far beyond anything envisaged before 1939. Its policy is now emphatically a positive one. Does this mean that the quest for national unity is over, and that it need no longer be the one overriding Canadian interest? Lester B. Pearson, who served for a decade as Secretary of State for External Affairs in the government of Louis St. Laurent, evidently thought that this was so:[2]

> "... Our society of two cultures has by now reached the more mature stage where foreign policy can be formulated as a result primarily of a dispassionate analysis of the foreign situation.
>
> "In the '30's we were intensely preoccupied with the effect of our foreign policy upon the unity of our country. But in the '50's we are also concerned with the connection between that policy and the unity of the coalition against aggression in which Canada is playing an active part. Hence the problem of seeking unity has been vastly enlarged in scope and complexity."

Whether Mr. Pearson was right or not about the maturity of Canadian society, it does seem that the present active position of Canada is one which she is forced to assume, and that her vigorous international activity since 1945 has itself been one of the forces creating national unity. Whereas in the 1920's and 1930's it was possible for Canadians to repeat the shibboleth that they lived in a fire-proof house, far from any source of danger, in the 1950's they lived next door to a fire-trap (the United States) and not far distant from a potential fire-bug (the Soviet Union). The fact that the likely enemy is the Soviet Union has been, in itself, a force for

[1] Formulated by Escott Reid in an article in *Canadian Journal of Economics and Political Science*, 1937; quoted by L. B. Pearson in "Some Thoughts on Canadian External Relations" to the Canadian Historical Association, Winnipeg, June 4, 1954.

[2] *Ibid.*

unity: to French-Canadians the Soviet Union is the spearhead of "godless Communism"; to Canadians of German, Polish and Scandinavian extraction it is the country which has overrun or threatened to enslave their lands of origin. Also, the fact that the United States and Britain have been united in opposition to the Soviet Union, and in attempts to unify European resistance to Communist aggression, has meant the removal of another potential source of Canadian disunity, a choice between the other two points of the North Atlantic Triangle. As Mr. Pearson indicates, Canadian policy has been directed towards the unity of the anti-Communist coalition. This may now be taken as the major interest of Canada in world affairs, an interest demanding deftness and care in diplomacy and a high level of sophistication in the Canadian body politic.

Now, having seen the basic elements of Canadian relations with the United States, the background of Canadian disunity in the past and allegedly greater maturity today, and the awareness of Canadian governments of the need for Canada to pursue an active foreign policy, we are in a position to describe Canadian interests and see how these have fared in the attempt to make them effective; also to see what differences exist between the major Canadian political parties in their approach to foreign policy.

The major Canadian interest, as suggested above, is the unity of the anti-Communist coalition. There are several reasons why this should be so. One is the practical reason that Canadian security is more likely to be achieved by the deterrent effect of a Grand Alliance against Communist aggression than simply by reliance upon unilateral action by the United States, even though the striking force in any Grand Alliance must necessarily be mainly American. It is not only that a Grand Alliance provides a greater array of deterrent force, however; it is also that Canada gains in diplomatic manoeuvrability from being able to bargain with the United States within the framework of an alliance which includes other powers too. This is one reason why Canada was so prominent in the formation of NATO; another is that NATO symbolizes not only the unity of a North Atlantic Community but also the unity of British, French and other European elements within Canada's own population. Mackenzie King's careful quest for Canadian national unity is not really over. The seeds of dissension still exist in Canada; but they are inhibited by the obvious danger to Canada from a Communist power which all Canadians, in their different ways, can find reasons to dislike.

But Canada is not only an Atlantic country. She has also a Pacific coast. It is this which is primarily responsible for the postwar Canadian interest in Asia, and especially in good relations with new nations there. One can say, in fact, that the second major Canadian interest today is the avoidance of a war in Asia which might involve the United States and eventually Canada herself. The suggestion earlier in this chapter, that Canada has an interest in avoiding world conflict as such, is amply demonstrated by the postwar Canadian record in Asia. Not only have Canadian ministers and diplomats done their best to cultivate good relations with the Asian Commonwealth countries; they have also accepted commitments in Asia which indicated that Canada was prepared to go to considerable lengths to see that peace was kept there. While Canada has, on the whole, followed the American line in formal Asian relations—for example, she has not recognized the Communist government of China—in most of the Asian crises of the early 1950's she was much more in line with British policy than American. Over the crucial issue of the Formosan straits, in particular, she queried the good sense of a provocative American policy; and over the truce in Indo-China she showed herself ready to suffer American obloquy in order to provide a basis on which the truce might be made effective. It is clearly a major Canadian interest to avoid a war in Asia, and to do so by making friends with independent, uncommitted Asian nations.

Both the Canadian interests considered so far—the preservation of the Western coalition and the avoidance of war in Asia—have to do with the United States. Neither can be contemplated except in terms of Canada's relations with that country. It is impossible to imagine a catalogue of Canadian national interests which did not mention the United States at every point. Strategically, the two are bound together; it is a measure of the unanimity that binds Canadian parties in major matters that the radar warning lines built across Canada for mutual defence should have been undertaken by a Liberal government, and that one of the first acts of the Conservative government which took office in 1957 should have been to agree to the joint operational control of the air defence forces of the two countries. Nevertheless, as suggested earlier, the fact of geographical proximity to the United States does not determine precisely what Canadian interests are; it only makes urgent the careful delimitation of Canadian interests from American. The kind of delimitation which thoughtful Canadians have made goes somewhat as follows. They agree that, strategically, there is no separating the two countries, but say that this transfers attention from the fact of mutual defence to the occasion on which that defence might be needed: in other words, it creates a need for Canada to influence American policy at all points, so that the decision to fight may be taken, not only with Canada's concurrence (which is not held to be automatic), but also after Canadian influence has been exerted on American thinking. The Canadian position in this regard is akin to the British position on American bases in Britain. Britain welcomed these, but claimed the right of veto over the use of them to retaliate against the Russians with nuclear weapons. Similarly, Canadians claim the right to influence, if not veto, American use of nuclear weapons from bases on the North American continent. Canadian influence may, however, need to be exerted farther afield than North America; it may need to be exerted in Asia, for instance, in ways already described. In all cases the Canadian interest lies in damping down American excitement under provocation from Communist sources, and in seeing that nuclear war breaks out only when it is necessary and unavoidable. This is a tricky interest for a country of such a small population to pursue; yet it is vital to Canada's existence. It may be regarded as a summation of the two interests already discussed.

As indicated already, the reasons for wishing to assert Canadian interests which are separate from American are not only strategic. They are also economic and cultural, using the latter term in its widest sense. Canadians do not wish to be merged in the American economy, or to have no separate cultural life of their own. Nor do they wish to be regarded as an American satellite. This is perhaps why Canada has not attempted to join such bodies as the Pan-American Union or the Organization of American States. It is, in a way, anomalous that Canada, a characteristically North American country, should thus reject the symbols of the Monroe Doctrine, but it is understandable that Canadians should not wish to be regarded as on all-fours with what are dismissed as "banana republics" in Latin America. Indispensable to the United States, it is thus Canada's interest to assert independence from the United

States, and to demand, on all occasions, negotiation on a basis of equality.

It is now time to introduce the part played by the Commonwealth in the assessment of Canadian interests. Reference has already been made to the importance of the Commonwealth in former times in providing a framework for internal Canadian unity, and opportunities for the growth of Canadian national sentiment. That importance still remains. It was a source of pride and solidarity that Canada was a monarchy and could enjoy the presence of Queen Elizabeth, not as a stranger but as Queen of Canada, until her reception in Quebec in 1964 underlined the rift between French-Canadians and the rest. There is even advantage still in the anomalous fact that major provisions of the Canadian constitution can be changed only by the British parliament, and not directly by any Canadian authority; this entrenches the provinciality of Quebec and prevents, or at least delays, a nation-wide argument about how the constitution might be changed internally. But it is externally that the Commonwealth is of greatest advantage to Canada; and this in spite of the fact that Canada is not part of the Sterling Area.

Each of Canada's major interests in international matters is served directly by her membership of the Commonwealth. The preservation of the anti-Communist coalition is helped by Canada's close, easy, confidential relations with Britain; indeed, it is difficult to see how Canada could have been appropriately introduced into NATO without the assistance of Britain as well as of the United States. Without her Commonwealth connection, Canada would be irremovably a North American country, so tied to the coat-tails of the United States as to find it difficult to cut an effective figure in international negotiations. The gradual rise of Canadian diplomacy under the joint encouragement of Britain and the United States, but especially of Britain, has meant that Canada has been able painlessly to achieve the status of a major "middle" power. In atomic energy, in NATO, in disarmament talks, Canada is now accepted as a country that counts. She might be able now to throw off her Commonwealth connection without loss of prestige and significance, though this is debatable; but to do so would be to put herself outside the range of confidential discussion with Britain and thus into close connection with no power but the United States. As things stand, Canada can perform the function of go-between for Britain and the United States with little or no exertion: and this increases her status and capacity in diplomacy, while also committing her to no abatement of her own individual pursuit of her interests. It is perhaps the final proof of the efficacy of the Commonwealth relationship that no one in Canada questions this efficacy, that no one suggests that relations with the indispensable neighbour, the United States, would be improved if Canada were not in the Commonwealth, and that, whatever Canadians disagree about, they agree that Canada must continue to be the middle term between the other two points of the triangle.

In Canada's concern for Asian affairs, also, Commonwealth membership has helped to advance her interests. Even more than Britain herself, Canada has gone out of her way to cultivate the Asian Commonwealth members and to publicize the unique relationship in which she stands to them. At times when the United States seemed to have no other Asian contacts than the Philippines and Formosa, Canada has purposely drawn attention to the close and confidential relations in which she stands with India; and, like Britain, Canada was anxious to use India as a go-between with Communist China in fixing settlements in Korea and Indo-China. At the United Nations, Canadian representatives have gone out of their way to vote or abstain in ways and at times which would please the anti-colonial Asian members of the Commonwealth. From the Canadian point of view there is something almost providential in Canada being part of an association which not only has major uncommitted Asian states as members, but has the prospect of acquiring more. Before World War II, Canada had no interest in Asian affairs except that she felt it necessary to exclude Asians from permanent immigration into her territories. Now, however, it is a Canadian interest to woo Asian countries and see that Asia is kept free of general war; and to this end her Commonwealth connection with Britain and India, in particular, is held to be of major importance.

The importance of the Commonwealth in the pursuance of that most elusive of Canadian interests, good relations with the United States, is fairly obvious and has already been alluded to. The Commonwealth is something else for Canada to belong to—something other than the strategic and diplomatic association with the United States. It is one of the weaknesses of the Latin American states in their dealings with the United States that they are not associated with anyone but one another. The European states with which they might re-make relations are old, tired and unimportant. They are, in fact, isolated from all countries but themselves and the United States. Canada, on the other hand, can claim close acquaintance, through the Commonwealth, with states in Asia, Europe, the Pacific and Africa. She can advise the United States on the attitudes of countries with which U.S. relations are not the best. She can profess diplomatic *savoir faire* which no Latin American state could pretend to for a moment.

These are, of course, only marginal advantages. They are effective, not in the realm of power but in that of influence. There is no doubt that if the United States was determined to exert her power over Canada, Canadian objections would be of little avail. But, since both the United States and Canada are democracies, and since the United States values her reputation as a state which does not use naked power to gain its ends, it is the field of influence that matters most in negotiations between the two countries. Canada has, in any case, things to offer which the United States wants to have. Geography has seen to that. It is simply that Canada, because of her vulnerable position, wishes to attach more conditions to the sale of the goods than would ordinarily apply in such diplomatic transactions; and it is the freedom of movement which the Commonwealth affords her, the capacity to bring to bear the influence of *other* Commonwealth countries upon the United States if need be, and the promise of influence to be used elsewhere in the Commonwealth on behalf of the United States, that constitute the value of the Commonwealth as an ancillary to Canada's bargaining power.

Major Canadian interests thus resolve themselves into a series of aims, each of which is helped and not hindered by Canada's membership of the Commonwealth. This fact is appreciated by both of Canada's major political parties. Up to the fall, in 1957, of Canada's apparently perpetual government of the Liberal Party, the Commonwealth had bulked large in all the pronouncements of Mr. St. Laurent and Mr. Pearson. Both had made Asian tours in which they extolled the excellence of the Commonwealth in bringing people of different races within the same association. Both had used Commonwealth contacts extensively during the various diplomatic crises of the postwar decade. Both were startled and shocked by the lack of British consultation over Suez; it is significant that Mr. Pearson's lamentations over the event were directed mainly to the bad effect it would have on the Asian members' opinion of the Commonwealth. Both tended to bring the Commonwealth into their speeches when emphasizing Canada's independence of the United States. They were, in fact, convinced of the reality of Canada's interests, and the part the Commonwealth might play in advancing them. But where they faltered, in the opinion of their Conservative opponents, was in not carrying their enthusiasm for the Commonwealth into the economic field.

When Mr. John Diefenbaker came to office as Conservative Prime Minister after the elections of 1957, he did so, agreeing wholeheartedly with the Liberal conception of Canadian interests on the political plane, but hoping to add to this conception Canadian interests on the economic plane which would enable Canada to lessen her dependence upon American money and markets and strengthen her association with the Commonwealth. In fact, this objective proved to be a chimera. But what is important is that the Canadian Conservatives, in spite of their background of hearty sentiment about the British connection, were as well aware as the Liberals of the diplomatic advantages which the modern, flexible Commonwealth bestowed upon Canada. When their Secretary of State for External Affairs, Mr. Sidney E. Smith, made his first statement in parliament on foreign policy, he spoke with fervour of the "thrill" and the "excitement" he had felt on first attenting a meeting of the Commonwealth group of ten nations at the UN, and of there being "something mystical in their adherence to common ideals"; but in his peroration he said: [1]

> "Canada is a middle power with roots in the three associations, in NATO, in the Commonwealth and in the United Nations. I think Canada has a special reason for avoiding an absolutely rigid dependence on any one of these organisations as the sole instrument or channel of its foreign policy."

[1] Canadian House of Commons, November 26, 1957.

Chapter Nine

INDIA

INDIA provides a marked contrast with Canada. Apart from the obvious difference in racial composition and geographical location, the two countries have had different problems to face as sovereign states in the postwar world. Canada had a slow and lengthy apprenticeship to the business of international relations, and gradually developed the equipment of a sovereign state; when she took her place as an effective "middle power" at the San Francisco Conference of 1945, she did so as of right. But India, on attaining independence in 1947, was pitchforked into international relations with little formal preparation. It is true that India had been a member of the League of Nations and of other international bodies before 1939, and that a certain amount of limited diplomatic activity had been carried on in her name. But all this had been under the strict tutelage of Britain, and had been attacked by Congress, the now dominant element in Indian government, as the subservience of Indian interests to British. The new Indian government was the product of an Indian independence movement of long standing, led by a commanding personality in Mr. Nehru. It brought to the business of foreign affairs little sense of continuity with past policies, but a burning sense of opposition to European colonialsim. The new India came into being in the full glare of international attention. She had no opportunity to feel her way slowly towards a clarification of Indian interests. At once she was called upon to take an attitude on such questions as Palestine and Indonesia. Soon afterwards, she was faced with a decisive change in Asian affairs when the Communist regime was established in China.

As a new nation of vast size and tremendous possibilities, India has been forced by circumstances to take a major part in international diplomacy. This has meant formulating a view of national interest which would not only cope with the immediate tasks of decision in foreign policy, but also act as a means of increasing national unity in India itself. Independent India began as a mutilated version of what the Congress had hoped would be its shape. The creation of Pakistan by the partition of the Indian subcontinent was accepted by the Congress with reluctance as the necessary condition for the departure of the British; it was still considered an affront to the ideal of an undivided India which Congress had striven to uphold. It may be said that the mutilation of the ideal India imposed an even greater obligation upon the India that remained to display a characteristic attitude in international affairs and to make a distinctively *Indian* contribution to the world's affairs. Thus it was not only the pressure of events in the world at large but also the pressure of events within the subcontinent itself that made the formulation of national interests so urgent. India had not only to present a characteristic image of herself to the world; she had also to make that image an effective one by diplomatic action, and to see that the interests she pursued were consonant with that image and effectively pursuable within the context of world affairs. One has only to read Mr. Nehru's speeches between 1946 and 1949 [1] to see how urgent was this sense of need for a conception of interests and policy which would be both appropriate and realistic.

There were various sources from which such a conception might have come. One was the series of diplomatic efforts which India had made while still under British tutelage—some of them aimed at preserving the security of India, such as those in Persia, Afghanistan and Tibet; some aimed directly at the welfare of Indians overseas, such as those in South and East Africa. As indicated above, Congress and Mr. Nehru had no particular reason to accept the estimates of Indian interests which had been current in the government of India before independence. They had been inclined to condemn Indians in the government as servile and as time-servers, and to condemn the external policies of the government as imperialism. But there were two factors which prevented Mr. Nehru's government from ignoring altogether the efforts of its predecessors. One was that, in spite of changes in political control in Asia, and in spite of new means of transport and communication, the physical facts of Asian geography remained the same, and so did the distribution of peoples on India's borders. The Imperial Government of India had been interested in Afghanistan and Tibet; Mr. Nehru's government could not help being interested too. Burma and Ceylon had both been British possessions, and there had been a free flow of Indians to those areas, as to

[1] Jawaharlal Nehru, *Independence and After* (Delhi, 1949).

East and South Africa, to seek their fortunes. Independent India would be bound to take an interest in these expatriates and their descendants. And once a new Indian government gained control of Indian defence forces, it would be certain to ask how those forces had been used before, what strongholds and weak points they had been intended to defend, and whether there was still something to be said for taking a strategical view of India's interests.

The second factor was that of personnel. Much as Congress might scorn the Indians who had entered the I.C.S. and helped to administer the policies of the Imperial Government, it was impossible to ignore the skill and knowledge which these civil servants displayed. The significance of this in regard to foreign affairs can be illustrated from the career of Sir Girja Shankar Bajpai, the first Secretary-General (permanent head) of the Ministry of External Affairs in independent India. He began his diplomatic experience in 1921, as secretary to the Indian delegation to the Imperial Conference, and went on to attend the Washington Conference and to make official visits to Canada, Australia and New Zealand. He was secretary to the Indian delegations to South Africa which, in the 1920's, discussed the condition of Indians there; he attended the Round Table Conference, the League of Nations and Imperial Conferences in the 1930's. In 1941 he became Agent-General for India in the United States, where he remained until being recalled to take charge of the Ministry of External Affairs. Thereafter he accompanied Mr. Nehru to the Commonwealth Prime Ministers' Conferences of 1948, 1949 and 1951, and represented his country at the United Nations' negotiations on Kashmir.[1] Such a man clearly brought with him a knowledge of international procedure and of the course of events which would be invaluable to a newly independent country whose government wished to play a prominent part on the world stage. But he must also have brought with him a number of assumptions about India's interests which could be harmonized with the other sources from which the conception of national interests was drawn. To say this is not to suggest that independent India simply repeated the actions, and resumed the assumptions, of the Indian Empire; but it is to suggest that a place could be found for these assumptions in the general discussion of national interest.

[1] Bajpai died in 1954. These particulars are from the obituaries in *The Times* and the *Manchester Guardian* of December 6, 1954.

A second source from which a conception of national interest might have been drawn was the Indian past, the long period before the conquest of India by Europeans. A national myth usually includes the romantic evocation of a golden age in which the country's glory was displayed, and which can be made to return if nationalist urges are given full play. The Indian independence movement was no exception to this. Its difficulty was, however, that India had a long history in which a variety of conquerors had ruled over India, and distinctively Indian modes of life and thought had been disseminated to other countries by the movement of peoples rather than by acts of policy. The difficulty was complicated by the fact that, while Congress was avowedly a secular body, its principal support came from Hindus and its main opposition from Muslims. The most coherent historical example of Indian unity was the Mogul Empire in its prime; but the Moguls were Muslims. To find a Hindu equivalent it was necessary to go back to the almost legendary empire of Asoka, centuries before Christ. Nevertheless, it was possible to do this, as can be seen from K. M. Panikkar: [1]

> "Our vision has been obscured by an un-Indian wave of pacificism. *Ahimsa* is no doubt a great religious creed, but that is a creed which India rejected when she refused to follow Gautama Buddha. The Hindu theory at all times, especially in the periods of India's historic greatness was one of active assertion of right, if necessary through the force of arms. . . . Apart from the Buddhist and Jain heresies which the good sense of the Hindus rejected long ago, it is not known what religious basis there is in Hinduism for the form of pacificism which has come, for some strange reason, to be associated with the Hindus. Once we are free from the effects of this idea, and are thus enabled to look facts in the face, it will be clear that Indian freedom can be upheld only by firmly deciding to shoulder our share at all costs in the active defence of the areas necessary for our security. To the Indian Ocean we shall then have to turn, as our ancestors did, who conquered Socotra long before the Christian Era and established an Empire in the Pacific which lasted for 1500 years."

Such statements as this could stimulate national pride, but they could do little to provide policy. Furthermore, too much emphasis upon the past unity of India would draw attention to the existence of Pakistan, and might be interpreted as an argument for Indian

[1] K. M. Panikkar, *India and the Indian Ocean* (London, 1951), p. 16.

action against that country. In consequence, it does not seem that statements about the past extension of Indian power and influence have played much part in Indian propaganda. But it is likely that a policy-maker who was searching for an excuse for a policy conceived on other grounds might find the Hindu past ready to hand.

A third source from which independent India would be likely to draw its conception of national interest was the preconceptions of the nationalist movement itself. Congress had always been primarily interested in independence in its domestic context, but had discussed foreign affairs also from time to time. Indian radicals had consorted with left-wing and revolutionary elements in England, in Asia and in Europe; there was no lack of theories about international diplomacy, and, if there had been, the various Communist fronts, such as the League against Imperialism, would have seen that they were supplied. Congress's principal sentiment was a burning hatred of imperialism, which it interpreted as essentially the extension of European power over coloured peoples. Its solution to the problem of imperialism was independence. Indian nationalism was essentially an assertion of India's right to become a nation-state; the nationalists wanted what Mr. Nehru called "the full-blooded words: Power, Independence, Freedom, Liberty".[1] In the late 1930's Congress was inclined to take the Popular Front line over China, Abyssinia and Spain, and to press for international action, but this was not allowed to obscure the need for Indian independence; indeed, it was held to complement the struggle for independence: "The challenge of fascism and nazism was in essence the challenge of imperialism. They were twin brothers, with this variation, that imperialism functioned abroad in colonies and dependencies, while fascism and nazism functioned in the same way in the home country also. If freedom was to be established in the world, not only fascism and nazism had to go but imperialism had to be completely liquidated."[2]

Such a sentiment in the independence movement was to be expected; it was and is common form in such movements. Its logical outcome was rebellion. But the Indian independence movement had another sentiment peculiar to itself: the Gandhian doctrine that resistance to imperialism should be non-violent

[1] Jawaharlal Nehru, *An Autobiography* (London, 1942), p. 421.
[2] *Ibid.*, p. 601.

non-co-operation, and should be intended to shame the imperialist into a realization that his conduct was wrong. Gandhism was a creed admirably suited to the task of welding India's masses into unity, and providing an effective protest against British rule; as Gandhi's uncertainties in World War II showed, it was not so easily applicable to international conflict. But the immense prestige which Ghandi's doctrine and example had gained in India ensured that, when Congress came to power, it would do so with a sense of conscience that power ought to be used in ways which could themselves be defended on moral grounds. Mr. Nehru called Gandhism "the spiritualisation of politics", and said that it meant the use of means "which satisfied my moral sense and gave me a sense of personal freedom".[1] Such ideas were, and still are, common among Indian leaders. Their effect upon the conception of national interest in independent India has been that, no matter how much Indian sentiment might wish for the liquidation of imperialism, there has always been the sense of obligation to use non-violent methods and to seek peaceful solutions. Anti-imperialism and non-violence are thus ideas which the struggle for independence bequeathed to India; they have proved to be the basic ideas on which the Indian conception of national interest has been based.

A final source from which that conception might be drawn has been the course of international events themselves, the pressures exerted on India by the movements of other countries. As suggested earlier, this is always a potent source of interests; India has been no exception to the rule that a country makes and changes its interests as it goes along. Each of the major developments of the postwar world, described in Chapter Six, has had its effect on India. Indian interests have had to be defined in relation to the policies of the Great Powers, the advent of nuclear warfare, the world economic climate, and the changes taking place in Asia.

Of these four sources, all but the second (the Indian past) have obviously contributed to the Indian government's formulation of interests. The influence of the Indian past has been more subtle. The government has, on the whole, frowned upon suggestions that it should use the more violent aspects of Indian history as inspiration for policy; even the comparatively modern example of the Indian Mutiny, a revolt of Indians against European control, was played down when its centenary came round in

[1] Jawaharlal Nehru, *An Autobiography* (London, 1942), p. 73.

1957. Yet the value of the Indian past as a means of asserting national unity and providing the common memory which a cohesive nation needs has been recognized. Indian schools have given more attention than before to purely Indian history. The almost mythical adventures referred to in the quotation from K. M. Panikkar are better known than they were. This kind of instruction may provide a national image, the need for which was always so strongly felt by Mr. Nehru. But it cannot do much more. It cannot set the course of Indian policy.

The other three sources, however, have fitted snugly together to provide a clarification of interests. From the pre-independence policies of India have been acquired a concern for India's frontiers and a continued concern for people of Indian origin, especially in South Africa—although it should be remembered that to the Indian government the crucial efforts on behalf of Indians in South Africa were not those of the Imperial Government but those of Gandhi. From the ideas of the independence movement has come, above all, the very idea of independence itself: the determination to keep India free from foreign domination, and enable her to work out her destiny for herself. From it, too, has come the emphasis upon non-violence and peace; though there is little doubt that the course of international events had strengthened this particular aim by indicating to the government that no other aim would consort with India's peculiar position in the world—until China became belligerent.

It is possible now to set down what seem to be the national interests pursued by India, roughly in order of precedence—precedence dictated by the amount of emphasis given to them in the utterances of the first Prime Minister. Although India has had to make up her interests as the tide of affairs has swept her along, this improvization was largely the work of one articulate man, Mr. Nehru, with the help of Mr. Krishna Menon; in no other Commonwealth country has the making of policy been so obviously in the hands of a single commanding figure. In concentrating upon Mr. Nehru's statements to show which interests India has pursued, I am not suggesting that Indian policy has been simply the product of his reason, his whims and his prejudices. I am suggesting rather that Mr. Nehru was the means of formulation of interests and policies which, given the situation of India and the kind of government which was to be expected after independence, could not have differed much from those which have, in fact, emerged. Mr. Nehru gave to them the particular stamp of his personality; since that personality was essentially an articulate one, concerned at all points to justify its actions, India's interests and policies have been understandably identified with Mr. Nehru, since they have been stated in his terms. But it seems likely that, without Mr. Nehru, a similar line might have been taken and very similar aims pursued. In other words, if one says India's policy was peculiar to its Prime Minister, one is correct to the extent that no one else would have put it in quite the same way, or given it quite the same emphasis; but it would be inadvisable to extend the identification of Prime Minister and policy to the point of believing that, if the Prime Minister had been changed, there would also have been a marked change in the policy.

Foremost among Indian interests is the preservation of Indian independence. It is true that all sovereign states strive to preserve that status, and to this extent independence is an interest of all countries; but in India there is the special reason that the personal image of Congress is of men who have won independence and wish to preserve and enlarge it. Although, in comparison with some other countries, India did not have to fight very hard for its independence, the language of the Congress is essentially the language of a struggle, of conflict and triumphant victory. To themselves, the Indian leaders are triumphant revolutionaries. By independence, Mr. Nehru and Congress did not mean Dominion Status; they meant independent sovereignty without any formal connection with Britain.

> "The Congress attitude . . . seeks a new State and not just a different administration. What that new State is going to be may not be quite clear to the average Congressman, and opinions may differ about it. But it is common ground in the Congress (except for a moderate fringe) that present conditions and methods cannot and must not continue, and basic changes are essential. Herein lies the difference between Dominion Status and Independence. The former envisages the same old structure, with many bonds visible and invisible tying us to the British economic system; the latter gives us, or ought to give us, freedom to erect a new structure to suit our circumstances."

Here Mr. Nehru [1] was expressing the attitude of Congress in the 1930's to the kind of Commonwealth relationship which existed

[1] *An Autobiography*, *op. cit.*, p. 418.

then, or which Indian militants thought was being extended to them under the Government of India Act. Both Mr. Nehru and the Commonwealth changed course. But the fact remains that the Indian government thinks of the independence which it gained in 1947 as different in quality from the kind of status which Britain offered to it before the war. A new State; a fresh start; a release from bondage: phrases such as these give the idea of independence a dynamic, mythical quality (in Sorel's sense of the myth) which is not present in the older Commonwealth members' views of their status. Independence so dearly sought must be fondly cherished; and it must be demonstrated. To some extent, the busy diplomatic activity of India is intended to indicate that independence is real.

> "Are we going to ask England to look after our foreign interests in other countries as Pakistan has done in many countries? Is that the type of independence that we imagine? What does independence consist of? It consists fundamentally and basically of foreign relations. That is the test of independence. All else is local autonomy. Once foreign relations go out of your hand, into the charge of somebody else, to that extent and in that measure you are not independent."

Mr. Nehru[1] said this in reply to complaints that the spread of Indian embassies was just a gesture to satisfy Indian vanity; but there is no need to go as far as this in order to suggest that the urge to demonstrate Indian independence is responsible for much of what India has done. Throughout Mr. Nehru's speeches there is the assertion that India *counts*—to some extent because of her geographical position and her size:[2]

> "Look at the map. If you have to consider any question affecting the Middle East, India inevitably comes into the picture. If you have to consider any question concerning South-East Asia, you cannot do so without India. So also with the Far East. While the Middle East may not be directly connected with South-East Asia, both are connected with India. Even if you think in terms of regional organisations in Asia, you have to keep in touch with the other regions. And whatever regions you may have in mind, the importance of India cannot be ignored."

—and partly because of the distinctive attitude which she has taken up towards foreign affairs. That attitude is often called

[1] *Independence and After*, *op. cit.*, p. 237. The statement was made in 1949 and would not now be true of Pakistan.
[2] *Ibid.*, p. 231.

"idealistic" or "moralistic", with the implication that it is not grounded in an appreciation of India's own interests. Mr. Nehru would constantly deny this. Indeed, he was careful to indicate to his Indian audiences that his policy always looked first to India's interests. In his first major speech on foreign policy to the Indian Constituent Assembly, he stated flatly:[1] "We are not going to join a war if we can help it: and we are going to join the side which is to our interest when the time comes to make the choice. There the matter ends." But he went on to indicate how the general interest of India was served by the kind of policy which is now recognized as distinctively Indian:[2]

> "Whatever policy you may lay down, the art of conducting the foreign affairs of a country lies in finding out what is most advantageous to the country. We may talk about international goodwill and mean what we say. We may talk about peace and freedom and earnestly mean what we say. But in the ultimate analysis, a government functions for the good of the country it governs and no government dare do anything which in the short or long run is manifestly to the disadvantage of that country.
>
> "Therefore, whether a country is imperialistic or socialist or communist, its Foreign Minister thinks primarily of the interests of that country. But there is a difference, of course. Some people may think of the interests of their country regardless of other consequences, or take a short-distance view. Others may think that in the long-term policy the interest of another country is as important to them as that of their own country. The interest of peace is more important, because if war comes everyone suffers, so that in the long-distance view, self-interest may itself demand a policy of co-operation with other nations, goodwill for other nations, as indeed it does demand."

From the basic idea of independence flow a number of the other interests which India pursues. Although it was essentially the independence of India itself which Mr. Nehru had wished to preserve, both he and Indian thinkers generally have enlarged the concept of independence to take in the rest of Asia in particular, and, in general, the other countries of the world which are or have been dominated by Europe. At the Bandung Conference of 1955, Mr. Nehru linked his policy of non-alignment and co-existence

[1] *Independence and After*, *op. cit.*, p. 200.
[2] *Ibid.*, p. 205.

with the pride of Asians in gaining and keeping their independence:[1]

"... are we, the countries of Asia and Africa, devoid of any positive position except being pro-communist or anti-communist? Has it come to this, that the leaders of thought who have given religions and all kinds of things to the world have to tag on to this group or that, and be hangers-on of this party or the other, carrying out their wishes and occasionally giving an idea? It is most degrading and humiliating to any self-respecting people or nation. It is an intolerable thought to me that the great countries of Asia and Africa should come out of bondage into freedom only to degrade themselves or humiliate themselves in this way."

Constantly, the achievement of Indian independence is linked with the anti-colonial movements in Asia generally, and the countries of Europe are rebuked for failing to recognize the great changes which have taken place in Asia. Among other attributes Asia was specially equipped, in Mr. Nehru's view, to be an exemplar of the "areas of peace" which he hoped would be established throughout the world:[2]

"I do not mean to say that we in Asia are in any way superior ethically or morally, to the people of Europe. In some ways I imagine we are worse. There is, however, a legacy of conflict in Europe. In Asia, at the present moment, at least, there is no such legacy. The countries of Asia may have their quarrels with their neighbours here and there, but there is no basic legacy of conflict such as the countries of Europe possess. That is a very great advantage for Asia and it would be folly in the extreme for the countries of Asia, for India to be dragged in the wake of the conflicts of Europe."

This creation of "areas of peace" by non-alignment with the blocs of powers already in existence was the second of India's interests, as pursued by Mr. Nehru; it was linked with independence because, in his view, independence and its possibilities in terms of a better life could be preserved only by non-alignment. He explained his position thus at Bandung:[3]

"We have to face the position as it is today, namely, that whatever armaments one side or the other might possess, war will lead to

[1] Speech before the Political Committee of the Asian-African Conference, April 22, 1955; in G. McT. Kahin, *The Asian-African Conference* (Ithaca, N.Y., 1956), p. 67.

[2] *Independence and After, op. cit., p.* 232.

[3] *The Asian-African Conference, op. cit.*, p. 66.

consequences which will result in, not gaining an objective, but ruin. Therefore, the first thing we have to settle is that war must be avoided. Naturally war cannot be avoided if any country takes to a career of conquest and aggression. But that is a different matter. Secondly, we countries of Asia have to consider whether we can, all of us put together, certainly not singly, prevent the great powers or big countries going to war. We certainly cannot prevent the big countries going to war if they want to, but we can make a difference. Even a single country can make a difference when the scales are evenly balanced. What action are we going to take? . . . The first step is to make our view clear that these things should not happen. So far as I am concerned, it does not matter what war takes place; we will not take part in it unless we have to defend ourselves. If I join any of these big groups I lose my identity. . . . If all the world were to be divided up between these two big blocs, what would be the result? The inevitable result would be war. Therefore every step that takes place in reducing that area in the world which may be called the *unaligned area* is a dangerous step and leads to war. . . . I submit to you, every pact has brought insecurity and not security to the countries which have entered into them. They have brought the danger of atomic bombs and the rest of it nearer to them than would have been the case otherwise."

Along with independence and non-alignment as interests, went opposition to colonialism and racial discrimination. These were seen as affronts to the dignity of man, but they were also seen as threats to peace, because they meant conflict:[1]

". . . there are two other issues in the world which, unless satisfactorily solved, may well lead to conflict and a conflict on a big scale. One is the issue typified by Indonesia, that is the issue of domination of one country over another. Where there is continued domination, whether it is in Asia or Africa, there will be no peace either there or in the people's minds elsewhere. There will be a continuous conflict going on, continuous suspicion of each other and continuous suspicion of Europe in the minds of Asia and, therefore, the friendly relationship which should exist between Asia and Europe will not come about easily. It is, therefore, important that all these areas of colonial domination should be freed and they should be able to function as free countries.

"The second important fact is that of racial equality. . . . If that is to continue in the world [i.e. the kind of inequality practised in South

[1] *Independence and After*, pp. 258–9.

Africa], then there is bound to be conflict and conflict on a big scale, because it is a continuous challenge to the self-respect of a vast number of people in the world and they will not put up with it."

The next interest which India has obviously pursued—so obviously that there is no need to quote Mr. Nehru in support of it—is that of India's own economic development. Mr. Nehru made more speeches on this than on anything else. Economic development is, of course, primarily a domestic matter, but it comes prominently into foreign affairs because of India's need for capital investment, and because Mr. Nehru was convinced that the realities of economics stood behind foreign policy, in the last analysis: "Ultimately, foreign policy is the outcome of economic policy, and until India has properly evolved her economic policy, her foreign policy will be rather vague, rather inchoate, and will be groping."[1] India's economic planning comes into foreign policy not only because of the need for foreign help in providing money, skill and equipment, but also because economic growth will make India stronger and better able to put her point of view before other countries. In a sense, this is another aspect of independence: India believes that she cannot be truly independent until she has mastered the problems of poverty and backwardness. Similarly, she cannot be independent if she is dependent for markets or money on the loaded favours of other countries; she must take aid without strings, or not at all.

The interests of India were summed up in the *Panch Sheela*, the set of five principles agreed between Mr. Nehru and Chou En-lai during the Chinese Premier's visit to India in 1954. India treated these as the basis of her relations with other countries,[2] and Mr. Nehru considered them her special contribution to world affairs.[3] They were:

1. mutual respect for each other's territorial integrity and sovereignty;
2. non-aggression;
3. non-interference in each other's internal affairs;
4. equality and mutual benefit;
5. peaceful co-existence.

[1] *Independence and After*, p. 201.
[2] *Report* of the Ministry of External Affairs, 1955–6 (Delhi), p. 43.
[3] *The Times*, September 19, 1955.

These principles are clearly repetitive. In fact, they amount to two principles only, non-aggression and respect for sovereignty. These in turn can be reduced to the maintenance of independence, which, as we have seen, is the basic Indian interest. Given the Indian view that independence is threatened by war, however war may occur, India's aims consist very largely of preserving and enlarging the independence she has won. To this, all of the four possible sources of interest mentioned earlier in this chapter contribute. It is the fourth of these, the actual course of events since India became independent, that accounts for the particular policies which India has brought forward.

The special problems which events have presented to India are those of Kashmir, the new China, Korea, Indians overseas, the existence of Pakistan, relations with such neighbours as Burma, Indonesia and Ceylon, and the general condition of the Cold War. None of these can be seen in isolation; each can be related to the possibilities of peace or war, and to the cultivation of friendship with countries which can help or hinder India's attainment of her aims. The way India has dealt with them indicates the special role which she wishes to play in world affairs. In the case of Kashmir, her emphasis throughout has been upon her legal right to Kashmir as an integral part of India, consequent upon the ruler's accession to India. To give up this standpoint would be to threaten the very basis on which the Indian Union was constructed. On this issue India has stood on the ground of her sovereign rights. But in regard to Indians in South Africa she has not hesitated to use the full resources of the General Assembly of the United Nations, in spite of South Africa's insistence that the treatment of Indians is a matter of that country's domestic jurisdiction. At the same time, India has made it clear that she does not consider Indians abroad to be under her special protection: Mr. Nehru's view was that their task is to make themselves citizens of the countries in which they live, and to play their full part there. Only if they are actively discriminated against will India take up their case, doing so in the same spirit as that in which she would take up the case of any other minority subject to racial discrimination. The emphasis here has been upon Indian sovereignty, and upon the sovereignty of other nation-states so long as they did not engage in active colonialism or racial discrimination. The case of countries holding enclaves on the Indian sub-continent was, however, one which India insisted on treating as special. Goa, in particular, was formally recognized as a Portuguese possession, but the Indian attitude was that a higher law made it an affront to humanity that European countries should continue to be sovereign on Indian soil. In general, the assertion of Indian independence has been a continual Indian activity, pursued at times by the strict rigour of international law, at others by appeal to historical destiny and the sword.

In her relations with her neighbours other than Pakistan, India formerly tried to make herself an indispensable friend. Her relations with Burma and Indonesia were good until her clash with China. Her relations with Ceylon have been continually complicated by the question of the status of Indians in Ceylon, and there has been much indignation in India over the reluctance of Ceylon to grant citizenship to these. But, largely because of Mr. Nehru's generous approach, India could previously assume the role of a benevolent uncle or cousin to these smaller, largely like-minded countries. The difficulties arose over China.

Mr. Nehru's approach was that China's Communism was not for export in the same way as Russia's, and that the more China was treated as yet another example of the vitalizing influence of Asian nationalism the less likely was a permanent coalition between China and Russia. India was alarmed by the continuance of the Korean War, fearing that it would set up a permanent conflict between China and the West, which would eventually involve Russia also. Her diplomacy went to great lengths to bring the combatants together and to use the influence of countries, like others in the Commonwealth which also wished to see the war ended, to press the United States to come to terms. Again in the case of Formosa, while the Indian attitude had publicly been that of a friend of China, striving to bring China into her "rightful place" both as UN member and suzerain of Formosa, India was in fact satisfied with a *de facto* recognition of "two Chinas", in order to preserve the existing position and not encourage war. Obviously, India must live with China in Asia; obviously, too, there would be competition between the two countries for Asian leadership—complicated by constant Chinese pressure on India's northern borders. Mr. Nehru seemed to think that, while there was ample justification for viewing China as a thrustful power, more harm would be done to Indian interests by opposing China than by negotiating with her: India had no special capacity to resist China, and to decide to do so would be to accept membership of the anti-Communist bloc in the Cold War.

Much of the argument of the preceding paragraph, so characteristic of Mr. Nehru, seemed effective in previous editions of this book, prepared before the 1959 revelations of Chinese incursions into India's northern areas, and before the Chinese frontier offensive of 1962 brought Indian troops into active and disturbing conflict with Chinese forces. It was an argument for non-alignment which could be pursued so long as China remained inactive towards other Asian countries and co-operative with the Soviet Union in combined hostility towards the United States. Its basis has now disappeared, in that China is regarded as the main enemy of India, India builds up forces to resist China, and the process of building up these forces is actively aided by the United States, the Soviet Union, and Britain. To the extent that non-alignment meant a refusal to accept military aid, India has now deserted non-alignment. To the extent that non-alignment was equated with lack of preparation for war, India has abandoned it. To the extent, also, that non-alignment was equated with the "Bandung spirit", embodying a strong emotional commitment against the West and a readiness to think the best of Communist countries simply because they were anti-colonialist, India has given this up too. The Cairo conference of non-aligned countries in 1964 was a very different one from Bandung: one side, led by Indonesia, adopted the Chinese line of outright defiance of the West; the other, led by India, Egypt and Yugoslavia, was sharply opposed to this. It is clear that non-alignment has been a failure so far as China is concerned. But the Indians still think it viable as between the United States and the Soviet Union: taking arms from both sides, they say, is an expression of non-alignment.

Given a bilateral alignment in world affairs, there is a case for Indian non-alignment on a strict "balance of power" basis.[1] If China can, as it were, be fenced off from the main struggle (though this is very doubtful), the peace of Asia might be enhanced if a significant middle power like India kept her own attitude uncertain, while continuing to build up her military strength; potential

[1] For a strong defence of India's policy in this respect, written before the threat from China was manifest, see G. S. Bajpai, "India and the Balance of Power", in *Indian Year Book of International Affairs*, Vol. I (Madras, 1952).

aggressors might be deterred if they did not know whether India was to be ranged against them. Whether the prospect of nuclear warfare renders this argument invalid is a matter of opinion. But it is possible to say with some certainty that if a country of vast area and population, with a highly articulate leadership and engaged in rapid economic development, were to ask itself which policy would bring it most in the way of notice, attention and favours from both sides in a Cold War, the answer would be something like the policy which India pursued before China attacked her. An awkward country like India—awkward in size, in economic power, and in the proved depths of its national fervour—can *afford* non-alignment in the pre-1959 Cold War situation. Whether it is equally applicable to other countries is another matter. But, as a policy worked out specifically to suit the needs of India it was a success from the standpoint of Indian national interests until China destroyed it.

What part does the Commonwealth play in Indian foreign policy? It was something of a surprise when India decided to remain a Commonwealth member, even to the extent of asking the Commonwealth Prime Ministers to recognize that a republic could be a member of the Commonwealth. The Congress had been strongly opposed to Dominion Status as that was understood in the 1930's, and Mr. Nehru himself had been a strong opponent of the Dominion Status solution to India's problems. It is true that in 1947 there was no alternative to Commonwealth membership as the form which independence would take; to this extent India was committed to the Commonwealth. But the commitment need not have been observed for long, as the example of Burma showed. India could have been in and out of Commonwealth membership in the space of a few weeks or less. Again, on the proclamation of a republic in 1949, India could have left the Commonwealth as Eire did. It is clear, therefore, that the Indian policy of remaining in the Commonwealth must have more behind it than either habit or constitutional laziness; on the face of things, Commonwealth membership seems to be something which India prizes and is prepared to retain for the advantages it brings.

When Mr. Nehru presented the conclusions of the 1949 Prime Ministers' meeting to Parliament in Delhi, he did not give details of any clear-cut advantages which India derived from the Commonwealth connection. He preferred to base his case for continued membership upon the fact that India had accepted no commitments and that "there is no law behind the Commonwealth".[1] India would lose nothing by remaining a member; there might be minor gains in such fields as military co-operation and easier arrangements for mutual citizenship, but the main reason for remaining in the Commonwealth was quite different:[2]

> "I wanted the world to see that India did not lack faith in herself, and that India was prepared to co-operate even with those with whom she had been fighting in the past; provided the basis of co-operation today was honourable, that it was a free basis, a basis which would lead to the good not only of ourselves, but of the world also. That is to say, we would not deny that co-operation simply because in the past we had fought, and thus carry on the trail of our past *karma* along with us. We have to wash out the past with all its evil."

To those who said that remaining in the Commonwealth would mean associating with imperialism, he said there was no such danger;[3] "if you talk of British imperialism and the rest of it, I would say that there is no capacity left for imperialism even if the will were there; it will not do". To those who said that it would mean joining a Commonwealth in which there was racial discrimination (with special reference to South Africa), he said that entering an alliance or an association with other nations did not mean accepting all their policies. In general, he pointed to the Commonwealth as an association which imposed no obligations but might do some good, if only because it represented an attempt to heal old wounds and further the cause of co-operation.

These have presumably remained among the reasons for retaining Commonwealth membership. In fact, it was not until 1957 that Mr. Nehru felt, for the first time, that India's membership might require further consideration; and this was under the stress of the British action at Suez, and, more particularly, the failure of other Commonwealth members to support India's case on Kashmir at the United Nations Security Council.[4] Even this pronouncement was not followed up. And before it there had been a number of occasions when Mr. Nehru had defended the Commonwealth link against critics in India.[5] So it would seem that he must have seen certain positive advantages in it, even though he did not define them. What can they be?

[1] *Independence and After*, *op. cit.*, p. 269. [2] *Ibid.*, p. 278.
[3] *Ibid.*, p. 289. [4] *The Times*, March 26, 1957.
[5] See, e.g., *The Times*, October 1, 1954; January 12 and December 6, 1955.

The most obvious seems to be that the Commonwealth has been of special advantage to India in carrying out its diplomacy. A country which is determined not to align itself in world affairs, yet wishes to be influential, must have channels of communication which enable it to find the ear of policy-makers in the Great Powers and to operate freely on the level of confidential discussion. This is especially so if the country in question does not possess substantial military force,[1] and must rely upon the suppleness of its diplomacy and the enlistment of friendly sentiment in the countries which it wishes to influence. In deliberately contracting out of the Cold War, India made it possible for herself to get a friendly, or at least a tolerant, hearing in Moscow and Peking—although it was not until 1954 that the Communist countries left off calling Mr. Nehru an agent of imperialism. The Communist side of the Cold War had made numerous attempts to woo uncommitted nations, and there was every reason to think that India, the biggest of all uncommitted countries, would be no exception so long as her policies did not obviously cut across the interests of Russia and China. Communication with these two countries was thus ultimately assured, even if it might have to be private and circumspect, and might mean that in public India must continually flatter them.

Communication with the other side in the Cold War, however, would have been extremely difficult, or at any rate only intermittent, if India had not been a member of the Commonwealth. The point has been put succinctly by Taya Zinkin:[2]

> "... Mr. Nehru's policies show how much he values the extra inches the Commonwealth platform adds to his stature. Mr. Nehru the Prime Minister of India talking to the free world—he never talks to the other—is a man whose voice is as loud as his guns: not very loud. The voice of Mr. Nehru, a senior partner of the Commonwealth, talking to the free world is as loud as the Commonwealth is wide: loud enough even to be heard in Washington through the London relay."

One lesson of the prolonged negotiations over Korea, Indo-China and Formosa was that India's membership of the Commonwealth gave her not only access to Washington through the London

[1] That is, in relation to the Great Powers. In comparison with these, India is militarily negligible. But it should also be recognized that, in relation to other countries in Asia (except China), she does possess substantial military force. The point is of special importance to her neighbours.

[2] *Manchester Guardian*, January 27, 1954.

relay but also easier access to Britain herself than might otherwise have been the case. Since the preservation of the Commonwealth is, as we have seen, a prominent British interest, Britain has usually taken special notice of what Commonwealth members said. India is the most populous Commonwealth country, and the most notable when Britain wishes to show the rest of the world that the Commonwealth is not only a free association but a multiracial one as well. Even if British policy on Korea, Indo-China and Formosa had not been broadly in accord with Indian, there would have been a strong British tendency to take account of India's views. The fact that the two policies ran along similar lines meant that India had special access to the British ear. But if India had not been a member of the Commonwealth, and if the give and take of constant consultation had not been customary between the two countries, Indian diplomacy could hardly have shown the flexibility and knowingness which it did show.

A similar point could be made about India's contacts with Canada and Australia. On various occasions—over Suez with Canada, over Indonesia with Australia—India has found the path of her diplomacy smoothed because she shared not only common interests with these countries but also the habit of informal consultation. As with Britain, the fact that consultation was a habit, and not something hastily put into effect to meet a particular crisis, has been of special advantage to India.

Commonwealth membership has thus been of some help in the carrying out of India's diplomacy, not only in day-to-day ways which are common to all Commonwealth countries, and figure as credit items in any assessment of the Commonwealth as an asset to them, but also in particular demands which a policy of nonalignment makes. It has enabled India to be of the Western camp, but not in it. No one can say for certain whether India would have been able to achieve this position without being part of the Commonwealth; quite possibly she could, since her power, personnel and policies would have been the same and could have been expected to work in similar ways. But there is no doubt that being in the Commonwealth has meant a flying start for any Indian initiative; and certain Commonwealth countries came first to India's aid in 1962.

There are also minor advantages which India receives from the Commonwealth connection. In the complicated field of citzenship, her migrants benefit from the status of Commonwealth citizen which some member-nations, notably Britain, provide. In the field of defence, India has open access to British training facilities (although this is not something confined to Commonwealth members) and also enjoys such facilities as the opportunity to carry out naval manoeuvres with the Royal Navy. India still retains her rights under Imperial Preference (although this again is not confined to Commonwealth members; Eire retains hers also).

Mr. Nehru has occasionally referred to the economic advantages which India gets from being in the Commonwealth. By these he presumably means Imperial Preference and membership of the Sterling Area. Retention of these advantages, as of those derived from the Colombo Plan, does not depend upon continuing membership of the Commonwealth. But the fact that the only kind of direction and control which the Sterling Area enjoys is that of the occasional Commonwealth meeting may well have something to do with India's remaining in the Commonwealth. The demands which economic growth makes on India's balance of payments constantly leave India with an acute need for foreign currency, and while she is customarily assisted by an international consortium, sterling is the basis of her currency. The Sterling Area's gold and dollar reserve is thus something which India may wish to draw on at any time. She could, of course, do this if she were a non-Commonwealth Sterling Area member, like Burma, Iraq or Eire; but her needs are so much greater than theirs that she might well hesitate before becoming a member of the sterling club who possessed no vote—for that is, in effect, the position of the non-Commonwealth members. As I have suggested earlier, there is no automatic control of Sterling Area policy by the Prime Ministers' Conference; but there is certainly enough of direction and emphasis about the Prime Ministers' role to make India wish to continue to be one of them.

India's advantages from the Commonwealth are further accentuated by the fact that she derives no disadvantages from it. Mr. Nehru was always careful from the beginning to emphasize that there was no room in the Commonwealth for any superior authority which would judge members' actions or resolve their disputes. This is why he so carefully refrained from bringing South Africa's treatment of Indians before the Prime Ministers' meetings, and why he always refused to allow the Kashmir issue to appear on the

Prime Ministers' agenda. The United Nations was available as a forum in which to indict South Africa; within the Commonwealth Mr. Nehru saw no room for indictments. India is thus armoured against the attacks of her fellow-members. She takes no responsibility for the policies of collective defence, colonialism and racial discrimination which some of them pursue, and feels free to criticize them at the United Nations and elsewhere. This point has proved somewhat subtle for some sections of opinion in India itself, which have persisted in demanding that India remove herself from an association which includes countries like Britain. Their view is that India should not touch pitch, even by implication. But the official view is that being in the Commonwealth means no approval or condonation of the policies of other members; and so far this has carried the day. It might also be argued that the presence in the Commonwealth of such a strictly anti-colonial power as India may have had effects upon other members with colonies. It is quite possible that the vigour of Britain's policy of colonial self-government has had something to do with the desire to keep India friendly and within the Commonwealth. But this cannot be demonstrated, and must remain a supposition.

From every standpoint, then, except that of the most ardent Indian nationalist, there is everything to be said for staying in the Commonwealth, and little or nothing to be said for getting out of it. The interests which we saw India pursuing are not harmed by membership. Her independence is guaranteed; her special type of foreign policy is not threatened, but is given extra opportunities to pursue its course; policies of anti-colonialism and opposition to racial discrimination can be pursued at the United Nations; economic development may get some help through Commonwealth good offices, and India has a say in the management of the Sterling Area. At the same time India is kept in an easy, informal relationship with Britain, so that the manifold unofficial and economic contacts which were made in the past can be continued without interruption. It is only natural that the Commonwealth relationship should be questioned in India from time to time, whether in relation to migration, preference or Kashmir. But the events of 1959 and 1962, leading as they did to a generally greater realism in India's view of the world at large, seem only to have enhanced the Commonwealth's position in Indian diplomacy; it is something of a tribute that this should be so.

Chapter Ten

AUSTRALIA AND NEW ZEALAND

AUSTRALIA and New Zealand are usually thought of as the most "British" of the member-nations of the Commonwealth. Indeed, it often turns out that when earnest British Conservatives and the Beaverbrook Press speak of "the Empire" or "the Commonwealth", they have in mind only Australia and New Zealand. The British-ness of these countries is held to show itself not only in their predominantly British ancestry, but also in their frequent approval of the policies of Conservative governments in Britain. In certain ways, this is a convenient shorthand method of describing their character in international society. But both countries have gone a considerable distance along the road towards national self-assertion, and both have pursued policies unacceptable to British Conservatives. The reason lies partly in occasional differences of emphasis between Labour governments in the two countries and Conservative governments in Britain, but much more in the development of felt national interests by Australia and New Zealand, under the pressure of circumstances.

Apart from their British-ness, there is much to be said for classifying the two countries together in such a book as this. They are located in the same quarter of the globe; they have developed societies with similar structures; both have grown rich on selling raw materials and food to Britain and Europe, and have attempted to consolidate their prosperity by the deliberate encouragement of secondary industries. They have similar political systems, and to outsiders their accents are often indistinguishable. Above all, they have been caught up in the same historical pattern. In this century, both have gone through the excitement and fervour of support for Britain in World War I, both suffered grievously in the Great Depression, both joined wholeheartedly in World War II in 1939, both were threatened by the Japanese in 1941–2, both have since been made apprehensive by the development of Chinese Communism, both have gladly become allies of the United States.

But there are also differences which need to be taken into account when one is considering interests and policies. The first is that of size. This operates in two ways. In the first place, Australia has a population four times as big as New Zealand's, but in the second place, the area of Australia is nearly thirty times New Zealand's. Australia is uncomfortably large, New Zealand tidily small. Although great areas of Australia, perhaps two-thirds, are unsuitable for settlement, the sheer size of the country on the map has induced in Australians themselves and in commentators overseas the conviction that Australia has vast empty spaces which she is not putting to good use. This means that Australians have a greater sense of haste and zeal about increasing their population than have New Zealanders, and a stronger sense of possible danger from Asia.

Here is a second difference between the two countries' outlooks: Australia is much closer to the outside world. New Zealand is not close to anything. It is the centre of the water hemisphere, and I have heard Wellington called the most unstrategic city on earth. It is not to be expected, therefore, that the two countries will display quite the same sense of urgency about their relations with Asia, or with other parts of the world. In general terms, Australia is a livelier performer on the international stage than New Zealand. Partly, this is a reflex of her size and her more strenuous internal political life. But it is also to be seen as the result of a position, in location and trade contacts, which forces her to be much more concerned with the world at large than New Zealand. This is especially noticeable in the field of trade. Both economies developed as heavy customers of Britain, and heavy suppliers to Britain; but now this role is retained by New Zealand to a much greater extent than by Australia, whose trade has become much more diversified. In 1956 New Zealand took 53% of her total imports from Britain, and sold 64% of her exports there; the comparable figures for Australia were 42% and 30%.[1] The combination of New Zealand's geographical isolation and her economic dependence on Britain has made her a distinctly more "British" country than Australia in the 1950's and 60's. Also, the traditional preference of Irish migrants for Australia over New Zealand (or New Zealand's lack of preference for them), and the far greater proportion of postwar European migrants into Australia, have given the two countries a significant difference in

[1] *The Commonwealth and the Sterling Area: Statistical Abstract No. 77, 1956* (H.M.S.O., London, 1957), pp. 76 and 87.

ethnic composition, not great enough to be immediately apparent, but sufficient to affect internal politics and to differentiate public attitudes towards Britain.

Taking these various differences, we can expect to find somewhat divergent concepts of national interest developing in the two countries, although it is reasonable to expect a broad similarity in comparison with India or even Canada. Certainly, however, the question of relations with Britain will bulk larger for these two South Pacific countries than for India or Canada.

Australia

The difficulties of Australia in the postwar world are best approached by regarding her (and New Zealand to a lesser extent) as an anomaly. Both are European branches on an Asian limb. Australia developed, and came almost to full stature, as a European settlement on the other side of the world, which remained European in its customs and manners because Asians were not sufficiently strong or free to affect it. In dramatic terms, its situation can be contrasted with that of Indonesia, also a geographical appendage of Asia, but much more heavily populated by its original inhabitants and less so by its European possessors; Indonesia, after centuries of Dutch rule, became an Asian country almost overnight. The differences between Indonesia and Australia are obvious. But what is ominously similar about them to discerning Australian eyes is that both developed as part of the extension of European power into Africa, Asia and Oceania from the sixteenth century to the twentieth. That power is now gone. As we have seen, the eclipse of Europe and the rise of new nations from colonial bonds in Asia and Africa are two of the great developments of the postwar world; if they continue, as they seem bound to do, they will make Australia even more of an international anomaly than it is now.

The anomaly gathers force not simply from the fact that Australia is an outpost of European settlement in a part of the world now being vacated by Europeans, but also from the extremely high standard of living which Australians enjoy. The standard is high in comparison with Europe; it is astronomical in comparison with Asia. It rests upon a combination of continued capital imports (mostly from Britain), good use of climatic conditions (as in woolgrowing), determined use of political opportunities, and native wit and drive. Australians think of it as the result of the contact between the riches of their soil and the strength of their hands. They have a strong sense of achievement and self-respect which is closely identified with their standard of living and the need to maintain not only the standard of comfort but the specific way of life to which they are accustomed. That way of life is based upon British precedents, in culture, religion, laws and government, but is aggressively Australian in its standards and its distinctive expression. Everyone who comes to Australia is expected to conform to it, whether he comes from Europe or Britain. It is the conviction that Asians would be unable to conform that gives the strength to the White Australia Policy and to the apprehension which Australians feel when they look northwards.

The composition of the population, the distinctive way of life and the high standard of living are three interlocking factors which help to form an Australian conception of national interest. The idea of the Australian as a unique and superior human being is not new; Australian nationalism, as a self-conscious expression, is not a contemporary product but a sentiment which has been brewing for a century, and which achieved what is now considered its classic expression in the 1890's. This nationalism, in its earlier years, had to make way against a strong feeling that, although Australians were superior people, they were superior primarily because they were British and that Britain ought to be recognized as the source of strength in national character as well as in its provision of defence through the Royal Navy. Throughout the twentieth century Australians have been inclined to discuss their external relations in terms of whether they ought to emphasize their independence or their British-ness. The two points of view—national and imperial—came to be identified with the two main political forces, Labour and Liberal, and to achieve some importance in policy-making. But the argument was largely false—not wholly so, since there were times when it acquired weight from being associated with real political issues, such as the devotion of Irish-Australians to Home Rule and the tendency of conservative interests in Australia to think of the imperial connection solely in terms of money and social sycophancy; but largely so because there has been no need to fight against British control. In spite of some heated arguments, Australia did not suffer the same permanent division of loyalties as occurred among white South Africans, and had nothing like the problem of a stubborn anti-British minority that the Canadians experienced. Resentment against Britain was strongest in Australia over two separate issues—the conscription issue of World War I, and the Great Depression of the 1930's with its cessation of the British capital flow into Australia—but in neither case was the resentment deep-seated or prolonged, and in both it was directed against Australian politicians and conservative forces even more than against Britain. In neither case did the British government attempt to alter Australian policy, although it gave advice. There was a slight return of anti-British feeling in World War II when it was felt that Britain was not giving enough attention to her commitments in Asia and the Pacific; but this was of little account in terms of sustained public opinion. However, there is still a certain force in the issue of pro- or anti-British, enough at any rate for it still to be used as a counter in Australian political argument.

The basic facts upon which any conception of Australian national interest must be based are the country's location, its distinctive standard and way of life, its aversion from organic connection with Asia, its economic links with Britain and Europe, and its experiences in World War II, when Australian safety demanded that the country hastily seek close alliance with the United States. Out of these, which have been given extra point by the events of the past decades, especially the rise of Communist China and of the new nations of South and South-East Asia, have come three main interests which Australian policy has pursued. None is new, but all are regarded as especially necessary in the conditions of today. The first is the preservation of Australian "racial purity" and the distinctive Australian culture; the second is the search for protection against an aggressive Asian power, together with good will among Asian countries generally; and the third is the expansion of Australian prosperity, especially through the increase of the Australian population.

I have deliberately used the term "racial purity", although many Australians would now wince to hear it. For long the term used by the Australian Labour Party to describe the results which it hoped would be achieved by the White Australia Policy, it now carries with it an embarrassing tang of discredited racialist theories, and the danger of offence to Asian countries which think their blood is as pure as the Australians'. But it still conveys much

BEHIND THE DOOR

(Copyright, Low and "Evening Standard")

of the feeling that lies behind the retention of the White Australia Policy. Even those Australians who wish to see the name of the policy dropped, and the policy itself relaxed so that small quotas of coloured people would be allowed to enter Australia as permanent settlers, are not advocates of miscegenation or even of the development of a plural society in Australia.[1] Apart altogether from the question of possible Asian immigration, there is continual debate in Australia about the wisdom of adding to the population from continental Europe and not simply from the British Isles. The Australian sentiment in this matter is not just a matter of colour. It is concerned with the whole texture of life, with the preservation of a quality and a character which have developed without much conscious planning but which are now recognized as distinctive. To Australians it is manifestly in the interest of Australia to continue to be as it is now, only more so. Even Australian intellectuals who are dissatisfied with some aspects of the life around them are appreciative of other aspects which they know cannot be dissociated from these. They think that drive, energy, inventiveness and solidarity in trouble, together with a form of practical social equalitarianism, are good value for the price paid in anti-intellectualism, intolerance and intermittent official puritanism. All this can be summarized by saying that Australians as a body are proud of their way of living and intend to preserve it, even though the movement of world events might seem to threaten it.

The search for protection against an aggressive Asian power has been a recurrent theme in Australian thinking about the world ever since there has been any such thinking. Before World War II the only Asian power which might be considered an actual threat was Japan; the war showed that aggression could become deliberate Japanese policy. In the 1920's and 1930's Australia was too young at the game of international politics, too inexperienced, too immature economically and in other ways, and too much dependent upon British sea power to frame any effective policy towards Japan. There were efforts towards one, ranging from paying part of the cost of the Singapore base to sending to Japan Australia's first goodwill mission. It is clear now that the only kind of policy which might have paid dividends would have been one of alliance

[1] See "White Australia—Today's Dilemma", in *Current Affairs Bulletin* (University of Sydney, 1957), Vol. 20, No. 12.

with the United States in an avowed determination to resist Japanese aggression, but this was quite impossible. The disinclination of the United States to make any commitments rendered it impossible at the start. Australian inexperience, insignificance and dependence upon Britain would have made it unlikely, even if the United States had shown any interest. The situation now is completely changed. The most likely aggressive power in Asia is China, to dangers from which the United States is thoroughly alive. It did not prove difficult for Australia in the 1950's to obtain the alliance which would have been impossible in the 1930's. But this does not dispose of the problem. There is no absolute assurance of prompt American assistance in the event of a Chinese drive southwards. In addition, China is not the only possible threat to Australian security, taking the long-term view which Australia, being securely anchored where she is, is forced to take. Japan is still in the picture; even more, Indonesia is an uncomfortable neighbour which, while militarily unpredictable, is so strident politically as to be the possible cause of a riot. It is not surprising, therefore, that Australian concern about future aggression from Asia remains alive. It is increased by the fact that "Australia" does not comprise only the island of that name; half of the island of New Guinea, immediately to the north, is either Australian territory or trust territory held by Australia with a conviction which no amount of United Nations resolutions would be likely to shake. The northern boundary of this territory is farther north than Java, and is only just south of Singapore. Australia is, in this regard, a colonial power, ranged alongside other colonial powers in the United Nations Trusteeship Council; but in her case the colonial area is contiguous to her own and is regarded by most Australians as a vital part of it.

Thus it is in the interest of Australia to be protected against aggression from Asia, and to scrutinize carefully the actions and protestations of all major Asian powers. But it is also in her interest to seek good relations with Asian countries, especially with those which are situated close to her own territory. Nothing will remove Australia from where it is, and wishing will not banish the hundreds of millions of Asians. As soon as the European tide began to ebb from Asia, Australian governments began to show their willingness to help friendly Asian governments. As an example, the Colombo Plan is, in essence, an Australian invention. Australia has struck numerous difficulties in her determination to advance this particular interest; but difficulties are implicit in the situation in which the country finds itself.

The third major interest, that of expanding Australian prosperity, is both domestic and external for Australia. If the country still has untapped resources, it is considered to be obviously in the interests of Australia to exploit them. A bigger population means more hands to work and more mouths to fill, a greater variety of skills and a bigger home market for the diversified products of the expanding Australian economy. In all these senses there are domestic reasons for pushing ahead with economic projects and for inducing migrants to come to Australia. Inextricably linked with these are the interests which Australia pursues externally. A bigger home market provides a more secure foundation for the Australian primary industries, but her increased production of secondary goods, and of primary goods also, provides a need for expanded markets abroad. It is in the Australian interest to seek wider markets while holding on to any tariff preferences she may already have. In the widest sense, it is in the interest of the country to have a rapidly growing population whose technical skills and standard of education are so high as to make them a match for any but the biggest and most determined military power. In a complex combination, domestic and external interests combine to push Australia on to seek more investment from overseas, wider markets and more people.

It should be emphasized that these various interests, although separated for purposes of examination and analysis, are not separate in the minds of Australians. More than with most countries, this is a case of the national image dictating both interests and policies. Australia as a continent is so vast, so lonely, so empty, many-sided and unique that any group of men who peopled it would be forced to assert their own importance and fashion a myth for themselves, like children in an empty house. It is a myth, not in the sense of being untrue, but in that of an embellishment of the past and an idealization of the future. From the Australian standpoint it is a prime necessity, not for national unity, as with the Canadians, but for national self-confidence.

It is one thing to recognize that national interests exist, and that they should be vigorously pursued in order to secure the safety of the country and to generate national self-confidence; it is another to express them in policy. Australian foreign policy has been vigorous but not always successful in its aims. It has been the subject of some party conflict; in fact, it has been caught up in the bitterness of party struggle to a greater extent than foreign policy in most of the other Commonwealth countries. This development is largely a product of the period since 1945. Before World War I Australians paid little attention to foreign affairs, although they were likely to view all external questions in terms of their attachment to Britain or their antipathy towards her. Since 1945 foreign policy has been a major issue in party discussions, although it has probably had little effect upon electoral choice. There have been differences between the parties, and also within one of them; and to see these differences against the background of Australian interests (which are broadly agreed upon by the parties) it may be useful to examine the attitudes of the parties towards certain problems of foreign policy.

Since 1949 the Australian government has been a coalition of the Liberal and Country Parties, led by Sir Robert Menzies. The coalition aspect of the government has had little effect upon foreign policy, the distinctive features of which have been provided by two Liberals, the Prime Minister and his Minister of External Affairs from 1951 to 1960. Both are politicians with long experience of foreign affairs: Sir Robert was a Minister in the Lyons government in the 1930's, attended the 1937 Imperial Conference, and was Prime Minister from 1939 to 1941; Lord Casey was the first Australian diplomatic officer of consequence, having been appointed in 1925 to represent the Australian Prime Minister in London. He was also the first Australian Minister to the United States, and was later British Minister of State in the Middle East and Governor of Bengal. Both are men of dedicated character and decided views. They have spoken for a government whose constituent parties are characterized by strong feelings of opposition to Communism, affection for the British connection, and admiration for the United States.

Opposed to the Liberal and Country Parties is the Labour Party, led until 1960 by Dr. H. V. Evatt, Minister for External Affairs in each of the Labour governments which held office from 1941 to 1949. During this period the party pursued a more active foreign policy than Australia had previously undertaken; it is usually considered that this owed much to the forceful personality and ideas of Dr. Evatt, although the country's perilous position during the war would have led to considerable activity in any case. The special features of Dr. Evatt's policy were enthusiasm for the creation of international institutions, assertion of Australian rights and independence, cultivation of the new nations of Asia, and an attempt to make Australia the spokesman and leader in regard to Commonwealth interests in the Pacific and its environs. Labour ceased to hold office at about the time of the Communist triumph in China, which changed the face of Asian affairs and set up new lines of force in the areas north of Australia. The Labour Party is normally an anti-Communist party in the same sense as the British Labour Party is anti-Communist, that of refusing Communist co-operation and campaigning against Communist tactics and policies. Since 1949, however, the party has been constantly racked by disagreements over the degree of opposition it should offer to Communism as a domestic political force and as an international phenomenon. Splits from the party have occasioned great bitterness; Dr. Evatt's leadership and policy were denounced by enthusiastic anti-Communists. The effect has been to make the leadership less strongly anti-Communist than otherwise it would probably be. Its avowed policy has sometimes been rather closer to that of the left wing of the British Labour Party than was the case when Australian Labour was in office. But it is still a strong advocate of the need for Australia to retain the protection of the United States. Once in office again, Labour would probably prove as close an associate of British and American policies as it was before.

Australia provides a spectacle which is not to be seen in any other Commonwealth country but Britain, that of a Government and Opposition, each of which not only has decided views on foreign policy but has had active experience of responsibility for foreign policy, and the leaders of which have shown particular concern with foreign affairs, and are inclined to see the country's interests as embodied directly in their own persons. This state of affairs did not recur in Canada until 1957, has some counterpart in New Zealand, but is unknown in the Asian or African Commonwealth countries, except perhaps in Pakistan, where the ordinary rules of party politics do not apply. In formal terms, as indicated, the same situation is to be found in New Zealand, but the temperature of New Zealand political life is well below that of Australia. Only in Britain and Australia has discussion on foreign policy been carried on by experienced, well-matched contestants with a determination to inflict damage on one another.

In 1955 Sir Robert addressed the House of Representatives at Canberra and stated certain objectives of Australian foreign policy, together with certain principles which his government considered it was adopting in pursuit of them.[1] The objectives were to seek for peace, providing it could be had with justice; if involved in war, to see that the country had powerful and willing friends; to defend not only Australian rights but also the rights of others; to seek to raise living standards not only for Australians but for other nations struggling towards a life such as Australians had enjoyed for a long time; and to live and let live, not interfering with the internal affairs of other people so long as they did the same. It will be seen that these objectives cover broadly the same ground as my statement of Australian national interests; but, as is understandable in a Prime Minister, they do not go into the same detail. Rather more attention to particulars is given in the "main principles" which Mr. Menzies said his government adopted:

1. We support the Charter of the United Nations, its structure and its procedures.
2. We support and closely co-operate with the British Commonwealth, which existed before the Charter, whose strength is vital to the maintenance of the peace, and which offers no challenge to the United Nations, since it has for years acted through that body and in conformity with the spirit of its Charter.
3. We work incessantly for the closest collaboration between the British Commonwealth and the United States of America who, between them, are the exemplars of peaceful pursuits and of high international ideals, contain the bulk of the military and productive power of the free world, and offer no aggressive threat to others.
4. We pursue "good neighbour" policies towards the Asian countries in this section of the world.
5. We encourage the development of the world's peaceful trade, including our own with other countries.
6. We will justify the co-operation of other nations by ourselves accepting obligations and doing what is necessary at home to make these obligations performable.

[1] The speech is reprinted in *Current Notes* (Department of External Affairs, Canberra), Vol. 26, No. 4, from which the quotations which follow are taken.

Such a list of principles would be acceptable to the Labour Party also, but the two sides in Australian politics differ in the emphasis and understanding which they give to such principles. It is possible to illustrate this fact, and also to indicate some of the main features of Australian foreign policy in action, by examining the Australian approach to a number of international issues of recent years.

First, one may take issues on which there has been no significant difference of policy between the two sides, in spite of differences of opinion about the exact line to pursue in particular circumstances. The first of these is the issue of association with the United States. The Menzies government was responsible for negotiating the ANZUS and SEATO pacts, the two instruments by means of which Australia is given as effective a guarantee of American assistance as can be provided in peacetime. The Labour Party protested against Britain's exclusion from ANZUS, but recognized the desirability of a defensive alliance which gave Australia some assurance of the kind of American protection which she had received in World War II. In the case of SEATO, Labour has been doubtful of the efficacy of the anti-subversion clauses of the Manila Treaty, and is concerned whether uncommitted Asian opinion (in particular, that of India) is likely to look favourably on what seems like interference in Asian affairs; it has also cast doubt on the status of Thailand, a SEATO member, as a democratic country. But it is unlikely that the Labour Party in office would attempt to withdraw from SEATO. To do so would be to invite the United States to dispense with Australian co-operation; and the Labour Party is basically aware of the need for American help. Indeed, it prides itself on having solicited this help in 1941–2, when its opponents might have felt that to do so would be un-British.

For its part, the Menzies government has been anxious to make the most of SEATO, both in protecting Australia's interests and in persuading uncommitted Asian countries that they are in no way threatened by it. Lord Casey made it plain when the Manila Treaty was signed that SEATO could not, in Australia's view, be directed against India. He said: "I wish to state categorically that the Australian government would never regard itself as being committed, contractually or morally, to military action against any other member of the Commonwealth."[1] Australia has also

[1] Statement in the House of Representatives, October 27, 1954, reprinted in *Current Notes*, Vol. 25, No. 10.

made much of the fact that among the members of SEATO are Asian countries such as Pakistan, the Philippines and Thailand. Although, in the first place, Australia intended to concentrate her economic aid to Asia in the Colombo Plan, the government decided in 1956 to provide a certain sum for economic aid to the Asian members of SEATO. The meeting of the SEATO Council of Ministers which took place at Canberra in March, 1957, was treated by the Australian government with great seriousness, in spite of the lukewarm support which it received from Britain. The whole emphasis of the discussions was on anti-Communism, in the sense that Communist subversion and potential Communist aggression were the main concern of the Ministers.[1] It was plain from the attitude of Australian Ministers at this meeting, and in all their statements about SEATO, that they had two main objectives. The first was to involve the United States as closely as possible, not only in a basic guarantee of help in an emergency, but also in detailed strategical planning. The second was to try to ensure that any war against an aggressor within the SEATO area—i.e. a war against Communist China—would be fought as far north of Australia as possible. The same reasoning lay behind the dispatch of Australian troops to Malaya in 1955, a matter which is dealt with below, since it proved a highly contentious act which was repudiated by the Labour Opposition. In spite of Labour divergence over Malaya, however, the government's attempts to implicate the United States in the defence of Australia, and its determination to block the path towards Australia which had been taken by Japan in 1941 were both likely to appeal to basic Australian sentiments.

The problem of Indonesia has been another on which, while there has been keen dispute between the parties about methods, aims have been much the same. In recent years it has taken two forms, those of what to do about West New Guinea and how to deal with Indonesian confrontation of Malaysia. The West New Guinea problem was an embarrassment to all concerned for many years. The Indonesians had no clear title to this territory, the status of which had been left undetermined when Indonesia was

[1] See *Current Notes*, Vol. 28, No. 3, for a full report of the meeting. There was some concern in Australia at the fact that, while the United States sent Mr. Dulles, its Secretary of State, to this meeting, Britain saw fit to send only the Earl of Home, Secretary of State for Commonwealth Relations, who was not considered by Australians to be a figure of comparable importance.

finally established by agreement with the Dutch. On the other hand, continued Dutch control, while acceptable to Australia, was progressively disowned by more and more of Australia's allies and associates, while continuing to be an offence in the eyes of the anti-colonialist bloc at the UN. In the end Indonesia gained its objective by the threat and partial use of force, Australia being almost the last country to support the Dutch. Although this dilatoriness led to some Labour criticism of the Menzies government, there had never been wholehearted Labour support of the Indonesian claim. Both Government and Opposition regard New Guinea as a vital area of Australian defence, no part of which should fall into weak or potentially hostile hands. In any case, it was widely felt that possession of other parts of New Guinea by the Indonesians might endanger the Australian presence in the eastern portion. Once Indonesia did get West New Guinea, Australia had to make the best of it.

When Indonesia began confrontation of Malaysia, there were already Australian troops in Malaya, sent there to help put down the Communist insurgents and to link with SEATO strategy. The Labour Party had been against their dispatch in its period of hostility towards SEATO, but had come round to a tacit acceptance of the position. Confrontation against Malaysia caused Australia to strengthen its military help to that country; again, there was Labour dissatisfaction with the means, but no real quarrel with the end. Both sections wanted continued good relations with Indonesia, Australia's nearest neighbour, but also wanted aggression countered.

Another field of policy in which the parties are agreed is that of the Colombo Plan. Australia has tackled this with particular zest, under the spur of two dynamic influences: one has been the anxiety of her government to show in deeds, and not only in words, the sincerity of its goodwill towards Asian countries; the other has been the rapid development of Australian productive capacity, which has enabled her to provide for Asia not only skilled training in many fields but also consumer and producer goods in great variety. The Colombo Plan has satisfied two major interests, those of making friends in Asia and of showing the potentialities of the Australian economy. Up to the middle of 1962, Australia had spent over £A10½ million on technical aid to sixteen Asian countries, and £A33 million on capital aid, either spent on equipment for Asian development projects or in the form of gifts of wheat and flour to be sold to provide development funds. More than 4,000 Asian scholars and officials had come to Australia for training, and nearly 500 experts had been sent to Asian countries.[1] The experience of being a donor in the Colombo Plan has had notable effects: apart from the fact that it indicates a certain maturity in Australia's development as a sovereign state, it has also meant that Australian governmental, educational and industrial authorities have been brought, for almost the first time, directly into touch with Asians and Asian ways.

A final example of bi-partisanship is trade and investment policy. Again there are disagreements over detail between the parties, but both are wedded to certain main lines of policy which can be summarized as the protection of Australian agriculture and manufactures; the preservation of Imperial Preference for the range of Australian exports which already receive it; encouragement of British and American manufacturers to come in under the shelter of the tariff and build up subsidiary companies to supply the Australian market; readiness to negotiate trade agreements with individual countries which are, or are likely to be, substantial buyers of Australian exports. Whereas in Britain it is widely considered that Australia is guilty of economic heresy in relying so much for foreign exchange upon wool, wheat and metals, sold on a free world market, while pursuing a narrow policy of protectionism in her own market, this policy makes good sense to all the significant elements in Australian politics: it seems to provide the best of both worlds, those of free markets and of autarchy. If the prices of Australia's exports were to fall and to remain low, both sides in Australian politics would look for agreements with Britain and other customers, involving bulk-buying and government-to-government contracts of one kind or another; but, in the absence of a permanent drop in prices, both sides agree on the need to expand the free market, and to make arrangements about reciprocal lowering of tariffs with any countries whose interests appear to coincide with Australia's.

Each of these fields of policy is of major importance for Australia. Each stems directly from her national interests. It can be assumed that something very like the present policy would be pursued by any government, regardless of party. But there are

[1] *The Colombo Plan* (C.O.I., London, 1963), pp. 67 and 76.

other fields, less obviously related to vital interests, in which sharp differences have appeared between the parties.

The first of these is the United Nations, which is not an object of much controversy in the other Commonwealth countries, except perhaps Britain. The main difference in Australia has been epitomized in Sir Robert Menzies and Dr. Evatt, and was most notably displayed in the debate between the parties over the Suez episode of 1956.[1] The essence of Sir Robert's position was that Australia should not decide her attitude in terms of whether the United Nations condemned or applauded the Anglo-French action at Suez; Australia should support Britain because it was in her general interest to do so, in spite of the fact that this meant going against the expressed opinion of the United Nations. Dr. Evatt's view was that enforcement action of the kind which Britain and France said they were taking should not be taken without the approval of the United Nations. The British and French action partook of the qualities of aggression; Australia ought to take account of United Nations opinion, since the United Nations' Charter was the principal law on which international intercourse rested. Behind these two attitudes to the United Nations position lay two different approaches to the whole question of international organization. Sir Robert's view has long been that the United Nations is not a suitable body to decide issues of foreign policy, partly because it was intended to operate on a basis of Great Power agreement which has not materialized, and partly because of the propagandist nature of the debates in the General Assembly, with their unreal assumption that all the members of the UN are of equal importance. Also, as his words quoted above indicate, he places more reliance upon the association of Australia with Britain and the United States than upon any other factor. He and his party are doubtful of the efficacy of international organizations, because of the possibility that these might limit the exercise of Australian sovereignty in such fields as trade and immigration, and because of the traditional attachment to Britain. Sir Robert has always been apprehensive about the aims of the Communist countries and anxious to be protected against them; he is also impatient of the pretentions of small

[1] See W. Macmahon Ball, "Problems of Australian Foreign Policy, July–December, 1956", in *Australian Journal of Politics and History*, Vol. II, No. 2, for an account of party attitudes on Suez.

states which set themselves up as judges of big ones. He does not like the suggestion that the United Nations represents in some way the conscience of the world. Dr. Evatt, on the other hand, an ex-President of the UN General Assembly, had been one of the most prominent figures at the San Francisco Conference of 1945, which put the Charter into its final form. As Minister for External Affairs, he was an enthusiastic supporter of the United Nations and of other international organizations, although he was careful to preserve Australian autonomy in such fields as immigration, trade and supervision of New Guinea. He was emotionally predisposed to international organization, because he deplored Great Power management of international affairs and wished the small and middle Powers to be accorded their due place in deliberation. He looked to the UN to bring law and order into the international anarchy, and accused his opponent of fostering that anarchy.

The differences between the two men on the UN should not be regarded as fundamental in party terms. They were largely temperamental, and were to some extent the outcome of the two personalities reacting on one another. On the Liberal side much more weight was given to the UN by Lord Casey, who had often been a delegate there, than by Sir Robert, who had not. There is no question of a Menzies government withdrawing Australian membership of the UN, although it might prove sensitive to criticism there. Australia does in fact participate fully in all UN activities. On the Labour side, Dr. Evatt's attitude is one which can be stated in large terms in the abstract, and when the party is in opposition; but it can hardly be sustained when the party is in power. Like the Liberals, the Labour Party is not prepared to allow the United Nations to decide vital matters, whether they be those of trade, immigration, colonial policy or war. But it is plain that a difference of emotional emphasis remains, one which, over the Suez affair, would probably have ranged a Labour government against Britain and with Canada and India.

Another field in which the parties have quarrelled is that of policy towards Communism in Asia. The attitude of the Menzies government has been fairly plain. It is that Communism is an innately aggressive force; that Communist parties are linked together in an organized plan of campaign; and that the object of Communist China is a conquest of the whole of Asia, with a possible future attack on Australia. The aim of the government has been to combat Communism by economic means, such as the Colombo Plan and by friendly actions towards uncommitted Asian countries such as India and Indonesia, and to buttress this non-military action with military action through SEATO and through the dispatch of troops to Malaya to help put down the Communist bandits there. In pursuing this policy the government has struck some awkward differences between the United States and Britain, with both of whom it has wished to be in accord. Taking such a strong anti-Communist line it has not recognized the Communist government of China, but continued to recognize the government on Formosa; this has given it prestige in the United States, but has signified a difference of policy from Britain. In the Formosa Straits crisis of 1955, the government's policy fluttered uneasily between support of the United States and support of Britain, although in the end it proved closer to Britain's policy. In the Indo-China crisis of 1954 it proved to be more of the British mind than the American. But on the general principle of identifying Communism as an aggressive force, and treating it as such, the Menzies government has gone farther than the British.

The question of Communism in Asia was certainly a major cause of the split in the Labour Party. Dr. Evatt and his supporters had tended to doubt the efficacy of SEATO and to condemn the sending of troops to Malaya as likely to be interpreted as "colonialism"; their views in the 1950's were much closer to those of Mr. Nehru than to those of either the British or the American government. On the other hand, their opponents within the Labour Party strongly approved determined action against Communism in Asia, stigmatized Communist China as an aggressor and loudly called for stronger Labour support for anti-Communist measures. Thus Dr. Evatt had continually to deal with dissidents in his own ranks whose line was very similar to that of the government to which he was opposed. This gave an extra virulence to his denunciation of the government's measures, although it is at least doubtful whether his own measures, as Prime Minister, would have been very different. The breakaway of his strongest critics, and his own retirement, have made the Labour Party less determined in such criticism.

It will be seen that the making of foreign policy in Australia involves not only a delicate balancing of advantages in deciding whether to follow a British lead or an American lead, or to take a separate Australian line; it also involves acute discussion at home of the implications of policy. The party struggle does not inhibit a government from following the policy on which it has decided; but it does mean that policy may be discussed in highly excited terms, especially if it relates to Asia and Communism, as much of Australian policy must. Australia's advantage in diplomacy lies in her high standard of living, with all the skills that go with it, her record in two wars, her energy and fertility of mind and the friendships which she had been able to cultivate. Her drawbacks are her relative smallness of population, her heavy dependence upon overseas trade, and her remoteness from likely allies, with the exception of New Zealand. Given all this, what is the significance of the Commonwealth in the making of foreign policy?

"The Commonwealth" as such has very little significance in Australia. Apart from the fact that Australians use the phrase to describe their own Federal government, and so must make a considerable adjustment of mind to use it about anything else, it is fairly clear that Australians think either of the attachment to Britain, which is of long standing and fully comprehensible, or of the fortunate connection with the Asian member-nations, but not of the two as being part of a whole. Relations with Britain are one thing; relations with the Asian countries another. Any discussion of relations with Britain is *sui generis*, to be taken on its merits as part of a long sequence of discussions extending over more than a century. The Asian members of the Commonwealth present a quite new and different problem which is not linked primarily with that of relations with Britain, but is part of the wider problem of learning to live with Asia as a whole. This fundamental dichotomy in the Australian approach to Commonwealth affairs must be appreciated if one is to make sense of what often seem to be remarkably naïve statements about the Commonwealth by Australian politicians.[1]

It is still true that most Australian thinking about Britain is based not upon any up-to-date appreciation of the nuances of the Commonwealth but upon the view that Britain is the motherland. This implies neither acquiescence in British policy nor acceptance of any British right of leadership. But it does mean that Australians have difficulty in thinking of Britain as simply an equal partner in an association of sovereign states. Australians are, to this extent,

[1] See Chapter Fifteen.

old-fashioned in their view of the Commonwealth. But they have more justification for being old-fashioned than the citizens of any other Commonwealth country with the exception of New Zealand. They are the descendants of British colonists, with a culture which is still unmistakably British in origin. To think of Britain as a mother is to include in one's thinking all the ambivalent sentiments commonly felt towards mothers; the one thing which one cannot do to a mother is to treat her as an equal. Thus it is noticeable that Australians concentrate upon the relationship with Britain when they are discussing the Commonwealth, and tend to expect other member-nations to have the same mixture of filial feelings as they have. When it is revealed that not only Indians and Malays, but Canadians too, are deficient in these feelings, Australians and New Zealanders have often been pained.

The practical effect of treating Britain as a motherland is that Australian sentiment, and, to a lesser extent, Australian policy, demands more of Britain than she can provide. In the field of migration, for example, Australia and New Zealand are the only two Commonwealth countries which assume that Britain has an obligation to provide them with more people.[1] In that of investment, Australian governments assumed for many years (and still assume to a lesser extent) that Britain should automatically provide whatever development funds were needed by Australia. In trade, Australians tend to assume that Britain will provide a guaranteed market for the food which they produce, but are reluctant to provide any guarantee of a market in Australia for British manufactured goods. In defence, in spite of disappointment at British inability to hold Singapore against the Japanese, it is still considered by Australians that Britain has some obligation to keep forces in South-east Asia and the Far East, and the Australian government was able to secure an assurance to this effect when Mr. Duncan Sandys, the British Minister of Defence, visited Canberra in 1957. At the same time, Australians tend to assume that British policy must be such as will create no difficult choices for Australia in her search for guarantees from the United States; one of the main Australian objections to the Suez affair was that it alienated Britain from the United States and made the Australian position especially delicate on account of this. In

[1] The same opinion used to be found also in Kenya and the Rhodesias. But that chapter is closed.

general, it may be said that Australian demands on Britain are heavy and constant, mitigated now and then by the realization that Britain is not able to do all that Australia might wish (as in the case of the trade agreement between the two countries in 1956 and the defence agreement in 1957), but perennially hopeful that Britain will see the wisdom of making Australia's interests her own. Australian demands that "a great British Commonwealth effort" should be made in this field or that usually prove to be demands that Britain should do something for Australia. In justification, Australia can, and does, point to the support which she has given Britain in two world wars, to the affection and respect in which the Crown is held in Australia, and to the close community of institutions from cricket to Cabinet government which the two countries share.

Such a background to the actual making of foreign policy means that there is a natural tendency for Australian policy, at the United Nations and elsewhere, to seek accommodation with British policy. Wherever possible, an Australian government and its diplomats prefer to act with Britain. In return, Britain shows some concern to keep in line with Australian interests. In cases where the two countries diverge it is possible to see basic national interests emerging: Australia's non-recognition of Communist China, for example, is a case of divergence from Britain because of the desire to emphasize the special circumstances of Australia in the Pacific and to retain the goodwill of the United States; the same has been true of Canada.

The link with Britain, then, is not seen in Australia as specifically a *Commonwealth* link. But the link with the Asian member-nations is. Under the Prime Ministership of J. B. Chifley, and with the enthusiastic concurrence of Dr. Evatt, the Labour Party welcomed Indian, Pakistani and Ceylonese independence, and India's determination to remain within the Commonwealth when becoming a republic. Lord Casey, with his experience as Governor of Bengal, had a close interest in the Indian sub-continent, and in the opportunity, which common membership of the Commonwealth provides, of access to Indian confidence. It was perhaps the Commonwealth link that made Mr. Nehru noticeably reluctant to castigate Australia as a "colonial" power in New Guinea; he usually limited his castigation to the Dutch, and made the distinction that the Dutch were European colonialists while the

Australians were rooted in the area in which they live. At all events it is common form among Australian commentators on international affairs, and Australian politicians and diplomats, to stress the importance of the Commonwealth link with Asia. Undoubtedly, the opportunity to discuss affairs informally at Commonwealth meetings has been an advantage to Australia in charting her Asian policy. But it would not be true to say that Australia has given Commonwealth opinion a veto over her Asian policy. SEATO is unpopular with both India and Ceylon; the fact that Pakistan, another Commonwealth member, belongs to it has not lessened its unpopularity. Nevertheless, Australian policy has been that SEATO is as necessary to the security of free nations in Asia as to that of Australia, and that this is a viewpoint which it is hoped India will adopt in due course.

The significant fact in this context is that, to Australia, it is Asia as a whole that constitutes the problem of foreign policy, not only selected countries in Asia. Here there is a difference from the Canadian position. Canada is so far away from Asia that access to a few selected Asian countries (i.e. those in the Commonwealth) is sufficient to satisfy Canada's needs for contacts with Asia. But to Australia every nation in Asia is a neighbour, and potentially a good or bad neighbour. The closest and most problematical is Indonesia, on Australia's doorstep. The value of the Commonwealth link with Asia is therefore different in Australia's case. It lies in being able to cultivate friendly, intimate relations with a number of important Asian countries, hoping that this intimacy and friendliness will spread to other Asian nations which are not members of the Commonwealth. There was reason to believe that Mr. Nehru's good offices had been used in regard to West New Guinea. Again, the Australian government hopes that Malaysia will continue to be basically anti-Communist in policy, and will eventually join SEATO or retain such close connections with Britain as will provide bases for joint Commonwealth military action. It hopes also that the continued existence of Malaysia will enable Australia to continue to rely upon the Singapore base. But similar hopes extend to other Asian countries, such as Vietnam, Cambodia, Thailand and the Philippines. The Commonwealth is a help to Australia in Asia, but cannot of itself solve the problem of Asian relations for her.

New Zealand

The formulation of national interests follows much the same pattern for New Zealand as for Australia, except that, as indicated at the beginning of this chapter, New Zealand is smaller, more remote, more homogeneous in opinion and less enterprising in foreign affairs. The effect is to make the New Zealand conception of national interests more limited, less tendentious and less affected by contemporary circumstances.

The first, and most obvious, interest is the preservation of the link with Britain. New Zealand politicians may no longer, like Sir Francis Bell in 1926, avoid any suggestion "that New Zealand was entitled to a voice in foreign affairs other than as a very, very small fraction of that great [British] Empire",[1] but they still think of the link with Britain as the determining element in New Zealand foreign relations. In an External Affairs debate in parliament in August, 1956, the Prime Minister, Mr. S. G. Holland, described his reactions when he heard of the Egyptian government's intention to nationalize the Suez Canal:[2]

> "I was able to tell Sir Anthony and Mr. Selwyn Lloyd that Britain could count on New Zealand standing by her through thick and thin. I am sure the House will applaud that announcement, as I am sure that we will not allow these people to get away with this. It was a very great man who coined the sentence, 'Where Britain stands, we stand'. I have said many times that we on this side of the House adopt that. I believe that that is the mood of the people of New Zealand. Where Britain stands, we stand; where she goes, we go, in good times and bad."

Mr. Holland was quoting the statement of the Prime Minister of New Zealand, Mr. Savage, at the outbreak of war in 1939. Although Savage belonged to the Labour Party and Holland to the Nationalist Party, the same sentiment is common to most New Zealanders, regardless of party. For New Zealand Labour, the connection with Britain does not have the same ambiguous overtones as it has for Australian Labour. The normal New Zealand position is to "follow Britain". The Labour governments which were in office between 1935 and 1949 did, at times, disagree with

[1] Quoted in F. L. W. Wood, *New Zealand in the World* (Wellington, 1940), p. 116.

[2] Statement in the N.Z. House of Representatives, August 7, 1956; quoted in *The Round Table*, No. 185 (December 1956), p. 71.

British policy, notably over "appeasement" and over the issue of the veto in the construction of the United Nations Charter. But they were in no sense so liable to independent diplomacy as the Australian Labour governments between 1941 and 1949. While the ANZUS agreement, from which Britain was excluded, was a startling break with New Zealand tradition, it was entered into with misgivings. In any case, its implications do not seem to have been clear to the New Zealand government. Only in 1955, four years later, did Mr. Holland announce that New Zealand had been released by Britain from what were considered to be her traditional obligations for Middle East defence, and would henceforward concentrate her military efforts in South-east Asia and the Pacific. The British link is fostered by New Zealand's economic dependence upon the British market, but is primarily a matter of sentiment and custom. To preserve it is to preserve an essential strand in New Zealand thinking.

A second national interest, however, is to have some guarantee of American protection. New Zealand adherence to ANZUS and SEATO is the outward sign of this. The fact that, not long ago, New Zealand's only Embassy was at Washington is an indication of the importance placed upon co-operation with the United States. Yet there is some difference in emphasis from the same interest as felt by Australia. New Zealand's connection with the United States in World War II was less intimate; it consisted largely of providing equipment and maintenance for Admiral Nimitz's ships, and New Zealand was not an extensive base for American land operations as Australia was. New Zealand's conception of American assistance must necessarily be primarily of naval help. The prospect of joint operations in Asia is more remote than for Australia. Contacts with Asia are fewer; New Zealand had until recently an Embassy only at Bangkok, consequent upon the need for an officer of high status at SEATO Headquarters—no other diplomatic representation in Asia. The possibility of an attack from Asia was demonstrated by the Japanese in 1941, and remains an important factor in moulding the New Zealand sense of national interest, but it does not have the same immediacy as for Australia. New Zealand has no neighbour like Indonesia.

The third obvious New Zealand interest (and that which bulks largest in day-to-day discussion of external affairs) is the maintenance and expansion of trade. The extremely high standard of living rests upon favourable prices for exports of wool, meat and dairy products. New Zealand manufacturing industries have grown, but are nothing like so ambitious as those of Australia. Farmers are a large and vocal section of the community. Also, the fact that New Zealand exports mostly go to Britain means that attention is continually focused upon the policies which Britain pursues in regard to imports and home production. The possibilities of the British market, the commitments of the British government to other interests than those of New Zealand, the complexities of GATT, the potentialities of Imperial Preference arouse more interest in New Zealand than elsewhere in the Commonwealth. It is difficult to diversify the country's exports, and difficult to find extra markets.

Given these interests, and given the small size of New Zealand, it is not surprising that the country's foreign policy has proved mild and limited in comparison with Australia's. To some extent this has been due to personalities, Sir Robert and Dr. Evatt being more flamboyant persons than Mr. Holyoake, Mr. Holland's successor as Nationalist Party leader, and Mr. Walter Nash, the Labour Prime Minister who took office after the elections of 1957. The Nationalist Party is a rough approximation to the Liberal and Country parties in Australia, blending the forces of middle-class feeling and private enterprise in city and country; the Labour Party covers much the same ground as its counterpart in Australia. Each is happier in dealing with a British government of its own way of thinking than with one of the opposite philosophy, but neither finds much difficulty in dealing with any British government. Neither has seen fit to expand New Zealand's diplomatic representation to anything like the same extent as Canada's and Australia's. By 1960 New Zealand had Embassies in Washington, Bangkok, Paris and Tokyo. She had confined her High Commissions to London, Canberra, Ottawa, New Delhi and Kuala Lumpur, along with a Commissioner in Singapore. Her representation extends only to areas in which she is directly interested. Such limited diplomatic resources abroad are matched by economy at home. New Zealand is one of the few Commonwealth countries to retain the old system of linking its External Affairs department to its Prime Minister's department; this is done by having the same permanent head for both. To the extent that a Commonwealth country's main external relations are with Britain, and these are carried on by the Prime Minister, such an arrangement has obvious advantages; but when external relations overflow into "foreign" countries a separation usually takes place. New Zealand is still achieving this kind of separation.

Given the small scale of New Zealand diplomacy, the main field of operation for her foreign policy has been at the United Nations.[1] Here she has played the part of a small nation with a determination to retain her self-respect while not offending her main connections, Britain and the United States. On small matters, such as the right procedure to adopt about the Guatemalan affair of 1954 and the treatment of Chinese Nationalist troops in Burmese territory, New Zealand has sometimes taken an independent line. She has been a model trustee in Samoa. She has given some verbal support to the idea of admitting Communist China to the United Nations; she suggested a UN Trusteeship for Formosa. She has shown enthusiasm for most UN projects; her representatives have usually been proud of New Zealand's energetic record in the League of Nations in the 1930's, and anxious to show that New Zealand is still a believer in international institutions. But in the vital matters which are considered to affect New Zealand security, she has not shown any inclination to allow the UN to affect New Zealand policy.

New Zealand's membership of SEATO is likely to involve her in closer relations with Asian countries.[2] The amount of military aid which she can provide is small, as is the economic aid; but since she has a tradition of skill and daring in military affairs and is far advanced in social services and rural science, she has something to offer to these countries. Also, although New Zealand does not admit coloured migrants, she has a good record of racial equality in her treatment of the Maoris and Pacific Islanders. There is thus some scope for New Zealand to cut a small figure in Asian relations if she wishes. But, as we have seen, circumstances unite to make her less inclined than Australia for such a role.

What is the significance of the Commonwealth for New Zealand policy? Even more than Australians, New Zealanders think instinctively of Britain as a motherland, rather than an equal

[1] See J. K. Cunningham, "New Zealand as a Small Power in the United Nations", in *Political Science* (Wellington), Vol. 9, No. 2.

[2] In spite of her lack of diplomatic representation, New Zealand has already had some experience of day-to-day relations with Asia through her efforts in the Colombo Plan.

partner. It is true that they are pleased to belong to an association of nations with the evident prestige of the Commonwealth. New Zealand Prime Ministers always attend the Prime Ministers' meetings in person. But the reality of the situation remains the link with Britain. In political terms, not even Australia matters very much to New Zealand; in spite of the two countries' apparent contiguity on the map, they are separated by more than a thousand miles of stormy sea and their economies are competitive. The Australia–New Zealand agreement of 1944, concluded between the two Labour governments of the time, has been a dead letter almost from its signing. In regard to some Asian member-nations, as we have seen, New Zealand does not show sufficient interest to appoint High Commissioners. Gestures of goodwill may be made at times towards Canada, but these amount to very little. To New Zealand, the Commonwealth is still Britain. In spite of attending Prime Ministers' meetings, and participating in the co-operative arrangements of Commonwealth countries at the United Nations (such as occupying the non-permanent Commonwealth seat on the Security Council when her turn comes round), New Zealand does not use the Commonwealth as a diplomatic instrument to the same extent as Britain, Canada, India or Australia.

However, there is little doubt that she will need to do so in the future. The appearance of Malaysia as an independent Commonwealth member, and New Zealand's participation with Australia and Britain in the defence of Malaysia, are bound to have an effect upon New Zealand's approach to the Commonwealth in Asia. She may be expected to cultivate closer relations with aligned and non-aligned states, and to exploit the Commonwealth link in much the same way as Australia. But it is likely that this development will be slow, in spite of the fact that the brief Labour government elected in 1957 proved to be more enthusiastic about it than a Nationalist government. Labour tends to be rather more benevolent towards the Asian member-nations than its opponents: this is partly on ideological grounds, and partly because Peter Fraser, the Labour Prime Minister of the 1940's, is remembered as having shown the same sympathy with the emergence of the Asian members as did Mr. Chifley, his counterpart in Australia. The change from a Nationalist to a Labour government might mean little more than a change of emphasis in foreign policy, and vice versa.

It is significant that the Commonwealth issue which agitated

Australia and New Zealand most in recent years was that of Britain's possible entry into the European Economic Community. Both saw danger to their exports of politically important foodstuffs. In Australia's case there would have been some disturbance to the economy but no fundamental hardship if the exports in question had declined; to New Zealand, however, the possibilities were potentially disastrous. Reactions to the situation were characteristic. The Australian government expressed itself strongly against the consequences of Britain's entry (although it admitted Britain's right to enter if she wished), and set up its own bargaining authority in Brussels to see that Britain got the best terms from an Australian standpoint and that Australian interests were kept well before the members of EEC. The New Zealand government seemed stunned at the possibility that Britain might be considering other sources of supply of its traditional exports; action was much less vigorous than with Australia, statements were less extreme, distress at British policy was much more evident. The impact of the whole affair was plainly greater in New Zealand.

The lesson we may draw is that the Commonwealth still has most significance in its traditional aspect in these two countries, and that economic ties provide the clearest evidence of the connection with Britain which both still prize.

Chapter Eleven

THE COMMONWEALTH IN AFRICA

SINCE Ghana became independent in 1957, the most important developments in the Commonwealth have taken place in Africa. Some of these have been in the sphere of new membership: Nigeria (1960), Sierra Leone and Tanganyika (1961), Uganda (1962) and Kenya (1963) have all gained their independence, and Zanzibar, on gaining it in 1963, united with Tanganyika after a local revolt to form Tanzania. Others again have concerned the attempt to form new groupings of colonies; the unsuccessful Federation of Rhodesia and Nyasaland is the most notable case. There was also the departure from the Commonwealth of South Africa, one of its foundation members. Over all has been the constant concern of Britain to divest herself of colonial responsibility in Africa without damaging her continued relations with the countries concerned. In the course of this effort, old assumptions have had to be cast aside. South Africa has become a foreign country, in spite of a long history of South African concern for the Commonwealth; Southern Rhodesia, set up as a self-governing colony in 1923 to go the way of earlier settler colonies towards independence under white control, has been called upon to retain subordinate status until African control is assured. In Africa the "new" Commonwealth has found its prime expression.

Yet, in spite of temptations to the contrary, it is important to recognize that all this activity has not been simply a Commonwealth matter, but rather a part of a massive anti-colonial process which has led not only to the removal of European control but also to the creation of a new sphere of international relations. There is now a politics of Africa which abuts on to general world politics and at times affects it greatly: the disturbances in the Congo, the constant arraignment of South Africa at the UN, and the increasing interest of Communist China in African affairs are examples. When other Commonwealth countries consider the Commonwealth situation in Africa, say in regard to South Africa, Southern Rhodesia or Ghana, they must do so, not simply in Commonwealth terms, but in terms of their own interests in Africa at large and of the influences it exerts elsewhere. This, in itself, has made the British task of disentanglement from colonial responsibilities even harder.

As the West African colonies began to prepare for self-government in the 1950's, it was not immediately clear that Africa as a whole would form an arena for international relations. Each colonial problem seemed unique: the different degree of development of each colony, the differing extent of white settlement, the regional and communal problems, all seemed to call for each African dependency to be treated on an *ad hoc* basis—as, indeed, its constitutional development was. But the process soon became one in which the British government made much the same moves in each case, with much the same responses; and by the time the independence of the East African colonies was being negotiated, there were already pan-African institutions which had to be kept in mind in assessing the proper speed and character of that independence. In 1964, when the question of Southern Rhodesia's status became urgent following the dissolution of the Federation of Rhodesia and Nyasaland, it was plain that pan-African politics was the principal element in deciding the attitude of the British government. Whereas the timing of independence had previously been regarded as essentially a British matter, not to be broached by other Commonwealth members, the question of Southern Rhodesia had to be decided very much in terms of what the other African Commonwealth members thought; and they in turn were acting within the ambit of the Organization of African Union and of the pan-African movements for independence which had preceded it. Nothing like this had happened in Asia, where, although the independence of India, Pakistan, Ceylon and Burma was clearly to be seen as a single process, no specifically pan-Asian pressure had been brought to bear on Britain to provide independence for the territories of Malaysia. Pan-Asianism had seemed to flare up briefly after World War II and then disappear. Its evanescence had made some observers sceptical that pan-Africanism could have a more robust life. Yet, as we shall see, pan-Africanism has proved to be a significant force, in spite of its not achieving all that its most fervent supporters had hoped for; and it is now the framework within which Commonwealth questions in Africa have to be discussed.

In this chapter I shall deal first with the growth of pan-African institutions, then with the appearance of new Commonwealth members in West and East Africa, and then with the problems of the settler areas of Southern Africa. This sequence is meant to emphasize the point already made, that Commonwealth questions must now be looked at in a general African context, and not simply in their own right; I intend to discuss the failure of the Federation of Rhodesia and Nyasaland, and the departure of South Africa, against the background of the new African politics.

The pan-African movement

There is a sense in which the Commonwealth should have been forewarned of the onrush of the pan-African movement, since President Nkrumah of Ghana, in his autobiography published as his country gained its independence, had this to say:[1]

> "I have never regarded the struggle for the independence of the Gold Coast as an isolated objective but always as a part of a general world historical pattern. The African in every territory of this vast continent has been awakened and the struggle for freedom will go on. It is our duty as the vanguard force to offer what assistance we can to those now engaged in the battles that we ourselves have fought and won. Our task is not done and our own safety is not assured until the last vestiges of colonialism have been swept from Africa."

Soon after independence, Dr. Nkrumah showed that he meant business by promoting, in April 1958, the first conference of independent African states, and in December of the same year the first All-African People's Conference. Since then the movement has shown a number of different developments. One has been the direct line of meetings of independent African states, culminating in the formation of the Organization for African Unity (OAU) at Addis Ababa in May 1963. A second has been the appearance and disappearance of rival African groupings, the "Casablanca" and the more militant "Monrovia" groupings. A third has been the formation of regional groupings, from the comprehensive Afro-Malagasy Union (UAM), designed to include all the French-speaking states of Africa, to the continuation of economic and other functional co-operation between the former British colonies in East Africa, and the appearance of an ambiguous Ghana–Guinea–Mali union in West Africa. A fourth has been the attempt to link African with Asian anti-colonialist movements, especially in the

[1] *Ghana, the autobiography of Kwame Nkrumah* (London, 1957), p. 290.

Afro-Asian Peoples' Solidarity Organization (AAPSO). Finally, we should note the concentration on specific African anti-colonialist objectives through the Pan-African Freedom Movement for East, Central and Southern Africa (PAFMECSA).

Any attempt to follow the fortunes of these various bodies demands constant study and considerable attention in detail. One may, however, extract from their recent history certain points.

The first is that, for better or worse, the existing African states, especially the members of the Commonwealth, are divided between those which are satisfied with their existing boundaries and those which consider that these must not be allowed to hinder the pressing need for African unity. The strongest proponent of the latter view is President Nkrumah;[1] but he has been unable to convince other leaders that a "Union Government of Africa" is a practical proposition. In particular, the Prime Minister of Nigeria, Sir Abubakar Tafawa Balewa, and the President of Tanganyika, Dr. Julius Nyerere, have shown themselves hostile to this headlong approach. All recognize a fundamental unity of spirit among Africans, but one side stresses the need for union while the other stresses the difficulty of obtaining it as things stand.

The second point which emerges is that, in spite of the variations in the approach to "unity", all independent African regimes share a distaste for European control, a conviction that it should cease in such areas as those now held by Portugal, a suspicion of Africa's being enlisted on this or that side in the Cold War, and a concern to increase Africa's importance in world affairs, especially at the United Nations. These are matters on which it is not difficult to agree, in spite of differences of opinion on *boundaries*, *trade pacts*, military arrangements and the like. Agreement has been greatly strengthened by experience in the Congo; here the African states have been faced with the prospect of weakness in Africa itself leading to intervention by bigger powers with lines of their own to pursue.

A third point is that, while some of the African organizations (especially the AAPSO, which is little more than a Communist front, and so was largely crippled by the Sino-Soviet quarrel) have been mainly concerned with propaganda, the more solidly-based bodies have begun to organize constructive schemes. The African Development Bank and the Commission of Mediation,

[1] See, in particular, his *Africa Must Unite* (London, 1963).

Conciliation and Arbitration (for settling border disputes), both set up under the OAU, are examples of schemes which have gone well beyond the paper stage. It is clear that a great deal of African inventiveness, application and intelligence can be harnessed in the service of these bodies, and that, while there is little likelihood of a single African state emerging, continued co-operation between the existing states is a genuine possibility.

Finally, there is the fact that the new African states have emerged at a time when they can make a relatively sophisticated approach to international life. Unlike the Asian states, they have escaped the evil consequences of the war in splitting states (such as Vietnam and Korea) between rival backers; they have also escaped that wearing period of the 1950's when the Soviet Union and the United States stood poised against one another, and the neutralist was attacked from both sides. The African states operate at a time when these two major powers recognize the need for negotiation in their treatment of non-aligned countries. Multi-lateralism is the main feature of the Communist world. While the threat of Chinese intervention in other countries' affairs grows stronger, it is necessarily much more remote from the new states of Africa than from those of Asia. The African states function within an international system in which they are courted by the major powers (including Britain, France and Germany) and shown that their opinions matter. They will not have to fight for their lives, unless it be against one another. The advantages of co-operation are obvious; by showing a capacity to manage their own affairs (e.g., in the Congo), they will encourage aid without strings from the richer countries. Nobody would maintain that all is set fair for the African states; but they can command more knowledge in more favourable conditions than their Asian and Middle Eastern counterparts in the 1940's and 50's. Their common efforts are more likely to survive.

All these points have relevance for the Commonwealth. They show that, although the Commonwealth can carry much the same advantages for African as for Asian states, their need for these may not be so great; they may get more help from their own growing African institutions without the risk of being dubbed the victims of neo-colonialism. At the same time, however, they may be expected to use the Commonwealth relationship for all it is worth; along with the UN and the specialized agencies, it is one of the instruments ready to hand for a new state, and capable of being used for African purposes. Once again, the contrast with the new Asian states in the period after World War II is instructive. These came into the UN and the Commonwealth when both bodies were heavily weighted in favour of European and American concerns; it took them some time to accommodate themselves to the new surroundings, and to try to change these to suit their own purposes. In contrast, by 1964 African states had a good half of the votes in the UN General Assembly, and constituted a little less than half of the membership of the Commonwealth; they were operating within institutions which had to take full account of them or face dissolution. The significance of these facts for the Commonwealth is obvious. In the 1960's it has had to give full weight to African interests. The Africans could do without the Commonwealth; it is doubtful if the Commonwealth could do without the Africans.

We may test some of these points by considering the particular circumstances of some of the African member-states.

West Africa

Nigeria and Ghana are the two important Commonwealth states in West Africa; Sierra Leone is too small and too much occupied with domestic problems to be of much significance in international affairs. The same will probably be true of the Gambia after independence. Nigeria and Ghana, however, are likely to continue to contest the position of dominant state in the area.

For this contest, Nigeria's natural advantages are great. She is the largest state in population in Africa; her economy is prosperous; the Nigerian people have reached a high level of education and sophistication in comparison with those of many other states in Africa. The realities of domestic politics, however, dispose Nigeria towards moderation in foreign policy, and deep suspicion of Russian and Chinese intentions in Africa; they also incline Nigerian leaders towards the West, but without the close attachment which characterizes states such as Malaysia or Thailand. Nigeria is thus a non-aligned country with its government's sympathies clearly directed towards the Western side in what remains of the Cold War; at the same time it is strongly African in its preoccupations, and has joined in the search for African solutions to African problems.

Domestic politics in Nigeria centres on the latent conflict between the less developed North and the more developed East and West. The bulk of population is in the North, and Northern influences have predominated in Nigerian politics since the Federal government was set up. It is likely that this predominance will continue. Basically, these regional differences rest upon ethnic differences; but Nigeria is so large, and contains such variations in climate, occupation and modernity, that they must be regarded as having something of the same permanence as cantonal differences in Switzerland or those between states in the USA. As Nigeria neared independence, there was much speculation on whether the dominant political forces of the East and West, as represented by the two political parties, the Action Group and the National Council for Nigeria and the Cameroons (NCNC), would combine to balance the force of numbers of the North, embodied in the Northern People's Congress (NPC). Instead, a coalition was organized between the NPC and NCNC, and the Action Group became increasingly the odd man out; in the end its leader, Chief Awolowo, was imprisoned, and the coalition was consolidated. Dr. Azikiwe, the early leader of the movement for Nigerian independence and the leader of the NCNC, has been Governor-General and President of the new state, and an NPC leader has remained Prime Minister.

Provided there is continued Northern dominance, a generally conservative position will characterize Nigerian foreign policy. The government will strive to keep up with the pan-African movement, and to co-operate fully in such bodies as the OAU; but it will not encourage movements towards over-all union, and will retain its suspicion of Ghanaian pushfulness. In general matters it will try to rally other conservative African states to its own line, and will retain its considerable reserve towards Russian and Chinese initiatives.

Such a government (which may not last if the balance of domestic forces is upset in Nigeria, but has shown good staying power in existing circumstances) is likely to find the Commonwealth a useful adjunct to its foreign policy. There are the advantages, which we have seen in other cases, of British assistance in setting up diplomatic machinery, providing technical aid, and otherwise smoothing the way towards an easier life as a sovereign state. There is the special economic assistance available as a Commonwealth country.[1] Above all, there is the continued connection with Britain, the country from which Nigerians expect to draw most of their help and to whose ways they are accustomed. In world affairs generally, the British line is broadly acceptable to the Nigerian government. This was so much the case that when Nigeria became independent, a defence agreement was arrived at between the two countries; after a year of its operation, however, it was abrogated by joint decision of the two governments, on the ground that its scope and purposes had been "widely misunderstood". "In particular," the two governments stated, "fears have arisen that in consequence of the agreement, Nigeria's freedom of action might be impaired and that she might even be drawn into hostilities against her wishes. The text of the agreement shows that these and other anxieties which have been expressed are wholly without foundation. Nevertheless, in order to end misunderstanding, the two Governments have thought it wise to reconsider the need for a formal agreement." They did, however, go on to say that they would afford each other "such assistance and facilities in defence matters as are appropriate between partners in the Commonwealth".[2] It is fairly clear that the Nigerian government was forced into abrogation of the agreement by hostile demonstrations within the country and by slighting statements from other African countries, which asserted that Nigeria could not be properly non-aligned if it had a defence agreement with Britain. But none of this has changed the general inclination of the Nigerian government towards British policies in the broadest sense.

Ghana is a different story. As the Gold Coast, Ghana was the first British colony in black Africa to be trained for independence; much was expected of a country in which British influence had been so strong and which had prospered so considerably. Dr. Nkrumah's attitude to Britain, once he became Prime Minister, was an ambivalent one in practice, whatever may have been his inmost thoughts. He has plainly never trusted British intentions; he regards partition of colonies, on a "divide and rule" basis, as a

[1] The 1960 meeting of the Commonwealth Economic Consultative Council inaugurated a Special Commonwealth African Assistance Plan (SCAAP), under which the developed Commonwealth countries provide financial and technical aid to the African ones. Most of the aid comes from Britain.

[2] The agreement and the statement on abrogation are in Nicholas Mansergh, *Documents and Speeches on Commonwealth Affairs 1952–1962* (London, 1963), pp. 581–3.

normal British practice; and his whole approach to the question of "neo-colonialism" suggests that he regards Britain as essentially an exploitative force.[1] At the same time, however, he has maintained a formally correct approach at all times to questions of Commonwealth connection, and has defended Ghana's Commonwealth membership on the ground that it does her no harm and does not inhibit her freedom of action.[2] While his rhetoric often suggests that he has adopted the whole corpus of Leninist theory about colonial relationships, he has evidently recognized that Ghana's progress demands the continued use of British specialists (including British officers in the military and police forces), and he has availed himself of whatever advantages he could get from Britain in fields such as education and technical assistance. His actions often lead observers to the view that he is cynically getting what he can where he can; but there is residual ambivalence in his actions and utterances which suggests that he has more respect and affection for the British connection than he is prepared to admit. However, for public consumption in Ghana and on the African stage at large, he is the most resolute of pan-Africanists, the foremost opponent of European intervention in the Congo, the leader who talks most like a Communist (although the Communist Party is banned in Ghana), and the target for attacks from other African leaders on the ground of the subversion which he is said to introduce into their territories. Against the caution and conservatism of the general Nigerian approach, he poses militancy and adventurism.

It is possible to treat Ghanaian foreign policy as largely an expression of President Nkrumah's personality, since that is what it is. Ghana has steadily become a one-party country in which the President's Convention People's Party (CPP) is the embodiment of his personal rule. Rivals have been removed; the free expression of alternative opinion has been mortally affected by a combination of anti-government conspiracies and the narrow evangelism of the government itself. Nevertheless, there remains a sub-stratum of interests which would probably be recognized by any Ghanaian government. These derive partly from Ghana's geographical position—surrounded by former French territories in which the dominant opinion has been hostile to President Nkru-

[1] See especially Chapters 2, 7 and 18 of *Africa Must Unite*.
[2] *Ibid.*, pp. 185–6.

mah's, and inclined towards co-operation with France in particular and Western Europe in general—and partly from her economy: in spite of aspirations towards industrialism and diversification, Ghana, like other countries in West Africa, remains dependent for income on the export of certain cash crops, and is deeply committed to the sale of these in traditional markets. There has been some help from the Soviet bloc, but Ghana must still look to Britain for most of the sinews of economic advancement. Moreover, there is the question of competition with Nigeria: the economies of the two countries are similar, and investment from abroad has the choice between the two.

It is thus plausible to suggest that Ghana remains in the Commonwealth because it does not exact penalties for the constant Ghanaian fulminations against colonialism, it does not commit Ghana to policies which she might resist, it offers some leverage in Britain for Ghanaian aims, and it enables the Ghanaian government to keep an eye on other African Commonwealth governments, especially those, like Nigeria and Tanganyika, which have taken a contrary line to Ghana's in many of the pan-African discussions. One might also expect Ghana to use Commonwealth facilities to further her government's general African plans. Since the French-speaking African states are brought together in the UAM, and can there concert their policies if they wish, it is quite likely that English-speaking African states will use the Commonwealth for something like the same end, though not to the same extent. At all events, there is some parallelism between the position of Ghana and its English-speaking rivals in Africa, and that of India and Pakistan: in each case neither party can afford to let the other monopolize access to whatever the Commonwealth can provide in the way of influence, persuasion or largesse.

East Africa

The situation has been less clear-cut in East Africa, where the level of development was generally lower among Africans before independence, where local settler interests were a significant factor, and where the links with the Middle East and Asia are more obvious than in West Africa. The three former British colonies of East Africa are Kenya, Uganda and Tanganyika.[1] Each of

[1] It seems better to leave the third name in this form, in spite of the fact that the official name of the union between Tanganyika and Zanzibar is Tanzania. The two parts of the union were still fairly distinct entities in 1964.

these has taken a prominent part in the movement for pan-Africanism. There is no clear distinction between them on grounds of caution and militancy; each has a regime in which the two elements are mixed. There are acute tribal problems in each one, in addition to potential difficulties involving Arabs and Indians. The three territories are relatively poor, requiring heavy expenditure in both productive and social investment. Each is very much caught up in the tide of pan-African sentiment; both the Congo and the countries of the former Federation of Rhodesia and Nyasaland are closer to these East African territories than to the West African Commonwealth states. Moreover, the nearness of the southern Sudan, and the necessary diplomatic links with the United Arab Republic through the various pan-African organizations, provide these three countries with surroundings that are potentially explosive.

It does not seem desirable here to attempt to deal exhaustively with the possibilities facing each of the three, since they are very young as sovereign states, have only just begun their diplomacy, and are still under the regimes which gained independence from Britain. Each of these regimes may well suffer significant change before long. Such leaders as Dr. Nyerere in Tanganyika and Mr. Kenyatta in Kenya have the charismatic appeal of men who have symbolized their countries' struggle against colonialism; but each faces discordant elements within his own government, some arising from immediately local conditions of tribal and personal conflict, some from the strains and stresses of the pan-African movement (in which cross-currents of allegiance have already appeared), and others from the intervention in African affairs of the Soviet Union and China. Tanganyika had, in 1964, the most immediate problems of this nature. The revolt in Zanzibar in 1963, immediately after that country had obtained its independence, substituted for a relatively traditional Arab minority rule the regime of African revolutionaries, impelled by the local grievances of a majority deprived of influence, and imbued with confused notions of general African solidarity and of friendship with the major Communist powers. This situation was transformed by the union of Zanzibar and Tanganyika in May 1964, under the headship of Dr. Nyerere. Conditions in Zanzibar remained tense, however, and the united government found the extension of its authority difficult.

Just as the union of Tanganyika and Zanzibar emphasized the divergent element within the new state of Tanzania, so one can see similar elements present in the other two East African states. As in West Africa, there is a basic conflict between moderates and extremists, between those wishing to get ahead with local development and remain basically friendly towards Britain and her associates, and those impatient of such gradualism and anxious to push on quickly with the liberation of territories still under European control and with closer connections with the Communist powers. To state the basic conflict in this way is to over-simplify it for many persons and situations: such matters as the Congo, relations with the Arab states, and the Sino-Soviet split have greatly affected this basic conflict, sometimes uniting the participants on the one side, sometimes altering alliances for tactical reasons. But the basic conflict remains; and it is to be expected that much of the political future of the East African territories will centre round struggles for power with pan-African issues as the source of argument and the rallying-points.

Meanwhile, there are solid problems of domestic concern, especially the preservation of the common services which the countries shared before independence, and the problems of defence. Earlier talk of federation between the three collapsed because of their differing degrees of economic development; as with the Federation of the West Indies, there were fears that the richer members might have to carry the poorer. Common services are, however, being maintained, and it is likely that the wisdom of keeping these will be recognized by whatever governments emerge. There is no such co-operation in defence, although it would be logical to extend existing common arrangements to include it. Following army mutinies in each country soon after independence, British troops were requested in order to maintain stability; after they left, arrangements were made between Britain and both Kenya and Uganda for further British help in building up local forces, but this sort of aid was rejected by Tanganyika. An agreement between Britain and Kenya in 1964 provided for assistance in training Kenyan forces, and for the retention of certain British rights of over-flying and maintenance of naval and air depots. Kenya's disputes with Somalia over part of her northern province made the agreement highly desirable from the standpoint of Mr. Kenyatta; but, as the Nigerian, Burmese, Ceylonese and Libyan cases show, such agreements may not last long if subjected to keen local criticism, as this one may well be.

In general, the future of the East African Commonwealth countries is highly uncertain. While they remain members they will undoubtedly wield considerable influence. Mr Nyerere's threat not to seek Commonwealth membership for Tanganyika if South Africa remained in the Commonwealth was an element in hastening South Africa's departure; the friendship of Kenya is a matter of importance for any British government seeking to maintain military force in the Indian Ocean. As already suggested, all three countries are deeply involved in pan-African affairs, especially those concerning territories still under European control. Their attitudes have been, and will continue to be, highly relevant to British policy towards Rhodesia.

Central Africa

The collapse of the Federation of Rhodesia and Nyasaland, which led an embarrassed life between 1953 and 1963, was the major failure of British colonial policy in the postwar period; yet it cannot be called a failure of the Commonwealth. It might have been so if the Commonwealth, as an institution, had stood for the right of white settlers to decide the political rights of native peoples who outnumbered them. This seemed axiomatic to most of the white settlers of the Rhodesias; but it did not seem axiomatic to anybody else, even to the British cabinet, which, while it put political control of the Federation into the hands of the settlers, retained detailed control of two of the three constituent territories (Nyasaland and Northern Rhodesia) in the hands of the Colonial Office, and ultimate control of the destiny of the Federation in its own.

From the beginning, the Federation was a victim of indecision by Britain. There might have been a case for letting the white Rhodesians go their own way, so that they could either amalgamate later with South Africa or face their own insurgent native peoples without responsibility resting with Britain; this would have been a nineteenth- rather than a twentieth-century solution, but it would have been clear-cut. Alternatively, there would have been a case for serving notice on the white Rhodesians that, since ideas about settlers' rights had altered with the passage of time, they could not expect independence on their own terms, but must accept the inevitability of control by the native majority, and seek the best terms they could get. This too would have been clear-cut. The solution which the British government adopted and later revoked gave the settlers immediate but limited control on the vague understanding that they would strive for "partnership" with the natives; "partnership" was never defined by anyone of importance, and on both sides, British and Rhodesian, the impulse to accuse each other of bad faith was consequently allowed to grow. The Federation was, in fact, constructed on a basis of immediate expediency in which concessions to minority white settlers were mixed with elements of British paternalism towards native peoples. In a sense, it was the victim of an historical hiatus: in 1953, when it was started, no black African state had achieved independence from colonial control, and there was sufficient plausibility in the dying notion of white men's superiority over Africans to make the scheme credible to those who constructed it. By 1963, when it was wound up, black states were common form throughout Africa, and the element of white domination in the Federation had become an anomaly and an embarrassment. By this time the whole thrust of the Commonwealth was towards assertion of native rights to independence. The Federation was a mistake which had to be rubbed out. From it emerged two Commonwealth members, Zambia and Malawi, the new names of the former dependencies of Northern Rhodesia and Nyasaland. Southern Rhodesia, the core of the Federation in that it was governed by white men on a basis organized as long ago as 1923 and transferred to the Federation, was refused independence but showed increasing white militancy in the face of the enmity of the black states around it. Inevitably its leaders turned towards South Africa as its only sympathetic neighbour.

It was a measure of the changing character of the Commonwealth that when, in 1964, the Southern Rhodesian government of Mr. Ian Smith looked for support in its claim to attend the Prime Ministers' meeting and to decide its own future, it found none among Commonwealth member-states, even those, such as Australia and New Zealand, which some people might have expected to sympathize with settler democracies. Its failure to gain support may be regarded as the definitive end of the concept of "white men's countries". Southern Rhodesia and Kenya had both been developed within this concept in the early part of the century;

now one was being refused entry into an association (the Commonwealth) originally composed only of white men's countries, while the other, under a black government, was among those which had the right to deny it entry.

The end of the concept showed that the Commonwealth was now essentially a link between white and coloured, not a white association to which coloured countries were admitted as a favour—as it had seemed to be in the immediate postwar period, when the Asian members were first brought in. It does not require much imagination to work out why Britain, Canada, Australia and New Zealand should not have wished to support Southern Rhodesia's demands. They were now on the defensive in Commonwealth relations, to the extent that their need for good relations with the new African states was greater than any lingering loyalty which they may have felt towards settler communities. Their own wide-ranging diplomacy (not to speak of that of the United States, their ally) demanded that they come to terms with the constituent elements of pan-Africanism, and gain what friends they could among the new states. To set themselves flatly against the dominant African temper on the ground that Southern Rhodesia had been given self-government under white control in 1923 and was therefore entitled to independence on the same terms, would have been to confirm, in the leaders of the new African states, the suspicion that white men's protestations of friendship were only skin-deep, in the sense that they had to give way to the demands of other white men. The political realities of Africa, especially as these had developed in the seething complexities of the Congo, called for clear affirmations from the white countries that they were not racialist in their basic sympathies. With the force of pan-African effort directed against the Portuguese and South African regimes, and plainly hostile towards Southern Rhodesia, Britain and the other "old Dominions" could not afford to be neutral if they wished to retain any African goodwill at all.

Central Africa is thus an area in which other Commonwealth members are willy-nilly called upon to take an interest, because of its significance for African and world politics. The new Commonwealth members there have their own domestic problems to solve (such as their lack of access to the sea, and Zambia's relations with the great copper companies); Southern Rhodesia remains at the time of writing a dilemma for itself and those connected with it.

"CLEAR OUT, YOU LOT! THE COMPOUND IS ROUND THE CORNER"

(*Copyright, Low and "Evening Standard"*)

South Africa

The Union of South Africa left the Commonwealth voluntarily in 1961, after having been a Dominion since 1910 and thus a foundation member of the Commonwealth. If she had not left of her own accord, she would have been expelled or other members would have given up their membership.[1] It is no longer necessary, as in earlier editions of this book, to discuss South African interests and the relevance of the Commonwealth to them, since South Africa is now outside the range of Commonwealth connections, like Eire and Burma. South Africa's departure was, however, an event of importance in the life of the Commonwealth as theirs were not. Apart from the fact that South Africa had been a foundation member, she had contributed a great deal to the lore of the Commonwealth, through both political activity and the efforts of publicists. The Statute of Westminster owed much, as we have seen, to South African prompting; the possibility of South African neutrality in World War II strengthened the trend towards acceptance of the divisibility of the monarchy. On the side of public discussion, South Africa had been, in some ways, the most prominent Commonwealth member. General Smuts had given the term "British Commonwealth of Nations" its greatest impetus as a replacement for "British Empire" in describing the relations between Britain and the Dominions; the granting of self-government to the Boer Republics in the first decade of the twentieth century was widely regarded as a forerunner of the Commonwealth process in action; the voluble Lionel Curtis and others were drawn into discussions of the Commonwealth's future through their experience with Lord Milner; from the Abe Bailey chair at Chatham House to the Beit and Smuts foundations at Oxford and Cambridge, British discussion of colonial and Commonwealth affairs leant heavily for many years upon money made in South Africa. Yet there was always difficulty in the use of South Africa as an example of the Commonwealth image.

The main trouble arose from the lack of acceptance of the whole Commonwealth mystique by a substantial section of the South African public, in spite of the fact that much of this mystique was

[1] See Mansergh, *op. cit.*, pp. 306–99, and articles in *Journal of Commonwealth Political Studies*, November 1961 and November 1963, for material on the event.

fashioned to fit the special circumstances of South Africa. The militant Afrikaners never forgot what they regarded as the injustices of the Boer War, and never gave credit to Britain for sincerity in her grant of status to South Africa. They were hostile to Botha and Smuts and later to Hertzog, in spite of these men's efforts to accommodate Britain and South Africa. They were against the influence of British capital, and against fighting in Britain's wars. They were suspicious of British intentions in native policy, fearing that Britain would give natives in her own African territories opportunities which might later be demanded by the natives of South Africa. The tenacity of the nationalist Afrikaners had its reward in 1948, when Dr. Malan's electoral victory began a period of apparently permanent Nationalist governments, generally hostile to the British connection.

There were two other reasons why South Africa was a bad choice as pattern Commonwealth nation: the position of the English-speaking South Africans, and the certainty of growing hostility to South Africa on racial grounds, as the peoples of Asia and Africa gained their independence. The English-speaking South Africans proved incapable of envisaging effective political symbols of their own, or of adapting the Commonwealth mystique to their own circumstances. Instead of developing a form of South African nationalism which would satisfy their Afrikaner neighbours' hunger for local symbolism, they clung to the British monarchy, the British flag and the British national anthem until these became empty symbols which their opponents derided and to which they were themselves unable to adhere when South Africa became a republic. At the same time, they showed no sympathy with those aspects of British colonial policy which were leading to eventual membership of the Commonwealth for black African states: most of them were as harsh towards Indians in South Africa, and towards native aspirations for citizen rights, as their Afrikaner fellows. The continued refusal of the British government to hand over the High Commission territories of Basutoland, Bechuanaland and Swaziland to South Africa, in spite of promises implied in 1910, showed the divergence between British and South African notions of native rights; there was no appreciable distinction between English- and Afrikaans-speaking South Africans on this particular issue.

From the time when the Imperial government in India began

to complain about South African treatment of Indians, South Africa was a symbol to articulate Afro-Asian nationalists of the racial discrimination which they wished to abolish. Almost as soon as the United Nations was established, complaints were made about racial policy and about the South African administration of South-West Africa. In the General Assembly and the Trusteeship Council, Britain, Australia and New Zealand found it increasingly difficult to side with South Africa on the issue of domestic jurisdiction, in spite of their wish to preserve this principle in regard to their own territories. As the pace of colonial self-government quickened, South Africa fell farther behind. In spite of her government's professed anti-Communism, South Africa was shunned by other Western countries in their formation of alliances; the Simonstown naval base, long used by the Royal Navy, was handed over to South Africa in 1955, and while remaining available to the R.N., was recognized as a South African affair in the future. The massive business connections between Britain and South Africa, especially in the mining industry, naturally impelled the British government towards moderation in its approaches to South Africa; moreover, there were the High Commission territories to be thought of, since these were heavily dependent on South Africa for their economic life. At the same time, however, the demands of black nationalism in West and East Africa were increasing; the idea of a successful Federation of Rhodesia and Nyasaland was posited upon an essential difference between "partnership" there and *apartheid* in South Africa; and little or no support for South Africa was forthcoming from other Western countries with which Britain was normally associated. Within Britain itself a significant movement of opinion was gathering against South African racialism. In all these circumstances it is not surprising that, when the challenge came to South Africa in the Commonwealth Prime Ministers' meeting of 1961, the British government should have considered South Africa's departure a reasonable price to pay for the retention in the Commonwealth circle of the African and Asian members. Only from Australia, New Zealand and the Federation of Rhodesia and Nyasaland was there support for South Africa's remaining a member, and this support did not go to the length of daring the Afro-Asians to resign.

South Africa's departure from the Commonwealth did not, of course, mean the snapping of the links between her and Britain, any more than Eire's had. Trade preferences were retained because they had been established on a bi-lateral, not a multi-lateral basis; South Africa had to leave the Commonwealth Sugar agreement, however, since this was a multi-lateral affair. South Africans in Britain were treated much as before. South Africa remained a Sterling Area country, and the flow of funds between the two countries did not cease. The Simonstown agreement remained in force. But, from the British standpoint, the Commonwealth system undoubtedly became easier to operate when South Africa left. It is hardly likely that the 1964 Prime Ministers' meeting would have been practicable if the question of South African membership had not been settled beforehand. It was possible for British policy in Africa to go forward with much less hindrance, and for Australia and New Zealand, in spite of their discontent with the treatment of South Africa in 1961, to begin to elaborate their own African policies, free of an embarrassing encumbrance. From the standpoint of the African Commonwealth countries, the removal of South Africa from the Commonwealth was at best a propaganda victory; they looked forward to international boycotts and sanctions against South Africa, and eventually to the displacement of its government by one representing the black majority. It was unlikely, however, that Commonwealth machinery would be used to this end, unless the remaining white Commonwealth members considered it unavoidable.

Africa and the Future

It will be increasingly difficult to separate Africa in the Commonwealth from Africa in the world at large. The African members will not make such a separation; they are likely to be glad of their continued connection with Britain, for obvious reasons, but will not let Commonwealth conventions take the place of African objectives. The intensity of internal African politics, so different from the nationally isolated politics of the Asian members when they gained independence, is likely to dictate the use of the Commonwealth as a means to satisfy not only domestic demands but also the requirements of the pan-African movement. However, in spite of the formidable achievements of pan-Africanism, we should not fall into the error of treating it as a monolithic force which will be able to use the Commonwealth as it chooses. As we have seen, there are substantial differences of outlook between the African members of the Commonwealth. Their various alignments are likely to bring them into conflict on a number of issues. They will find it easy to unite on demands such as the outlawing of South Africa, but the settlement of their own differences will require forbearance which their more impatient politicians are not likely to display. Only if the other Commonwealth members show themselves as stubborn as South Africa are they likely to be used as pawns in the African political game.

It would also be an error, however, to consider that the only part which the non-African members can play, or might wish to play, is that of a pawn. Each of them necessarily has its own interests to maintain in Africa. British interests are clearly the greatest: not only does Britain still have unsolved colonial problems in Africa, but she also retains considerable investment and trade in the countries which have become independent. In addition, any British hopes of a significant role in world affairs at large rest upon a capacity to influence events in Africa and in the Indian Ocean; without friends among the independent African states, and their influence for goodwill in pan-African and Afro-Asian counsels, British capacity would be small indeed.

The interests of Canada, Australia and New Zealand are less obvious than Britain's, but tend in the same direction. While they have little or no direct economic interest in Africa, they are directly affected by the stability or instability of the continent, and its effect upon international relationships in general. In particular, they are likely to be very much concerned about increased Chinese and Russian penetration, and to wish for non-Communist African governments inclined towards friendship with the West. In this their interests largely parallel those of the United States. The Commonwealth, as a ready-made instrument for collaboration with African states, is likely to appear more valuable to them as Africa bulks larger in their general calculations. At the same time, it will probably prove to be a source of trouble: if they seek the friendship of African states, they can hardly remain aloof from those states' demands, whether in such fields as the denial of weapons to South Africa and Portugal, or represented by an inquisitive interest in their own colonial possessions in the Pacific and elsewhere. Acute tension could arise if African members proved to have direct and open connections with the Communist states. It seemed that this might happen after the Zanzibar revolt,

Zanzibar having previously been accepted as a Commonwealth member; but the union of Zanzibar with Tanganyika, a state less inclined to direct collaboration with the Communist world, averted this particular embarrassment. If it occurs again, diplomacy within the Commonwealth may prove as delicate as it can be anywhere.

All the same, there is good reason why the new African states should wish to keep the Commonwealth in something like its present condition, even if it does not provide all the things which they want. None of the remaining white members is obnoxious in the sense that South Africa was. There is no need for spectacular crusades against British or Australian colonialism; both these countries are striving to end their colonial responsibilities in a dignified and responsible way, and neither enshrines racial discrimination in her laws in the way that South Africa did. It is possible, of course, that the exigencies of pan-African politics might set the African members competing against one another to prove their militancy; but most of them would find this unwelcome, and would probably try to stop its breaking out. They have plenty to do already, without trying to destroy the Commonwealth. It is not an essential element in their diplomatic armoury, but they would be worse off without it. Their association with Britain is still useful to them. The example of Ghana, the most strident of the African states and yet the one which has been longest a Commonwealth member, suggests that African states will think hard before pushing the Commonwealth relationship to the point of rupture.

However, it is clear that the growth in numbers of the African members has already changed the character of the Commonwealth's discussions and will continue to do so. As indicated in an earlier chapter, Commonwealth Prime Ministers' meetings are now very much concerned with the issues which matter to African states. The pressure upon the more affluent members for assistance is strong. The demand for positive action against recalcitrant colonialists such as the Portuguese and South Africans is difficult to resist. Britain may be expected to accede to pressures of this sort, though not so thoroughly as the African states might wish, and to counsel her non-African Commonwealth fellow-members to do the same. They are not likely to wish to go so fast as Britain, since they do not have so much at stake. But it is in the interests of all of them to maintain good relations in Africa; and the Commonwealth provides a means, flexible in this as in its previous functions.

Chapter Twelve

PAKISTAN, CEYLON AND MALAYSIA

PAKISTAN, Ceylon and Malaysia are grouped together here to indicate the varied interests which it is possible for Asian Commonwealth countries to have, and the choice of policies which lies before them. Each seems a minor power in world affairs, Pakistan because of its backwardness and lack of national unity, Ceylon and Malaysia because of their smallness; none takes the spotlight so readily as India. For this reason there is a tendency to assume that India normally represents Asian opinion in the Commonwealth. Frequently this is so, but not always. The three countries also offer an extended opportunity of seeing what Commonwealth membership may mean to an Asian state.

Pakistan

Pakistan is, in terms of population, the second biggest member of the Commonwealth, with a population of over 80 millions. She is an anti-colonial country, in the sense that she is a member of the Afro-Asian bloc at the United Nations, and makes the appropriate statements of opposition to European colonialism on such occasions as the Bandung Conference. She has no special reason to like the Western world, and might be expected, in the ordinary course of events, to take up a position like India's or Egypt's. Since 1954, however, Pakistan has been connected with the United States, and a partner in the military alliances of CENTO and SEATO. She is the only Asian Commonwealth country to belong to either of these. The explanation is her hostility to another Commonwealth country, India.

Suspicion and fear of India are at the base of nearly every aspect of Pakistani foreign policy. To say this is not to suggest that dislike of Pakistan plays no part in the foreign policy of India; in fact, it is clear that India makes no concessions to Pakistan, and derives pleasure and satisfaction (even if it is only the satisfaction that comes from superior strength and status) from Pakistan's discomfiture. Indo-Pakistani relations are important to India, but they are all-important to Pakistan. India has nearly five times the population of Pakistan; she is in a position to cut land communication between East and West Pakistan at any time she likes; she has superior military strength; she plays a bigger part in world affairs and is listened to more attentively; and she is in possession in Kashmir, the principal area in dispute between the two countries. Further, the world has hardly recovered from the assumption that undivided India was a nation in embryo, and that the making of Pakistan through the partition of undivided India was in some way a marring of destiny. India—which many Pakistanis refuse to call by this name, considering that India should remain a geographical expression—has inherited much of the prestige which undivided India possessed, just as she inherited India House in London; and this remains a source of offence to Pakistanis. India can have a horizon which includes Pakistan but includes many other nations too; it is difficult for Pakistan to prevent India from filling her horizon.

The sources of friction and antipathy between India and Pakistan have often been stated,[1] and need to be mentioned only briefly here. First in point of time is the memory of Hindu-Muslim conflicts in undivided India, of the growth of the Muslim League under Mr. Jinnah, of the demand for Pakistan as the recognition of a nation already in existence in undivided India and entitled to its place in the world as a sovereign state, and of the fierce opposition of Congress to any suggestion of partition. There would be no Pakistan if Indian Muslims had not been persuaded that their status in an independent, undivided India would be an inferior one, subject to deliberate discrimination from the Hindus. This feeling was the impulse that forced the creation of Pakistan upon an unwilling British government and a hostile Congress. It is natural that such a feeling should remain: it was the myth[2] that lay behind the creation of the nation, and the leaders of Pakistan have naturally tended to resurrect it whenever they wished to foster national unity. To the extent that Pakistan has failed to acquire unity, dignity and self-reliance, so the sense of hostility to India has increased.

[1] In particular, they have been stated extremely well by Professor Keith Callard in *Pakistan: A Political Study* (London, 1957), to which this chapter is much indebted.

[2] The demand for Pakistan is an almost perfect example of Sorel's idea of a revolutionary myth, "not [a] description of things, but [the] expression of a determination to act"; incapable of being refuted, because "at bottom, identical with the convictions of a group", and unmixed with politicians' Utopias or blueprints. See Georges Sorel, *Reflections on Violence* (London, 1925), pp. 32–3.

It has been fed by the disputes over Kashmir, the Indus waters, evacuee property, currency agreements and the like. In each of these Pakistan has had a good case. But she has been convinced, all the time, that whether India had a good case or not would be less influential with other countries than the likelihood that India would, or would not, support them in international dealings of one kind and another. This Pakistani view that India is at an advantage, and Pakistan at a disadvantage, in international influence, is sometimes true and sometimes false; but it is true sufficiently often to embitter Pakistan towards India. It has caused Pakistan to base her whole system of alliances and international friendships upon the extent to which they seem likely to enable her to exact justice from India. The Pakistani Prime Minister, Malik Firoz Khan Noon, declared in the National Assembly in March 1958, that he had heard "rumblings" that in 1959 the United States would stop delivery of arms to Pakistan under pressure from India. That, he said, would be the time to reconsider the situation; and if Pakistanis found their freedom threatened by India they would break all the pacts in the world to save their own freedom, and "go and shake hands with people whom we have made enemies for the sake of others".[1] The prophecy came true within a few years, when Pakistan, observing India's discomfiture on its border with China, began to draw closer to China. Pakistanis believe that India is a danger. This being so, we can say that the principal felt interest of Pakistan is that of security against India. It is an interest attributable partly to geographical location, but even more to political memory; it precedes in time such issues as the Kashmir question, but is confirmed and reinforced by them.

Geographical location provides Pakistan with another major interest, that of stable relations with Afghanistan. Since partition the Afghan government has proved, on the whole, hostile to Pakistan, unwilling to accept her frontiers, opposed to her entry into the United Nations, and, in its association with the Russians, a possible source of invasion of Pakistan. In regard to the boundary, Afghanistan has refused to recognize the Pakistan government as the legitimate successor to the British government in treaty relations. Afghanistan has proved a disturber of the peace for Pakistan, in that she has encouraged the Pushtu-speaking people

[1] *Manchester Guardian*, March 10, 1958.

of West Pakistan to hope for a new state of Pakhtoonistan. This is a constant source of friction. But more serious has been the belief that the Russians, who are closely linked with Afghanistan and support her with economic aid, would be prepared to give her military help if war broke out between the two countries. The awkwardness of relations with Afghanistan is increased for Pakistanis by the fact that the Afghans are Muslims.

The belief in Muslim solidarity, which was an essential prerequisite of the campaign to establish Pakistan, is one which carries over naturally into the international sphere, making it seem obvious to fervent Pakistanis that Muslim states should show the same sense of common purpose as Muslims in undivided India are supposed to have shown. Another felt interest in Pakistan, therefore, is the fostering of unity among Muslim countries, not only in order to glorify and strengthen the faith but also to demonstrate that the driving force behind Pakistan itself is one which derives from Islam and is not simply an outcome of the special conditions of the Indian sub-continent. The myth of Pakistan demands that every effort should be made to bring out the latent unity of Muslims throughout the world. In any case, Pakistan is almost the biggest Muslim state, and it is easy for Pakistanis to believe that it should also be the leader.

The interests which Pakistan pursues are thus very much the product of her dominant religious faith and of her association with India, both in the present condition of two sovereign states resulting from partition and in the memories of relations between Hindus and Muslims in undivided India. The desire for security and the desire for Muslim leadership are the concerns which lie behind Pakistani foreign policy. In its particular incidence, however, that policy has been affected by other influences also. Among these the most important has been the character of the men making it, i.e. of the leaders of Pakistan since partition.

The internal politics of Pakistan are unlike those of any other Commonwealth country. The country completed ten years of independence without having had a national election. Its Prime Ministers seemed to come and go with little apparent reason; its Governor-General (transformed, on Pakistan becoming a republic, into its President) had, and wielded, far more power than any similar official in other Commonwealth countries; its first national parliament was dissolved in ignominy; its politics displays little or nothing of that "respect for parliamentary government" and "belief in the democratic way of life" which were so often, and so unctuously, claimed to be the common portion of members of the Commonwealth. Pakistan is, in fact, an oligarchy tempered by free criticism and independent law-courts. It is not a parliamentary democracy at the national level, although it had some of the characteristics of democracy at the provincial level. "In Pakistan politics is made up of a large number of leading persons who, with their political dependents, form loose agreements to achieve power and to maintain it."[1] While the number is large in the sense that a nation of 82 million people can provide lucrative and significant jobs for a large number of men, it is small in regard to national policy. The names of a few dozen men have appeared and reappeared at the head of Pakistani affairs since independence; they have moved from ministries to Constituent assemblies, to governorships of provinces and chief ministerships in them, to posts as ambassadors and in and out of the civil service. The opportunity for personal politics occurred partly from the lack of acceptable public figures and experienced politicians when Pakistan was created, and partly from the confused nature of political parties. The Muslim League, which was supreme at the beginning on account of its leadership in securing partition, and the fact that Mr. Jinnah was its controller, soon broke up into sections and lost the power of unity which, in India, has been kept in spite of vicissitudes by the Congress. The absence of elections at the national level gave the politicians every opportunity of making personal pacts and bargains; the fact of elections at the provincial level led only to disruption and ignominy for the Muslim League. It is not surprising that when Mr. Ghulam Mohammed, as Governor-General, summarily dissolved the Constituent Assembly in 1954, General Iskander Mirza should have said:[2]

> "What we need is one good, strong man like our Governor-General, Mr. Ghulam Mohammed, at the helm of affairs to look after law and order. You must have someone to prevent people from destroying themselves."

Nor is it surprising that General Mirza, as Mr. Ghulam Mohammed's successor, should have fallen to General Ayub Khan.

[1] Callard, *op. cit.*, p. 67.

[2] *Manchester Guardian*, October 30, 1954.

In the present state of politics, effective decisions in government, and especially in foreign policy, are taken by the equivalents of a monarch and courtiers rather than by ministers who are responsible in the British sense of responsible government which is found elsewhere in the Commonwealth. There is less direct contact with public opinion, less opportunity for public opinion to form and direct itself on major questions, and less likelihood that ministers will be able to secure effective support either in the political system or in the country at large. A country in a condition of court politics is likely to display rapid shifts of policy without apparent explanation, and to make pacts and alliances with little obvious preparation of the public mind. It is also liable to desert these alliances in favour of others, if it seems to the small group of men at the head of affairs that better terms can be obtained elsewhere. All of these characteristics have distinguished Pakistani foreign policy.

In the period immediately after partition the country's policy was broadly the same as India's, except for the obvious rifts between the two states; that is, the outlook which Pakistan presented to the world at large, and especially the Western world, was that of an uncommitted country anxious not to be mixed up in the cold war. Pakistan was also foremost among the anti-colonial countries at the United Nations and in other international gatherings. She seemed for a while to wish to keep out of "power blocs". But in 1954 Pakistan signed a Mutual Defence Agreement with the United States, and joined SEATO. In 1955 she became a member of the Bagdad Pact. It is fairly clear that the objects in view were American defence aid and security against India. The fear of Russian pressure through Afghanistan was also present. The result was to intensify Indian intransigence in negotiations over Kashmir and the other issues between India and Pakistan. In addition, there is reason to believe that the extent to which Pakistan was assured of outside aid in the event of hostilities between herself and India was very limited; the aim of her beneficiaries was to secure her co-operation against Communism, not against India. There is little doubt that Pakistan's adherence to these pacts, in association with "colonialists" such as Britain, France and the United States, was defended within the country on the ground that it brought security against India. When it became clear that Pakistan's partners were not interested in defending specifically Pakistani interests against India (except perhaps at the United Nations, over Kashmir), but were concerned to defend the whole of South Asia and the Middle East against Communism, enthusiasm for the pacts diminished. The country was, however, in no position to denounce them, since this might mean the end of American aid and would leave her without any friends. The solution has been found of continuing the pacts but setting up a special relationship with China, to put the West in its place.

Pakistan's disappointment over pacts with Western countries has been matched, and perhaps exceeded, by her disappointment over attempts to develop the unity of Muslim states in international affairs. Pakistan has consistently carried out the obligations of a Muslim state at the United Nations: she has refused to recognize Israel and given full support to Indonesia in its contests with the Dutch. But the intense rivalries of the Arab world have defeated her, in that she has been able to make no headway as a leader of Muslim opinion and has found that her only effective collaboration with Arab countries—in the CENTO pact—has come about as a by-product of her co-operation with Western powers. Egypt, the major Arab state, has proved more interested in India's anti-colonialism and good offices than in the Muslim unity offered by Pakistan; to a lesser extent, so did Indonesia. In spite of numerous conferences and ambitious plans for cultural and political unity among Muslims, Pakistan has found that India's big battalions carry more weight with other Muslim countries than her own efforts. In any case, the stubborn fact of Afghanistan's hostility has proved the essential lack of unity of Islam as a factor in international politics.

Taken in general, Pakistan's foreign policy has not been successful in achieving the ends which it set out to achieve. Pakistan has not been guaranteed any kind of security against India; it can be argued that she became a client of the United States without any real advantage, except assistance in balancing her budget at the level of arms which she wishes to sustain. At the same time, by joining the CENTO Pact she has ranged herself on one side of the split which divides the Arab world and made herself the object of bitter attack from Egypt and Syria. Her membership of SEATO seems to have lessened the chances of an agreement with India over Kashmir and the other matters in dispute between the two countries. As against this, it can be cogently argued that she has been given better security against a Russian or Chinese attack than she could ever have got on her own; but her later association with China suggests this is not something she fears.

What part has Pakistan's membership of the Commonwealth played in her foreign policy? She has had the advantages which accrue to every member-nation, those of general consultation at an informal level with other members, and of access to discussions in which she might not otherwise participate. It is impossible to gauge the effect of these upon Pakistani policy. But it seems clear that Pakistan has been disappointed at the failure of other Commonwealth members to bring pressure upon India to make concessions over Kashmir. Broadly speaking, the opinion of most other Commonwealth governments has been with Pakistan on the question of a plebiscite in Kashmir: India promised such a plebiscite, yet seems to have laid down increasingly arduous conditions for its being held. On this issue (not on the general issue of whether Kashmir should go to India or Pakistan), the strength of Commonwealth opinion has lain with Pakistan. But it has not been pressed to the point where India need take account of it. So far as we know, neither the British nor any other government in the Commonwealth has asked India to amend its policy as a matter of Commonwealth duty. Until 1964, Kashmir had not been discussed at the official meetings of Prime Ministers. Whenever it has been raised at the United Nations, other Commonwealth countries have either abstained from judgment or, in recording their votes, have emphasized that they did so only within the context of existing United Nations resolutions on the matter and only in order to facilitate mediation and a settlement. They have not espoused either side. And whenever India seemed aggrieved by the direction of other Commonwealth votes, her fellow-members have hastened to assure her that they were not making a judgment on the issue as a whole. All of this has been deeply unsatisfactory to Pakistan. Nor has she derived any more satisfaction from her association with other Commonwealth countries in SEATO and CENTO. Kashmir is outside the geographical limits of SEATO; as we have seen, the Australian government has indicated that it will accept no obligations which force it to fight with one Commonwealth country against another; and Britain is of the same mind.

The only obvious advantage which Pakistan derives from the Commonwealth is, paradoxically, that India is also a member of it. If there should be any softening of the Indian attitude, the Commonwealth connection is available to facilitate discussion between the two countries. If India should prove aloof and intransigent, the Commonwealth makes available plenty of go-betweens to restore the situation. If India should prove actively hostile and menace Pakistan with military force, Pakistan would receive, not military, but moral and diplomatic support from the other members of the Commonwealth. These advantages might not amount to much. But Pakistan's position is an awkward one in which trustworthy allies are hard to find, and in which the countries to which religion and geography draw her are highly unreliable. She can derive good offices from the Commonwealth; perhaps she can also derive some material advantage from those fellow-members who are ranged beside her in SEATO. Her misfortune is that she should be seeking protection against India, the Commonwealth country which Britain, Canada, Australia and New Zealand are anxious to placate up to the point where she might actively threaten their interests. If it were any other country, Pakistan would probably find that her Commonwealth connections were much more useful to her. But, given her situation, good offices may be some help; and, if she falls out of favour with the United States, there is still the possibility of co-operation with Commonwealth countries which recognize that an Asian country of Pakistan's size is a useful associate.

Pakistan's foreign policy may be regarded as that of an Asian country which is basically anti-colonial in sentiment, but which has tried to balance alliance with the West against association with China. It is complicated by the fact that Pakistan's greatest difficulties are not with a Communist country, but with India, whereas her Western allies wish to cultivate India and oppose Communism. Pakistani policy gains some flexibility by reason of the small circle of men who make it and their comparative freedom from the pressure of public opinion and effective opposition; but it is restricted by the greater size and strength of India, and by the virtual certainty of India's ability to seize East Pakistan if war should break out between the two countries. The Commonwealth gives Pakistan some extra international stature, and access to a number of countries outside Asia. It also gives her backstairs access to India, if she should want it. But the Commonwealth has proved a disappointment to Pakistan because of the refusal of the other members to judge between her and India and to bring any more than token pressure to bear on India over Kashmir. Pakistan rebels against a basic feature of the Commonwealth association. But she is in no position to change it, and must adjust herself to the fact that Commonwealth members, for a variety of reasons, will not judge between one another.

Ceylon

Ceylon presents a quite different picture from Pakistan. It is far smaller in size and population; its background of communal strife is much less serious than that which divides Pakistan from India, although certain communal issues do cause difficulty between it and India; it is not afflicted by division into two artificial areas; it had an easier journey towards independence; and it has no claims to be a leader in international affairs. Above all, it is not subject to military threat from any power. Since it is so small, its opportunity of influencing other countries is slight; but, since it is not hemmed in by potentially hostile neighbours, as are some other small Asian states, it can exercise a good deal of freedom in its international associations. This is the main reason why Ceylon was able to make an apparently radical change in her foreign policy when Mr. S. W. R. D. Bandaranaike's government was elected in April 1956, without disturbing her membership of the Commonwealth and without any great alteration in Ceylon's association with other countries. The change was represented at the time as a swing away from the West towards neutralism; but the only major difference from the previous situation was that the new government arranged for the British government to vacate the naval and air bases which it was occupying in Ceylon. The British withdrawal was to take from three to five years to complete; such a slow withdrawal, arranged in such an atmosphere of amity, hardly indicated a sharp reversal of previous policy. In any case Ceylon had not been a member of any security pact; she was not receiving defence aid from the United States, and had been one of the more prominent countries at the Bandung Conference, as resolutely anti-colonial as her "neutralist" neighbours. It is true that Mr. Bandaranaike's predecessor, Sir John Kotelawala, had been outspoken in criticism of Soviet colonialism, saying that it was as bad as that of the West; but this implied no necessary sympathy with either Western colonialism or Western military pacts.

Ceylonese national interests are few and simple. They are to improve the formerly high standard of living, by sustaining the condition of the existing export industries, achieving self-sufficiency in foodstuffs and encouraging manufactures; to develop friendly relations with other Asian countries and with those non-Asian countries which have something to offer Ceylon; and, above all, to exploit the relationship in which geography has placed Ceylon and India. The economic interests are largely a matter of internal concern, although they have had some significance externally through the trade agreement which Mr. and Mrs. Bandaranaike's predecessors made with Communist China and which was enlarged and renewed in 1957. The interest in friendship with other countries was developed by Ceylon's earlier governments through the Commonwealth link, and through the Colombo and Bandung meetings of Asian powers. Ceylon was not admitted to the United Nations until December 1955 on account of Soviet opposition. In consequence, she had less opportunity to take an obvious part on the international stage than her neighbours, India, Pakistan and Burma, all of whom had been members at least since independence. The Bandaranaike government thus had the task of defining Ceylonese policy within the ambit of the United Nations. It did so mainly by following the Indian lead on most matters. Its main expansion of diplomatic activity, however, was in its recognition of a number of Communist countries with which previously Ceylon had not had diplomatic relations. Through these moves Ceylon benefited from offers of technical aid from China, East Germany and Czechoslovakia. Ceylon also receives economic aid from the United States and the donor countries of the Colombo Plan. She is in the fortunate position of having all men wishing her well, and showing their goodwill with gifts.

The main aspect of Ceylonese foreign relations must, however, always concern India. No Indian government would be pleased to find Ceylon a tributary of any potentially hostile power. Ceylon is, in fact, as much a responsibility of Indian defence as the Isle of Wight is of British, or Tasmania of Australian. From the Indian standpoint, Ceylon is safe so long as the Ceylonese government does not provide bases or other opportunities to an enemy of India; if there were any prospect of this in a situation of danger of war, India would probably act swiftly to secure the co-operation of Ceylon, either by agreement or by coercion. As things stand, there is no need for India to worry about this possibility, and Ceylon can proceed with her own foreign and defence policy, aware that, in the long run, she will be protected by India.

Seen in such terms, the relationship with India seems idyllic. But the internal position in Ceylon causes difficulties between the two countries which have so far proved impossible to remove, although they have not caused an open rift. The difficulties take two forms, both arising from the fact that, of Ceylon's population of eight millions, just under a million are "Ceylon Tamils" (Ceylon citizens of Tamil—i.e. South Indian—origin) and a similar number "Indian Tamils" (citizens of India, many being illegal immigrants into Ceylon). One form is the language issue within Ceylon itself. The Tamil minority is united in wishing to see Tamil made equal with Sinhalese as an official language; Ceylonese politicians vie with one another to show their loyalty to Sinhalese. Much of Ceylon's politics is taken up with argument over this issue. The second form is that which concerns India: it is the issue of citizenship for the Indian Tamils. They were deprived of citizenship before the 1952 elections, because it was alleged by Ceylonese politicians that they had exercised a disciplined communal influence out of all proportion to their numbers at the previous elections. Early in 1954 an agreement was made between the two governments, with the intention of settling the question of citizenship, and eventually ensuring that the million Indians in Ceylon acquired citizenship in one or other of the two countries. Later in the year the Ceylonese government complained that the Indian High Commissioner had been interfering in Ceylon's domestic affairs by demanding that the Ceylonese constitution be amended to make certain provisions about citizenship for people of Indian origin.[1] Such complaints strained the relations between the two governments, as did Indian complaints that the Ceylonese government was proving slow and unnecessarily selective in granting citizenship. The matter is of relatively little importance to India, but of great importance to Ceylon, because of the explosive part which the communal question can play in Ceylonese politics. No matter how much a Ceylonese and an Indian government may

[1] *The Times*, July 10, 1954.

agree on external policy, their day-to-day relations must necessarily be coloured by the problem of the Indian Tamils.

It is not difficult to see what membership of the Commonwealth means to Ceylon. It gives her stature which other small Asian states, such as South Vietnam and Cambodia, do not possess. It eases relations with Britain, which might otherwise prove difficult when a radical government in Ceylon talks of nationalizing tea plantations or ending British occupation of naval and air bases. Its main effect, however, is to give her an artificial but useful equality with India. Another small state with which India has common boundaries and close relations, Nepal, cannot claim anything like the same equality. This is very largely because of Nepal's backwardness and geographical location. But it is also, to some extent, because of the fortunate circumstance (from Ceylon's standpoint) that Ceylon, as an ex-British dependency, is an equal member with India in a Commonwealth in which members are treated as in no way subordinate one to another. When the Prime Ministers come to London, a Bandaranaike or a Senanayake will get almost as much of the spotlight as a Nehru; this is good for Ceylonese self-respect, and it may have some effect upon the relative positions of the two countries when they enter into diplomatic negotiations. But it would be foolish to assume that the equality of members of the Commonwealth will always apply between India and Ceylon. It is, at best, an artificial equality, kept alive, like that of sovereign states in international law, because it suits certain purposes of all concerned when they are in a condition of mutually acceptable relations. But, just as the equality of sovereign states at large tends to disappear in times of stress, so might that of Asian members of the Commonwealth. To say this is not to suggest any hostile intent on the part of India towards Ceylon; it is simply to recognize the fact that Ceylon, like Nepal, might in conceivable circumstances prove so necessary to India's security that her equality disappeared and she became a client state. This would, of course, be bitterly resisted by the Ceylonese and would be unpalatable to the Indians. The present relationship satisfies both. It does not depend entirely upon common membership of the Commonwealth, but that common membership gives it dignity and stability which might otherwise prove difficult to maintain.

Malaysia

The Federation of Malaya (Malaysia's predecessor) became independent in 1957; Malaysia was established in 1963. There is complete continuity in foreign policy between the two. Broadly speaking, this policy took up a position between those of Pakistan and India. Unlike Pakistan, Malaya is not in SEATO and has not signed a treaty with the United States. Unlike India, she did not embrace non-alignment but has continued previously existing defence arrangements with Britain, Australia and New Zealand, and has shown a preference for anti-Communist countries in Asia, such as Thailand and Vietnam, rather than the countries which have refused to be counted on the anti-Communist side. Such a policy may not last, any more than Sir John Kotelawala's did in Ceylon; an electoral avalanche might overwhelm it as his was overwhelmed. But there are certain features of the Malaysian situation which suggest that the country's interests, as conceived by its first responsible government, may prove fairly durable. A further point of interest about the developing position of Malaysia is that its defence arrangements with Britain, Australia and New Zealand are styled *Commonwealth* arrangements. This means only that they have been entered into by governments of Commonwealth countries, and not that they commit the Commonwealth in general. But it is a notable example of the flexibility of Commonwealth relations that the name can be given to these arrangements, in spite of the generally atomistic character of Commonwealth membership.

The interests of Malaysia, as acted upon by her first government, have been shaped very much by the position of the country at the time of its achieving independence. Malaya was in the unique position of having fought a Communist rebellion for a decade by means of British troops, and, in the later years, Australian and New Zealand military aid. The Communist leadership had shown little or no readiness to give up the fight on the attainment of Malayan independence. Whether prompted by Communist China or not, the Malayan Communists acted as if they were: their attitude was that the independent government of Tunku Abdul Rahman was an agent of the Imperialists, and that Malaya would not be free until they (the Communists) were in control. In addition, the Communists continued to be mainly Chinese in membership, and to intrigue in the Chinese schools against the predominantly Malay government. The unsolved internal problem of Malaysia is that of bringing the Chinese population into full active citizenship, and of rendering sterile the emotional and other links which they retain with Communist China. The Chinese of Singapore, Malaya and Sarawak are balanced by Malays, Indians and various Borneo peoples, but only just; the Chinese are vigorous. Tunku Abdul Rahman's Alliance Party does bring together elements of the three racial groups of Malaya—Malays, Chinese and Indians—but its weakest hold is among the Chinese. It is obvious that such a government will have different feelings towards Communist China from those of a Ceylonese or Pakistani government. Whereas they can view it as a government to be wooed, or, at the least, to be treated as an Asian government of a different complexion but potentially friendly, the followers of Tunku Abdul Rahman must see it as a source of internal disaffection and a potentially hostile power, which might find willing allies among Malaysia's population if the two countries were involved in war. The burden of adequate defence against the Communist rebels would, in any case, be crippling if Malaysia were to shoulder it alone. If Malaysia can take advantage of helpers who are already on the spot, and who share a common attitude towards the rebels and towards Communist China, why should she not do so? This was the reasoning which lay behind Malaya's defence treaty with Britain; the same applies to the Malaysian treaty.

That treaty does not commit Malaysia to more than her own defence, that of the Malayan peninsula, Singapore and Borneo, plus Brunei and Hong Kong. She is not a member of SEATO, and so is not committed to action within the wider SEATO area. She need not even come to the help of Australia and New Zealand if they should be attacked. Malaya's earlier commitment to the remaining British colonies in Asia meant that she had underwritten British colonialism. But each of these colonies, except Hong Kong, is close to Malaya and most have become part of the wider Malaysia. For Malaya to make this link was for her to ensure some goodwill in the areas which she hoped eventually to influence. A further aspect of the situation is that the various parts of Malaysia owe much to British capital for their development, and there is no reason to break the connection.

The reasons for continuing the treaty with Britain were strong between 1957 and 1963, when the Federation of Malaya was the beneficiary; they became even stronger in 1963, when Malaysia was being launched as a combination of the Federation, Singapore, Sarawak and Sabah (formerly British North Borneo). It was plain that Indonesia under President Soekarno was hostile to the new state, and that Indonesian confrontation, beginning as diplomatic hostility, might move on to infiltration and armed attack. Not only the groups behind the Tunku, but also those behind the Prime Ministers of Singapore, Sarawak and Sabah, were glad to welcome the reassertion of British military interest. Indonesia, with nearly 100 million people and twenty years of active military experience, was a formidable foe for a newly unified country of 11 millions. Moreover, she showed every intention of using dissident Malaysians on her own side. The British guarantee was eagerly accepted; alone among those which British has given recently to newly-independent ex-colonies, it was needed immediately against an enemy.

The military help which Malaysia gets from Australia and New Zealand is valued too, because it smacks less of a continuance of British rule than does military aid from Britain. The Malaysian government presumably recognizes that Australian and New Zealand forces are on the spot because their governments consider that their interests are thereby served; but this does not imply any wish to dictate to Malaysia, and it can be treated as the kind of mutual aid which allies customarily extend to one another. The title Commonwealth Reserve which is given to the combined forces dates from before independence, but it can reasonably be said to carry some of the overtones of Malaysian membership of the Commonwealth now that that is an established fact. In many ways, then, continued Malaysian association with Britain, and Malaysian membership of the Commonwealth, are obvious advantages to the new state.

But it is possible that later the position may shift somewhat. One can imagine circumstances in which Malaysia's Commonwealth associates might seem embarrassing in their role as military allies, and might be asked to resume the kind of Commonwealth relationship that exists between Ceylon and her fellow-members. If, for example, the Communist rebels were finally liquidated or came to terms, while the Chinese government decided on a long-term policy of appeasement of non-Communist states in Asia, Indonesia meanwhile giving up confrontation and extending (under a new government) the hand of friendship and co-operation to Malaysia, the Malaysian approach would necessarily be different. It is difficult to imagine all of these things happening together, and difficult to imagine some of them happening at all, but they are brought in here in order to show that changed circumstances could substantially alter the present conception of Malaysian interests. In those circumstances, there would be other influences to detach Malaysia from alliance with Western countries. Whatever government eventually became dominant in Indonesia would, for example, wish to exploit the close ties of religion and culture between Indonesians and Malays, and would presumably wish to lessen Western influence in Malaysia. The incalculable force of Islam, which has proved so defective in forging links between Pakistan and other Muslim states, might operate differently in this case; it already provides links between Malaya and Sumatra, though not many with Java. Disunity is a very real possibility in the new state; confrontation keeps it at bay for the time being, but if confrontation stopped there would undoubtedly be tension between Malays and Chinese. Possibilities of this kind need not be regarded as immediate; but it would be foolish to consider the foreign policy of a new country as set by the circumstances of its first few years of independence, and Malaysia will have to face considerable changes in South-east Asia. In any event, a policy of non-alignment along the same lines as Ceylon under Mr. Bandaranaike might seem attractive in Malaysia, provided that the danger of Indonesian war had gone. The difficulty would be that, unlike Ceylon, Malaysia has no non-Communist protecting power to the north and has already had the experience, in 1941, of invasion from there. So long as the Malaysian government remains predominantly Malay, and has to cope with hostile Communists, it is likely to preserve its present commitments.

In such a situation, Commonwealth membership is a considerable advantage. It gives Malaysia access to the principal non-aligned country, India, along with the formal equality which she shares with her allies—Britain, Australia and New Zealand. It spares her the isolation which would encourage Indonesia. It soothes the British investor, and gives Malaysia a bigger influence over the Asian policy of the British Foreign Office than she would otherwise be able to exert. For a country whose present extent and associations must necessarily be regarded as provisional, these are all advantages worth having. The only disadvantage is the abuse which Indonesia can throw at the government as a continuing associate of Britain; and this would presumably be thrown in any case, whether Malaysia were in the Commonwealth or out of it.

Indian Ocean Commonwealth?

The suggestion is sometimes advanced that Britain should promote a common defence arrangement in the Indian Ocean, basing it upon the East African friendship of Kenya and perhaps Tanganyika, the anti-Chinese sentiment of India and the anti-Communism of Malaysia, and the dependable but so far defenceless west coast of Australia. Such an arrangement could come about if China's expansionism were feared by all these parties and proved sufficiently menacing to allay the anti-colonialist views of most of them. It would also require a guarantee of Britain's ability to maintain forces in the area. But if it did come about (a possibility which would have seemed far-fetched in 1960, but seems less so in 1964), the machinery of the Commonwealth could be used to ease its birth, and perhaps in due course, Ceylon and Pakistan might be induced to participate.

Chapter Thirteen

CYPRUS, THE WEST INDIES AND THE PACIFIC

THE variety of circumstances of Commonwealth members is now bewildering. As we have seen, it has assumed increasing complexity. In the days of the "old Dominions" there was something straightforward about the situation, in spite of the special circumstances of South Africa, Canada, and, for a while, Eire. The addition of the first Asian members provided a new sort of Commonwealth, but it was possible for a time to think of this as fairly stable in character; an Asian extension was made to the existing European-type structure, as it were. The rapid growth of African membership has given the Commonwealth a new dimension, the consequences of which are still to be discovered. These three widening circles of Commonwealth membership—Dominions, Asian, African—are not, however, the only ones, although they are very much the most important. The Commonwealth also has meaning in the Mediterranean, the Caribbean and the Pacific. In this chapter I am concerned with examples of what might be called "difficult" Commonwealth membership, actual or potential, outside Africa. They show not only the variety of the Commonwealth today, but also how Commonwealth questions have become embroiled in, and often subsidiary to, world politics. This latter lesson is not new, but it is worth underlining.

Cyprus

Cyprus has been the principal Commonwealth problem in the Mediterranean.[1] Under British control since 1878 but not formally annexed until World War I, Cyprus was a fortress territory in which British culture, language and institutions made little headway against the Greek and Turkish loyalties of the inhabitants.

[1] The purpose of this book is not to provide exhaustive treatment of every Commonwealth country, however small, so I am leaving out consideration of Malta, which became independent and a Commonwealth member in 1964. As a British colony it had had a tumultuous past in the 1930's and again in the 1950's and 60's, while maintaining its importance as a British naval base until economies and new forms of warfare made it no longer essential to the Royal Navy. Independence was, in this case, a second-best solution, following an attempt at union with Britain, which ran aground on the entrenched position of the Roman Catholic Church in Malta.

Little effort was made to make Cyprus "British" in any significant sense except that of sovereignty. The Greek Cypriot majority retained its unity and ecclesiastical loyalties, cemented under the long period of Turkish control; the Turkish Cypriot minority saw British rule as a protection against the union with Greece which the Greek majority was emotionally inclined to. From the British point of view, the inclinations of the Cypriots had never been a matter of great concern, since the British mission in Cyprus had not been one of pacification or civilization or trade; it had been solely military. Cyprus was a way-station to India, later an alternative to Egypt. Its importance arose solely from British conceptions of where and how Britain might have to fight abroad.

The loss of the Indian Empire would have reduced the significance of Cyprus in British military thinking if ideas of a continued British role in the Middle East had not given it an extra importance. Even now, with Suez far behind and Aden and South Arabia the remaining British preoccupations in the Middle East, Britain retains two areas, totalling 99 square miles, which are British sovereign enclaves in the Republic of Cyprus, subject in no way to Cypriot law. These are bases for military use. Much of the difficulty over Cyprus in the period before independence was gained in 1960 was due to the fact that, whereas the question of *enosis* with Greece was one with which Britain would, in the natural course of Mediterranean relationships, have wished to have nothing to do, British military considerations prevented this question from being tackled in its logical form, as one between Greece, Turkey and the Cypriots. It is a matter of note that an interim solution was achieved in 1960 (interim in the sense that, although it created an independent state of Cyprus, it did not solve the local communal problem) only with the co-operation of Greece and Turkey, the benevolent intervention of the United States, and the use of a treaty between Britain, Greece and Turkey to determine the future of the island. Although, as with other British colonies attaining independence, a British Act was needed to give Cyprus sovereign status, it was clear that this was occurring only because Greece and Turkey had been persuaded to agree to it. Without their approval, communal peace would have been impossible, and Britain would not have been able to hand over power to any sort of agreed Cypriot government.

Cyprus thus set a new example among British dependencies in

gaining independence because two foreign countries gave their approval and joined with Britain in military guarantees of it. A further precedent was set by Cyprus in opting for Commonwealth membership, not on attaining independence, but nine months later, and doing so in terms of a five year trial period dating from 1961. It is fairly clear why the Cypriots, both Greek and Turkish, agreed to Commonwealth status: Cyprus's economy was heavily dependent upon British military spending and upon special trade ties with Britain, and there were no obvious alternatives to these. In the Cypriot view, Britain was more likely to retain both military and economic ties if Cyprus joined the Commonwealth than if she did not. The decision was given to the Cyprus House of Representatives to demonstrate the agreement of all parties to the arrangement.[1] In no other case has the Commonwealth been chosen with quite such cool calculation.

The Commonwealth played no part in the attempts to settle Cypriot communal strife before independence, nor did it exercise any obvious influence or example when this strife flared up again in 1963. Cyprus is essentially a European and Middle Eastern problem, complicated by its geographical location near Turkey, the Greek origins of the great majority of its citizens, and the position of Greece and Turkey as members of NATO and possible foes of the Soviet Union. When Cypriot quarrels embroiled Greece and Turkey in support of the two sections, the United Nations, not the Commonwealth, was called in to try to restore order. This was another manifestation of the fact that the Commonwealth is not a super-state and cannot be expected to settle either the internal difficulties of its members or disputes between them. But in the case of Cyprus one can assume that the Commonwealth was even less relevant than in other cases in which Commonwealth mediation has been suggested. It is difficult to imagine what the Commonwealth means, if anything, in the mind of Archbishop Makarios; but it is fair to say that it cannot mean so much to him as to men like Mr. Kaunda or Dr. Banda or Tunku Abdul Rahman. To them, the Commonwealth connection is essentially an extension and rationalization of the connection with Britain, which, while it has been a colonial connection, has also been one with massive overtones in local institutions in such fields

[1] For some relevant documents, see Nicholas Mansergh (ed.), *Documents and Speeches on Commonwealth Affairs 1952–1962* (London, 1963), pp. 276–9.

as education, law, representation and language. In Cyprus the British connection has been simply one of administration on military grounds. Cypriots can hardly feel the affection for certain British institutions that other Commonwealth peoples can feel. The Archbishop, as leader of the Greek Cypriots, has been the expression of Greekness, which is a different thing in this context from representing Indian nationalism, a Malay majority, or the African personality.

It is little wonder, then, that Cyprus's entry into the Commonwealth should have proceeded with such calculation, or that the Commonwealth should seem so insignificant in Cyprus's affairs. Any formulation of national interests for Cyprus must necessarily centre on the Greek–Turkish conflict. As things have developed, there can be little common ground between the two sections. Increasingly, the Greek Cypriots have made *enosis* their aim, in spite of the provision in the 1960 Treaty of Guarantee between Cyprus, Britain, Greece and Turkey that the Republic "undertakes not to participate, in whole or in part, in any political or economic union with any State whatsoever". Even if *enosis* should not be achieved, the aim of any likely Greek Cypriot movement would be an international position aligned with that of Greece, and the closest connections with Greece. The British situation is essentially that of a country trading military bases for employment and economic assistance; these do not in themselves create any Cypriot disposition to adhere to British positions in the world at large. Cypriot membership of the Commonwealth is an interim arrangement until some final settlement of the Greek–Turkish problem can be made. If no such settlement is possible, Cyprus will presumably remain independent and a Commonwealth member; but its preoccupations will be those of the Eastern Mediterranean, and wider issues will acquire importance to the extent that they affect this area.

The West Indies

In recent years the countries of the British Caribbean have raised certain problems for any theory of the Commonwealth. They have illustrated the difficulties of bringing together separate territories in any sort of integrated association, the importance of specific national interests in the case of even small countries such as Jamaica and Trinidad, and the fact that no automatic measure can decide when a colony is ripe for independence in the political sense.

A Federation of the West Indies (not including British Guiana, British Honduras or the Bahamas) was established in 1957. It was one of the weakest federations ever constructed: the Federal government had almost no means of independent finance, there were still barriers to migration from one section of the federation to another, and there was no common customs tariff. The federation was an attempt on the part of both Britain and West Indian leaders to find a way of ensuring suitable conditions for independence. The problems of the islands were obvious: they were separated by vast areas of sea, none had a big population, and all were poor in relation to the developed countries, although there were substantial differences in standards between them. At the same time, they were essentially British in orientation, and unattracted towards other independent states in the Caribbean.[1] Moreover, they were countries with well-developed representative institutions and an intense local political life. Unlike other postwar candidates for independence, which had seen their central parliaments grow with the demand for sovereign status, the West Indies were trying to develop national consciousness and national institutions long after local institutions had been firmly established.

In no sense could they be said to have tried very hard. The realities of the situation were against the creation of central institutions, except to satisfy certain demands (as for a university and a court of appeal) which could be satisfied by co-operation between the existing administrations. Neither the central parliament nor the central civil service acquired much power. Meanwhile, substantial economic development was taking place in both Jamaica and Trinidad, the two largest and richest of the constituent colonies. Quarrels over the finances of the federation were endemic, as was rivalry between the leaders of the various colonies. After only three years of federation, and before there had been any grant of independence, resistance to federation in Jamaica grew to the point where the government of that colony put the question of continued membership to a referendum, which resulted in a majority against federation. Jamaica immediately set about withdrawing from the federation and seeking independence on its own

[1] British Honduras, with its involved relations with Guatemala, would be an exception if this statement were intended to relate to all British colonies in the area; but British Honduras was not a member of the federation.

account. Trinidad followed suit, arguing that it would not participate in a federation of the remaining units of the existing one, but would be prepared to accommodate them in a unitary state in the future. Both Jamaica and Trinidad became independent and members of the Commonwealth in 1962, the federation having been dissolved in the meantime. There was not much to dispose of.

The failure of the West Indies federation was a warning to those, in Commonwealth circles and elsewhere, who had insisted that integration of disparate neighbouring countries was the way to viability. Like the Federation of Rhodesia and Nyasaland, the West Indies federation was handicapped from the start: it was deliberately kept short of power because the separate elements insisted on retaining vital authority in their own hands, and had popular support in doing so. Behind both federations was the vague idea that integration in itself, accompanied by the institution of certain common services, would engender a federal or national spirit. Comparisons were made with Australia, Canada, the United States and other federations. But no attempt was made effectively to parallel the circumstances of these countries as they had been when they federated; much was said about the difficulty of survival for tiny nations in the twentieth century, but not enough attention was paid to the entrenched position of established interests.

As exemplified in Jamaica and Trinidad, these interests were formidable, and remain so. They are not centred upon the international situation, but upon the economic condition of the islands and their prospects for future investment and growth. Clearly, neither wanted its standards affected by poorer neighbours which might, under federation, be in a position to call for fiscal subventions. There was little or no sense of common purpose; instead, the politicians of the two main islands recognized that their areas, recently emerged from poverty similar to that still being experienced by the others, could make better bargains with investors on their own than if they had to carry others with them. Any consciousness of West Indian identity was vague and formless; awareness of local advantage was immediate and concrete.

It is unlikely that Jamaica and Trinidad will attempt to exert much influence upon the world stage. Unlike the flamboyant ambitions of President Castro in Cuba, the aims of West Indian politicians are limited and local. Moreover, there is little anti-colonialism in the West Indies[1] as that has been understood in Asia and Africa. Britain may have been a neglectful steward in the Caribbean; she has not been a harsh one, and her lead is likely to continue to be welcomed. The men who govern Jamaica and Trinidad have no natural antipathy towards the United States, although they may be distressed from time to time by American treatment of Negroes. American investment is a prime aim in both Jamaica and Trinidad. Unless great changes take place in the governing elite, opposition to British and American policies in the world at large is not likely to develop. The Commonwealth is a natural and proper resting-place for the two countries which have emerged from the wreck of the West Indies federation; ultimate American protection is guaranteed to them by their geographical situation.

It remains to be seen, however, whether the Commonwealth is the proper resting-place for British Guiana. This turbulent colony, convulsed by communal strife and political hubbub for many years, has provided problems not only for Britain but for Afro-Asian opinion. The 1964 Commonwealth Prime Ministers' Conference, which contained more ardent anti-colonialists than any previous meeting, showed in its references to British Guiana how great a puzzle that country provided. The Prime Ministers "expressed concern at the political rivalries in British Guiana which had led to disorder and inter-racial strife and had prejudiced the attainment of independence"; while expressing several different views among themselves about what should be done, "a number of Prime Ministers expressed the hope that the political leaders of British Guiana would seek urgently a basis for collaboration in the interest of their fellow countrymen of all races in order to restore mutual confidence among the races and to strengthen a spirit of national purpose and unity. Only in these circumstances could British Guiana hope to sustain true independence."[2] This statement is, in effect, an endorsement of the conventional British approach to colonial independence, which is normally unacceptable to anti-colonialists. The communal troubles of British Guiana are not unique, although they may have proved more violent before independence than those of some other Commonwealth countries. They are, however, essentially troubles between Indians and

[1] British Guiana is another matter.
[2] *The Times*, July 16, 1964.

Negroes (both some generations removed from their origins), exacerbated by an excitable, Communist-favoured nationalist party led by Dr. Jagan. It would be impolitic for the Commonwealth Prime Ministers, however anti-colonial in theory, to choose between Indian and Negro communities. Moreover, there had been enough rumour about Dr. Jagan's Communist associations to make him unacceptable to a number of Asian and African members of the Commonwealth. In the circumstances it is not surprising, however ironic it may be, to see them falling back upon the classic British formulation of why independence is delayed for colonies in which there is communal strife.

The Pacific

Although there are territories in the Atlantic and Indian oceans which might conceivably achieve independence at some future time, the Pacific forms the main area of unsolved problems of Commonwealth status. While the colonies concerned are small and backward, there are lessons here for Commonwealth relations, arising from the size and location of the territories and the fact that Australia and New Zealand are involved, not simply Britain.

So far as the British territories are concerned, there is some surface similarity to the situation in the Caribbean. The islands are far-flung, with even less communication between them; and in Fiji, the one substantial colony (with nearly half a million people) there are the elements of a British Guianian dispute between native Fijians and Indians, although no Dr. Jagan has yet appeared to light the fires of conflict. Here, as in the Caribbean, simple-minded independence formulae are inapplicable. Fiji, in spite of its population and its high standards of living and education, has only just emerged from the most primitive kind of Governor's rule. The constitutional changes introduced in 1963 went no further than an increase in elected members in which official members still predominated; in the following year unofficial members were given the equivalent of ministerial responsibility for the first time in the Executive Council. In conventional terms, this represents the introduction of self-government at a snail's pace. Yet it is clear that there is little agitation for anything more, and that both the Indian and Fijian communities fear the introduction of more advanced institutions which might remove the arbiter between them. The fact that Fiji, if it attained independence, would also gain Commonwealth status, is neither consolation nor solution for possible problems of communal strife.

The other British islands do not possess the size, richness and advanced social institutions of Fiji. Their future is problematical. There have been suggestions that they might be united into some sort of federation with other island territories, but these schemes all seem utopian at present: again the analogy with the Caribbean is important, since the West Indies were closer together, more populous and further developed than the British Pacific possessions, and yet were unable to construct a viable federal power. There is, however, some possible precedent for Britain in the action taken by New Zealand over Western Samoa.

Western Samoa was a New Zealand Trust Territory, acquired through the Treaty of Versailles; before World War I it had been a German possession. Ties with New Zealand were close, although the distance between was substantial. In 1962 Western Samoa became independent, but without some of the normal appurtenances of independence. Under a treaty of friendship with New Zealand, the new state arranged for its external relations to be conducted for it, its defence to be guaranteed, and advisory services of various kinds to be available. Western Samoa did not join the United Nations; nor did it join the Commonwealth. It remained in much the same practical relationship with New Zealand as before independence, but with sovereign status and the approval of the UN for its new position. As a country largely insulated from contact with others, living its own life in a vast expanse of sea, it lacks nearly all the conditions which have produced nationalism and anti-colonialism in Asia and Africa. The solution it has found is a pragmatic one which might well be applied to British possessions in the Pacific, provided the exigencies of UN politics will allow it.

From the standpoint of this book, the interesting thing about Western Samoa is the fact that no effort has been made to join the Commonwealth. The reason presumably lies in the fact that Western Samoa has not had anything to do with Britain. The association with New Zealand is the extent of Western Samoa's contact with the Western world; it is sufficient in the sense that the Samoans seek no involvement with British investment, military strength, trade or migration, and so have no incentive to join an association which is essentially Britain-centred and has meaning for its members primarily in terms of continued association with Britain. No doubt, for the sake of ideological tidiness, some people would like to see Western Samoa apply for membership of the Commonwealth, on the ground that it was previously in a sense part of the Commonwealth, having been a dependency of New Zealand, which was a member. But this does not seem to have occurred to the Samoans themselves.

There has been some slight discussion in Australia of whether the Western Samoan solution can be applied to the two territories of Papua and New Guinea, which are administered together and will be referred to here simply as New Guinea. The Australian dilemma in regard to New Guinea is considerable. In area (over 180,000 square miles) New Guinea is by far the biggest colonial possession remaining in the Pacific in any country's hands; in population (about 2 millions) it is larger than any British colonial possession at the end of 1964, with the exception of Hong Kong and Southern Rhodesia. Political development has been slow. An elected assembly began its operations in 1964, but with ministerial control firmly in the hands of the Australian administration. Problems of economic and social development are probably greater than in any other part of the world in which independence has been an aim; development has been almost entirely with Australian money, most of it from the Australian government. Yet New Guinea is potentially rich, and its people respond quickly to Western ways. The problems of development might well be begun, if not solved, before Australia made a gesture of renunciation and gave up sovereignty over New Guinea. The main difficulty, however, is that most Australians (and clearly the Australian government) would regard New Guinea as vital to Australian security. It is geographically close, and shares a common frontier with Indonesia. The prospect of a hostile Indonesia, whether Communist or not, is very real. It is, in fact, too much to ask of Australians that they should be indifferent to the future of New Guinea, as the British might be towards that of Ceylon or Sierra Leone.

In such a situation, the attractions of the Western Samoan solution are obvious. If New Guinea independence could be gained on the basis of a treaty of friendship, whereby external relations, defence and development were largely looked after by Australia, this would preserve the essentials of the present position while freeing Australia of the stigma of colonialism. But the difficulties are equally obvious. It was in no Asian power's interest to oppose New Zealand's arrangement with Western Samoa, which is a territory remote from Asia and lacking any connection with the currents of world politics. New Guinea, on the other hand, is contiguous to Indonesia, which would certainly not be indifferent towards proposals for its future. Moreover, New Guinea, unlike Western Samoa, is populous, large and potentially rich. Its people are at present quiescent, occupied with local affairs and hardly aware of the world outside. The cornucopia of Australian aid in fields such as health, education, transport and agricultural assistance is sufficient to occupy their attention and satisfy their immediate demands. But the existence of an elected legislature, with the prospects of political education which it carries with it, ensures that wider horizons will become apparent. In such conditions the Western Samoan solution might be attractive at the start, but might not be able to withstand later pressures from within and without.

Again, the significant thing is that no one has mentioned the Commonwealth as a force which might be employed to settle the New Guinea problem, or as an international association which might suit New Guinea when independent. Australia has persistently failed to bring up New Guinea questions in any Commonwealth context. Like Western Samoa before independence, New Guinea is no doubt "in" the Commonwealth in some technical sense, but no attempt has been made to apply the Commonwealth mystique to it. If New Guinea did not accept a version of the Western Samoa solution, and became independent without special links with Australia, the idea of Commonwealth membership might be brought in as a last resort to retain some sort of connection; but this is unlikely in a context in which the Commonwealth has not previously been mentioned.

The examples in this chapter show that, while the Commonwealth has been a sound solution to the problems of relations between Britain and most of those ex-colonies whose affairs have been considered in previous chapters, there are certain places for which the Commonwealth solution is either irrelevant or likely to be accepted in only limited terms. They also show that by the 1960's Britain had begun to reach the awkward edges of the colonial problem: the massive problems of Asia and Africa had been tackled, but irritating oddities remained.

Part III

THE NATURE AND FUNCTION OF COMMONWEALTH RELATIONS

Chapter Fourteen

THE COMMONWEALTH IN ACTION

So far we have seen how the Commonwealth developed, what common institutions it has, and what interests and policies are characteristic of its members. We should now be in a position to examine more closely the nature of the Commonwealth, and to seek out reasons why it persists as an international association. We have seen enough of the history and policies of the individual members to know how different they are from one another, and how important are national self-respect and national self-assertion in their lives as sovereign states. At the same time, we have seen that in various fields they find membership of the Commonwealth a convenient weapon in their diplomatic armoury. Now we can look for common elements between them, and test some of the assertions often made about the nature of their mutual relationship. The title of this chapter, "The Commonwealth in Action", is not meant to suggest that the Commonwealth can be viewed as a unitary body with common purposes and a single source of direction. It is meant rather to indicate that the Commonwealth is, in point of fact, a going concern. The chapter is intended to investigate the reasons why the Commonwealth keeps going. It begins with an attempt at classification of the interests of the members, as we have seen those displayed, and proceeds to suggestions about the main force of Commonwealth connection.

Preliminary Classification: Settlement and Administration

When we view the overseas members as individual states, the most obvious classification is into those which were British colonies of settlement and those which were British colonies of administration. The former are those to which British settlers went in large numbers; the latter those to which British traders and officials went, but not as permanent settlers. Both got their institutions from British administrators, but in the former case these were soon replaced by local people. The term "colonies of administration" seems more suitable for the second group than the more usual "colonies of exploitation", since the word "exploitation" is capable of many meanings and overtones, and does not effectively describe the kind of division which I wish to emphasize. If by "exploitation" we mean the use of British investment to unlock the natural resources of colonies, then all former British dependencies, whether settled by British people or not, were colonies of exploitation. If we mean the degradation of the local inhabitants in the interests of British investors, the term does not apply to any of the countries which are now Commonwealth members: all have had their standards raised by British investment and all are anxious for more. "Exploitation" is thus a liability if we use it to describe the relations between Britain and the countries which are now Commonwealth members: it can be used to describe either none or all of them, and so is useless as a means of classification. On the other hand, the contrast between settlement and administration has some effective relationship to the actual polities of the countries in question. To the countries of settlement British people took their own institutions of parliament, land tenure, law and religion, and gradually developed these to suit the special circumstances of their new lives. The institutions were brought out under official supervision, and were, in their early stages, administered by British officials of one kind and another; but they were not alien to those who lived in and under them. Even in the cases of French-Canadians and Afrikaners, the British institutions were not wholly strange, since they fitted into certain broad European traditions of conduct. To the countries of administration, in contrast, British institutions were brought as the gifts of an imperial overlord. Only gradually did they replace the existing institutions; in many cases, both sets of institutions continued side by side, one form of law with another, Christianity with paganism or Hinduism or Islam, elected local government with hereditary chiefs. British ways were superimposed upon ancient civilizations and tribal practices, the combination being kept together by benevolent and disinterested civil servants. This process was common to British dependencies in Asia and Africa. Its result was to make British institutions familiar and practical without their becoming indigenous. In the colonies of settlement they became indigenous. We can expect, therefore, to find things in common between those Commonwealth members which belonged to either group, at least so far as their political systems are concerned.

The countries which developed as colonies of settlement were

Canada, Australia, New Zealand and South Africa; those which were colonies of administration include India, Pakistan, Ceylon, Ghana, Nigeria, the East African states and Cyprus. The ill-fated Federation of Rhodesia and Nyasaland, intended as a shining example of the first category, when dismembered belonged to the second. The West Indies are difficult to place in either. They are hardly colonies of settlement, since local white men play only a small part in their politics, and they have a long tradition of management by British administrators. But, at the same time, their reception of a number of British institutions is of such long standing and has been so thorough that they have many of the characteristics of the former colonies of settlement. The fact that they do not fit easily into the categories is no reason for abandoning these, since the other and more important countries can all be fitted into them.

What is immediately apparent from this division is that Britain, by definition, is on neither side of it. Britain stands apart in a special position, as the progenitor of one group and the moulder of the other. As we have seen, it is characteristic of British policy that it has a special concern for each group. The ties of blood are strong, but the ties of former responsibility and of pride in the continuance of association with formerly administered territories are also strong. In neither case, however, is sentiment the only connection. British investment has been busy in both kinds of country; British strategy has taken both into account; British foreign policy is concerned to retain friendly relations with both, since both contain countries which count in the assessment of British interests. If this analysis is correct, we need to make a preliminary three-way division of Commonwealth countries—into Britain, the former colonies of settlement and the former colonies of administration. Britain, as we have seen, has interests which embrace the other two categories. The division between this is based upon the origins of their institutions, and the kind of relationships which they had with Britain before they became sovereign states; does this mean that the two groups will necessarily have antagonistic interests in the world at large? We should be able to discover this by reference to the policies which the various countries have pursued. We can see whether the division persists in foreign policy by considering the approaches of the various Commonwealth countries to the two major issues of alignment in world politics, those of association with Communist states and of association with the United States.

In terms of association with the Communist bloc we can say that Commonwealth members divide into two groups—those whose policies are openly hostile towards Communism as an international phenomenon (i.e. as a force representative of the foreign policies of Russia and China), and those which are ostensibly neutral on this issue. The countries openly hostile are Canada, Australia, New Zealand and Malaysia, with Pakistan doubtful. They have made this plain by their membership of anti-Communist coalitions or by the special policies which their governments have pursued. The other Commonwealth countries profess to be non-aligned. Most of these, however, have proved hostile to Communism as a domestic development. The Indian government has suffered one Communist rebellion and put it down with severity; the Ceylonese government, until Mr. Bandaranaike took office, was strongly opposed to Communist propaganda and to relations of other than a trading character with Communist countries; and in Ghana Dr. Nkrumah's party was severely purged of Communists before independence was achieved.

In terms of association with the United States there is again a division—between those countries which are in military alliance with the United States and those which are not. The first group includes Canada, Australia, New Zealand and Pakistan; the second, India, Ceylon, Malaysia, the African states. In terms of economic aid, however, the position is different: except Pakistan, the countries of the first group are assumed to be advanced countries to which the conditions of economic aid do not apply. All of the second group receive it in one form or another, even if it is only Peace Corps assistance. They differ very much in their approach. Some, like India, cannot do without economic aid; others, like Ghana, say they can. Moreover, even when officially non-aligned, some take military aid from the United States; India after its China fright is the supreme example.

Two things are notable about this method of examination of the Commonwealth countries: its effect upon the original division into former colonies of settlement and administration, and the extent of similarity and difference which it reveals in members' policies. The effect on the former division is to show that, while it broadly persists in that we have put all the former colonies of settlement into the anti-Communist group and most of the former colonies of administration into the neutral one, there are two former colonies of administration—Malaysia and Pakistan—in the anti-Communist group, and one of these—Pakistan—in the group of countries in formal alliance with the United States. Also we have seen that the former colonies of administration are only a little, if at all, more tolerant towards Communism as a domestic phenomenon than the settler countries. None is an associate of Communist states, except in so far as India's and some others' aid from Russia and China might make them such; in India's case, though, the aid is directed against China, a Communist country.

There is no question of one group of countries being for Communism and the other against: the original distinction is blurred, in that the most vehemently anti-Communist countries come from both categories. No Commonwealth country is pro-Communist and all have systems, and dominant political parties, which are subject to Communist opposition and subversion. A man from Mars, looking at the Commonwealth members in the light of their individual policies on Communism, might well say that none was a Communist state; all were anti-Communist, but some carried their anti-Communism to the point of military alliance while others restricted it to domestic policies of varying degrees of intensity.

Similarly, he might say that they were all associated with the United States, although the association was closer and less complicated in some cases than others. He would notice that each of them assessed its connection with the United States in terms of its own security and advantage. To some, like Australia, this connection was basic; to others, such as India, it was something to be availed of at a time of national danger; to others, such as Ghana or Cyprus, it was largely a diplomatic counter, to be used to attain specific national ends but disowned if it seemed likely to prejudice the attainment of those ends.

What I am suggesting, in the name of the man from Mars, is that, on the major issues of association in world politics, the original division among Commonwealth members—a division based upon the origins of their institutions, the content of their cultures and other factors which are said to divide off "European-type" countries from "ex-colonial" countries—is inapplicable. If we take the main conflict as between Russia and China, on the one hand (whatever their quarrels), and the United States on the other, the Commonwealth countries are ranged either on the American side or in the centre; and those in the centre are mostly closer to the American side than to the Communist side. This is a matter of major importance. Just how important it is can be judged by trying to envisage a Communist state as a member of the Commonwealth. It is impossible to imagine the present relationships continuing, impossible to believe that Prime Ministers' meetings could proceed with anything like their present character. If the country were a small one, like Ceylon; if its government wished to retain membership of the Commonwealth; if the others considered that such a request might enable them to detach this country from the Communist bloc—some formal connection might be maintained. But to say this is to speculate beyond the limits which the facts which we have so far gathered warrant us preserving. When we look at the actual policies of Commonwealth countries, without any preconceptions, we see that they are countries which are either opposed to Communism or cool towards it while anxious not to offend it; and they are countries which are in either alliance or friendly relations with the United States. To say this is not to postulate identity of interests either among them or between any one of them and the United States. But it is to say that none is on the anti-American side. Further, to say it is to emphasise that the division between settlers' countries and formerly administered countries is not directly relevant to the major issues of world politics. It has, of course, a relevance elsewhere; and before we go further it would be advisable to see how this division fares in regard to the world conflict over "colonialism".

On the face of it there is a clear division here, based upon the origins of the states in question. On questions of trusteeship at the UN, for example, it is usual to find all the former colonies of settlement voting one way and the former colonies of administration the other. There are occasional abstentions, but the division persists. But we should be careful not to put too much weight on this. If we consider the conflict over "colonialism" to be one between those who think that every colony should be freed tomorrow (in the sense that European control would be immediately terminated), and those who think that they should never be freed (in the sense that European control should persist indefinitely, as a matter of right), then there is really very little division within the Commonwealth. South Africa was the only member likely to affirm the latter proposition. All the other former colonies of settlement have either endorsed colonial independence in particular cases or suggested some delay in granting it, on account of local circumstances; but none would be prepared to state flat-footedly that European rule was in all cases good for natives and should persist. Only the government of South Africa, now departed, adopted this belief. The others might have doubts and fears about particular colonies which it was proposed to make independent, but they would base these upon pragmatic considerations and not upon a belief in European destiny or superiority. Similarly, while the former colonies of administration would all affirm the need for existing colonies to become independent, they would not demand that this happen immediately. Their method of argument has usually been to maintain that the colonial power should set a target date for independence, and that this should take into account the preparation of the colony for life as a sovereign state. Mr. Nehru's tolerant attitude towards the British preparation for independence in Malaya is a case in point. The instances of colonialism about which the "anti-colonialists" have spoken with most vehemence have been those of French and Belgian and Portuguese colonies, in which the colonial power has shown no intention of willingly permitting independence to be an ambition. In other words the British colonies, which are those to which one might have expected most attention to be directed by Commonwealth members which were formerly British dependencies, have largely escaped attack, with the exception of "settler colonies" such as Kenya and the Federation of Rhodesia and Nyasaland. In these it is the local white men, and not the colonial power, who have been criticized.

The United Nations votes can mostly be explained by the fact that a false unity has been created among the former colonies of settlement because each of them except Canada has been a trustee. They tend to resist attempts to give orders to one trustee, on the ground that to establish a precedent might mean that orders were, in due course, given to the others. Also they have been anxious to avoid an extension of UN powers into the field of domestic jurisdiction, and so have supported one another—and Britain—in resisting attempts to stretch the Charter on the issue of colonialism. But this has not meant that their own policies towards Trust Territories were identical, or that they agreed with one another's policies: in fact, the South African approach to African questions was a perpetual source of embarrassment to the others. For the anti-colonial Commonwealth members, on the other hand, the apparatus of the UN has been an irresistible temptation to expound their creed at its most extreme and to claim the support of world opinion for it. In given cases of investigation of Trust Territories, and in relations with particular trustees (with the exception of South Africa) they have shown more prudence and restraint.

The Force of "Negative Agreement"

In sum, I think we can say that on major issues of association with either Communism or anti-Communism and of "colonialism" there is a broad measure of what might be called *negative agreement* between Commonwealth members. By this I mean agreement about what they do not want to happen. In the one case they do not want to see the world communized; in the other they all, with the former exception of South Africa (and Australia perhaps in New Guinea), do not want to see a perpetuation of European rule over coloured peoples. This negative agreement is weaker on the second issue than the first. This is to be expected. We have seen how pervasive is the element of myth in the collective minds of the former colonies of administration: all are liable to dramatize the past in terms of victory against a colonial oppressor, and all are likely to imply that subjection was heavier and more brutal than it was in fact. In each of them the ruling group gained its ascendancy by its struggle against the colonial power, and endeavours to keep that ascendancy, and to stimulate national unity, by recalling the struggle.[1] It is not surprising that they should cast other peoples in the roles which they have filled, and should dramatize others' situations even more than their own. But it is also the case that, as each ex-colonial country develops its independent life as a sovereign state, its government recognizes the difficulties of government as such and is likely to make some allowance for the problems of a colonial power—provided that that power shows a willingness to postulate self-government as the goal for its colonies. This kind of feeling is in conflict with the other kind, the national myth; to

[1] The positions of the ruling groups in Pakistan, Cyprus and certain other countries are all ambiguous in this regard, since they gained their status from struggle with their fellows rather than with Britain. This does not necessarily alter their sentiments, but it may well affect their policies.

some extent this explains the tergiversations of policy of newly independent states.

Nevertheless, there is a good deal of negative agreement within the Commonwealth over colonialism as it applies to colonies of Commonwealth members; and there is even more about Communism. It is true that there was a public division of opinion between India and the older members in the days of Mr. J. F. Dulles, who expected everyone to declare himself on this issue; but the two views are capable of a good deal of accommodation in particular cases, as we have seen. Negative agreement may not seem a very strong reason for supporting a common institution such as the Commonwealth. But its force can be shown, as I have already suggested, by trying to envisage a Communist state as a member of the Commonwealth. If the Commonwealth as it stands has any special characteristics, they are certainly not those of either a summit meeting or the United Nations. There is neither the open hostility and hard bargaining of the one, nor the emphasis upon protocol and hollow agreement of the other. Yet, if a Communist state were to enter the Commonwealth (or, more likely, if a Commonwealth member were to become Communist), the atmosphere of the Commonwealth meetings would inevitably become identical with one or the other of these. As the association stands, each member can treat each other as an independent state, with confidence that the term "independence" has some meaning. Each Commonwealth member is a sovereign state in the full sense of the term, and each is able to decide its own policy within quite broad limits. In the absolute sense of independence, that of having to take no one else's opinion into account, none is independent, not even Britain. But none is the servant of another country. The position of a Communist state is quite different. It is either a master, like Russia and China, or potentially their servant. It is essentially part of a *system*. Bringing a Communist state into the Commonwealth would mean bringing in part of a system which had its centre elsewhere, and which was bound together far more tightly and in far more detail than any of the alliances and associations which Commonwealth members at present have with countries outside the Commonwealth. It is the essence of the position of a Commonwealth country that it is not part of a system in the Communist way. It makes alliances, makes friends, gets help, does business; but it is neither a master nor a servant of other allegedly sovereign states. Commonwealth members would find that in practice they did not treat a Communist state as they now treat each other. The agreement which, I have suggested, is now negative, would quickly display its positive aspects. But the whole nature of the Commonwealth connection would have changed.

So far I have suggested that there is a substantial amount of negative agreement between the overseas Commonwealth members, now that South Africa has gone, on the issue of colonialism when that is presented in its most extreme form. I have said little or nothing about the position of Britain; yet the position of Britain is crucial, since it is with Britain, rather than with one another, that the Commonwealth members have their main contacts. Britain gives more time and energy to the cultivation of the Commonwealth than any other member. As we have seen, she has a number of interests which can be satisfied only by the continuance of the association. If her influence were exerted in opposition to this negative agreement—i.e. if she consistently pursued policies which offended Commonwealth members and which cut across the sort of negative agreement which I have suggested can be found between them—then either the notion of negative agreement as a force sustaining the Commonwealth would have to be abandoned or the Commonwealth would simply fall apart. But in fact Britain supports, and, to some extent, manufactures negative agreement on both the major issues with which we have been concerned. She makes it abundantly plain that she takes seriously the opinions of both the former settlers' colonies and the former colonies of administration. She makes it clear that the ties of blood are not to be taken as automatically ensuring British agreement with the policies put forward by Australia and New Zealand, for example; Mr. Harold Macmillan's Commonwealth tour of 1958 was in one of its aspects an attempt to impress on the Australian and New Zealand publics the importance which Britain places upon the views of the Asian members of the Commonwealth. A Labour Prime Minister would have been just as forthright, if not more so. And Britain has been careful to relate colonial policy to foreign policy when dealing with the Asian and African members.

In regard to the two major issues of world politics discussed above, the British position strengthens the degree of negative agreement which exists among the overseas Commonwealth nations. On Communism she is securely established as an anti-

Communist nation, a fellow-member with the United States in both SEATO and NATO; but her anti-Communism is worn with a difference, symbolized by her refusal to deny recognition to Communist China and the very great freedom of action which she allows to Communists at home. Anti-Communism with Britain is not so much defence against a noisome creed as it is with fervent anti-Communists in some of the other Commonwealth countries, but rather the present-day incarnation of the traditional British opposition to a potentially aggressive supreme power in Europe. Its ideological aspects are played down, its balance of power aspects played up. This is still in some contrast to the situation in the United States. Nevertheless, the American alliance is accepted by all parties in Britain, and made the pivot of British external policy. In the case of countries like India, which wish to remain non-aligned and are inclined to criticize the United States for its pushfulness, Britain is concerned to emphasize the common aims of free nations. She is also prepared to use non-aligned countries as listening-posts and information centres in the Communist world, as the use of India during the Korean War showed. The British role is, in fact, to emphasize the degree of common agreement among non-Communist countries and not to stress anti-Communism as a creed—certainly not to carry it to extremes.

In regard to "colonialism", the British position is similar. Britain is committed to self-government for her colonies, and to their graduation to Commonwealth membership in cases where the viability of the colony can be assumed. She is the only colonial power (except the United States in regard to the Philippines and Puerto Rico) to have publicly announced that independence is her aim and to have made this policy a reality. Thus she wears her colonialism with a difference, too. Her approach to Dutch, French and Portuguese colonialism, and to the designs of the South African government, has usually been sufficiently ambiguous to enable her to retain connections with these countries without committing herself to their policies. As I have suggested, British colonialism is not often under fire from anti-colonialists in other Commonwealth governments.

We can say, then, that if negative agreement of the kind that I have suggested exists between Commonwealth members, British policy helps it and does not hinder. How far can we take this negative agreement? We should not try to find too many instances of it; so long as it applies to two or three major matters of world politics and is not displaced by continuous disagreement on a number of important issues, it can be said to act as a reason for staying in the Commonwealth and keeping that association together. The Commonwealth countries do not want general war to occur; they do not want colonial wars (as in North Africa) to continue; they do not want Communist regimes established in their countries, or on their doorsteps; they do not want to be so utterly beholden to the United States as to forfeit their freedom to disagree with American policies. Even South Africa and India used to agree on these negative desirabilities; and they are of the very essence of British foreign policy. We need not be surprised that even the tortuous platitudes of the communiques issued after meetings of Prime Ministers can be interpreted to state this kind of negative agreement. But, if we consider that negative agreement is the main characteristic of Commonwealth members, at least in their external policies, we should be surprised to find them co-operating closely as a group in any more than a spasmodic way. It is a mark of negative agreement in politics that it does not lead to continuous common action. To hope to avoid something is not such a goad to action as to hope to bring something about. A campaign against war is always more ragged and inefficient than a campaign to win a war; men are more easily brought together to get rid of an existing evil than to stave off an impending disaster. There is always the possibility of something else turning up. In any case, policy to prevent something happening is much less easy to formulate than policy to stop something which is already happening. In politics, in addition, the persons or states which are joined in negative agreement are pulled apart, at the same time, by the positive demands which each has and may share with some of the others but not with all. This is very much the state of affairs which prevails among Commonwealth members. They all have special interests which demand individual diplomacy and special forms of treaty and alliance; sometimes these involve other Commonwealth members, as with Canada's place in NATO or Australia's and New Zealand's in ANZUS, but they rarely involve all the others. But, all the same, the member-nations do have certain negative interests in common, and have found that the Commonwealth association is a means of forwarding these.

One objection which would probably be made to this line of

argument is that, even if the Commonwealth members are joined in a loose form of negative agreement, this is hardly likely to survive such bitter internal quarrels as those between India and Pakistan and between Ghana and Nigeria. The only answer to such an objection is that these countries do remain together in the Commonwealth, in spite of their hostility, and that it is difficult to postulate any solid *political* reason for their doing so, apart from some form of negative agreement on wider issues of world politics. (Economic reasons are discussed below.) The bitter disputes between members are prevented from tearing the Commonwealth apart by the determination of nearly all concerned to treat them as separate matters which are not susceptible to general Commonwealth adjudication. From time to time there are feelers from India, Pakistan and elsewhere that this state of affairs should be changed; but they are not taken up and they quickly disappear, for the reason that even the country advancing them is quickly reminded that it gains advantages from the same rule of Commonwealth relations as its opponent seems to be profiting from for the moment. If there are times, for example, when Pakistan wants "justice" against India, there are other times when she is grateful that the Commonwealth as a whole has no means of judging her ties with China. The fact that the Prime Ministers' meetings have stuck resolutely to the rule of not discussing members' domestic affairs, or what a member said were domestic affairs, has meant that discussion could be concentrated upon those issues in which all members might be likely to take an interest. This has brought even the warring members into some kind of harmony. Pakistan and India may be at daggers drawn about Kashmir, but they may have a common interest in not being shut out of the Common Market in Europe; India and South Africa could both agree on the dangers inherent in a forward policy in Egypt by Britain and France unsupported by the United States. The Commonwealth in action, then, is seen in a number of unrelated, and sometimes panicky, joint reactions to events and circumstances which seem to threaten some result which all the members of the Commonwealth are united in hoping will not happen. This is perhaps a disappointing view of things, but it has the merit of not assuming agreement for which there is no evidence.

Perhaps, however, we have been starting at the wrong end in seeking the reasons for the continuance of the Commonwealth in the common elements of foreign policy among the members. There are two other reasons sometimes given for the persistence of the Commonwealth: one is that the members possess "a common sense of values and ideals",[1] and the other that they are held together by common economic interests. Both these contentions require examination.

"Common Values and Ideals"

The first is often put in a form of this kind: "Among the factors that link the ten Member States of the Commonwealth none is more fundamental than their common possession of the institutions of parliamentary government based on United Kingdom practice."[2] This is undoubtedly correct, to the extent that the members have versions of these institutions, and that they all derive largely from British institutions. But this is, in itself, insufficient to explain membership of the Commonwealth. The Union of Burma and the Republic of Ireland both have such institutions, but they did not remain in the Commonwealth. Again, in at least one member-nation (Pakistan) the operation of parliamentary institutions has hardly accorded with the British pattern; only the Courts could be said to have followed out that pattern. In the newer African states parliamentarism has had to give way to charismatic leadership. Elsewhere the British model has incorporated federalism of the American or Swiss kind; and federalism is a form of government which great British writers on constitutional matters, notably Bagehot and Dicey, have persisted in regarding as distinctly un-British. In South Africa the dominant party looked not to the British parliament as the model which it hoped eventually to copy, but to the legislatures of the Boer Republics. In fact, it is possible to find a great deal of divergence within the parliamentary institutions of the Commonwealth, even though one need not challenge the main point that these institutions derive broadly from British ones, and that Erskine May is an authority abroad as he is in Britain. The real difficulty of giving credit to parliamentary institutions for sustaining the Commonwealth bond is that it is hard to see how these institutions, in themselves, are likely to create the "common sense of values and

[1] *What is the Commonwealth?* Central Office of Information Pamphlet No. 15 (H.M.S.O., London, 1956), p. 2. Somewhat different in 1963 edition, p. 7.

[2] *Parliamentary Institutions in the Commonwealth.* Central Office of Information Reference Pamphlet No. 29 (H.M.S.O., London, 1957), p. 1.

ideals" which is said to go with them. Undoubtedly, they carry power in their bones; the adoption of the parliamentary model in India has already markedly affected the lines of development of politics there.[1] But the effect is more upon the tactics and logistics of politics than upon the ideals and aims in the service of which those are employed. One can be a scoundrel in parliament as well as out of it, and it is idle to believe that the mere presence of parliamentary institutions is a guarantee that government will be free, efficient and inspired by the same ideals as governments in other parliamentary countries. Egypt, Japan, Germany, Spain and Italy have all shown at different stages of their history that the presence of a parliament is no protection against tyranny. Again, parliamentary institutions may well exist as a cloak for truly dictatorial government; nearly all tyrannies maintain some kind of parliament as a means of deluding their own citizens and foreigners too.

It is true that if we take the term "parliamentary institutions" to include such things as the right of opposition, freedom of the Press, a non-political civil service and the rule of law, there is some guarantee that a country which accepts and operates all of these will be a free country and that tyranny will be difficult to sustain. But this is to stretch the term to the extent of making it equivalent to "British political institutions"; and such an extension is hardly justified. Not all British political institutions have been transplanted to Commonwealth countries, and not all which have been transplanted have survived. The governments of the Commonwealth are not simple replicas of Westminster and Whitehall. They contain indigenous elements; in most African members these have already become dominant. Even in such heavily British countries as Australia and New Zealand there are aspects of political institutions which would shock the purists in Britain—such things as unicameralism, party election of Cabinets, pressure from external party organizations, a different role for local government, and the right of courts to decide the constitutionality of parliamentary enactments. The atmosphere and temper of government in these countries are different from those of Britain; institutions which are ostensibly the same are found to be worked in quite different ways and to serve different purposes. If this is true of Australia and New Zealand, it applies to an even

[1] See W. H. Morris-Jones, *Parliament in India* (London, 1957).

greater extent to Commonwealth members which developed as colonies of administration and not of settlement. The point is that values and ideals can, at the best, be only *nourished* by political institutions. They can hardly be inculcated by political institutions, except in so far as there is a tendency towards them, inherent in the society to which they are being made to apply, and stimulated by religion, education, culture and social patterns. A parliament, for example, imposes certain basic patterns of political behaviour, especially if it is part of a system of responsible government: there is a government and an opposition, ministers must explain themselves to parliament, political debate is polarized around the activities of the ministry. To a certain extent, these patterns of behaviour will provide their own values: opposition has an opportunity to establish a position of some responsibility and not to be treated as treason; the practice of debate demands a certain courtesy and set of rules which imply respect for other opinions than the official one; ministers have some responsibility towards parliamentary opinion, and not simply to the electors or their party organizations. But, if these values are to be generally accepted, they must not only find answering sentiments in the community at large; they must also chime with the dominant values of the community. Parliamentary government was a failure in Germany, Japan and Italy between the wars, largely because its postulates offended against dominant social values; so it has been in Africa. My conclusion is that if we are to look for values and ideals which are shared between particular countries we must look for them, not primarily in similarity of political institutions, but in values inherent in the societies themselves.

To look for such values does not mean that we must assume them to be dominant throughout the societies, in the sense that each citizen can consciously describe them and say that he believes in them. It is enough, on a short view, if the persons in control of affairs or likely to be in control accept these values and tend to act upon them. If the politicians, diplomats, civil servants, businessmen and leaders of society generally hold them, that will be sufficient, for the time being, to ensure some common universe of discourse and a capacity to sympathize with the ideals expressed by others within it. And it is here that we find some similarity among the Commonwealth countries. In all of them the men in charge have some common sense of values, derived from the strongly British-centred culture which they share. The common use of English is an example; the prevalence of training at British universities or at universities of the British type is another. The traditions of English law have been a notable example of this common culture, shared by a large proportion of the active politicians of the member-nations. There was a sense in which an Afrikaner politician like Dr. Malan or Mr. Strijdom was more of a foreigner in Britain, more the product of an alien culture, than Sir Robert Menzies or Dr. Nkrumah or Mr. Suhrawardy: the Afrikaans language and the postulates of Afrikaner culture and religion were further away from British norms than those which the upbringing of the Australian, the Ghanaian and the Pakistani had led them to regard as normal and proper.

To a great extent, the governing elites of the Commonwealth share a common culture. This enables Prime Ministers, politicians and diplomats to converse with relative ease—i.e. with greater ease than they often find in company with their counterparts in countries outside the Commonwealth. It means that they have usually been exposed to British standards of conduct and measures of social value, even in cases (such as India and Pakistan) where potent local sources of values were also in existence. It is here that the significance of parliamentary institutions is to be seen. Parliamentary institutions are among the most obvious British characteristics. An elite in another Commonwealth country, which has been exposed to British culture, will have been, of necessity, exposed to parliamentary institutions and will, *ceteris paribus*, wish to copy them in setting up its own independent institutions. It may, indeed, have no option: India adopted parliamentary institutions because they were the only form of national government of which it had any experience. The prevalance of parliamentary institutions in the Commonwealth is thus to be explained by the direct transmission of them, with other British institutions, to the former colonies of settlement, and by the sense of familiarity with them acquired by British-educated elites in the former colonies of administration. The institutions have been accompanied by appropriate values, and, to this extent, it is possible to say, as I have said above, that they carry power in their bones.

But we must also ask whether that power is likely to continue beyond the point where the institutions are largely manned by members of the British-educated elite, by the survivors of the independence movements and their immediate followers. So long as these people remain in charge it is reasonable to expect that they will share some common standards and values derived from their pre-independence training and culture. But each national movement carries within it the determination to make its institutions as indigenous as possible, and to cast off survivals of its colonial past. In particular, an independence movement in the former colonies of administration often desires to replace English by some local language or group of languages—unless it is quite impossible to find a local language which can act as a *lingua franca* for the country as a whole. In India, Ceylon and Malaya this development has been particularly notable. Similarly, national movements carry with them resentments against the religion of the colonial power, and the seeds of established opposition to it. The speed with which missions have had to be dismantled in Asian Commonwealth countries may, or may not, be paralleled in the more widely Christian West African countries; but there will certainly be opposition to any special favours to religious institutions which have not taken on the full colour of the country.

Looking, then, at the prevalence of parliamentary institutions throughout the Commonwealth, one can say that these have resulted from direct inheritance or transmission through British administration; that they have been disseminated through the spread of a general British culture which the present elites of the Commonwealth member-nations share; that this common culture does embody certain broad values and ideals, especially in government; and that, so long as those elites remain in power, they will be able to talk to one another with considerable ease and understanding. But one must also recognize that this is not, in itself, sufficient to explain the cohesion of the Commonwealth. It is impossible to argue that common values and ideals pervade the various societies of the Commonwealth. It is also impossible to argue that parliamentary institutions, in themselves, constitute a bond sufficiently strong either to hold the Commonwealth together or to ensure a continuance of the present measure of common values which is shared among the elites. Rather, we can expect each country to become more indigenous, in that its institutions conform more and more to the special developing characteristics of its society. This process is by no means confined to the former colonies of administration. It is a process familiar to any student of life in Australia, Canada, South Africa and even New Zealand. Dominant social values make their way upwards as well as downwards in equalitarian societies such as these; and elites become increasingly the elites native to their own areas. To imagine that the present degree of common culture which Commonwealth leaders share will remain constant is an illusion. Even if the leaders wished it to remain (and many of them do not; they are nationalists who feel that they will be more at home with their own developed cultures), the pressures against it would be too strong.

This is not to say that certain broad elements of agreement will necessarily be swept away. Parliamentary government, for example, has more to recommend it than the fact that it was copied from Britain. So has the system of a non-political civil service. The independence of the judges can be justified in strictly pragmatic terms. It is to be expected that institutions such as these may retain some strength, no matter what relations with Britain and the Commonwealth may be. All that we need to say is that the existence of these institutions is not sufficient explanation of membership of the Commonwealth. It means only that the country in question has some claims to be a free country and not a tyranny; but this is true of a good many countries outside the Commonwealth which have had little reason to connect their institutions with Britain's. In so far as having free institutions means sharing certain broad values in regard to government, these values are shared, not only with Britain and some former British colonies, but also with other free countries in Europe, the Americas and elsewhere.

I think we can say that, while there is some reality in the notion of shared values and ideals, and of some mutual sympathy arising from the prevalence of parliamentary institutions, neither of these points has enough strength to explain the continuance of the Commonwealth. Shall we find sufficient strength in the economic ties between Commonwealth members?

Economic Ties

In considering the economic ties we must take into account three factors: imperial preference, British overseas investment, and membership of the Sterling Area.

As we saw earlier, imperial preference consists of a series of bilateral trade agreements between Commonwealth countries.

It is not multilateral in its operation, has not been subject to any sort of central direction, and in certain of its details has not been revised for a quarter of a century. Furthermore, the agreements do not cover the principal exports of a number of Commonwealth countries: wool, wheat, metals, jute, and other major overseas products do not come into them. For Britain, while imperial preference has been useful in giving British manufactured goods an advantage in Commonwealth markets over competing goods from Europe and the United States, it has been of less use in protecting British goods against local manufactures receiving favoured treatment. British exporters have been less concerned about their foreign competitors than about local, favoured, competitors in the Commonwealth countries where they have been hoping to sell. In so far as the system of imperial preference was ever supposed to provide a closed, or protected, system within which overseas countries would exchange their surpluses of primary products for British manufactures (and very few governments ever thought it could), it has been a failure. The Empire, and then the Commonwealth, proved unable to absorb all its own products; no member-nation was prepared to discourage local manufactures in the interests of Britain; and no British government (except in wartime) was prepared to resist the temptation of cheap food from outside the Commonwealth. The preference system would have been equal to its difficulties only if it had been centrally controlled and had had central development funds to allot to the component parts of the system. But nothing like this has ever occurred.

In view of the limited extent of the imperial preference system, it may be asked whether Commonwealth members derive any advantage from it at all, and whether it can be considered any serious reason for their cohesion as a group. The answer is that, while the system provides very few advantages in major fields of trade, it does give opportunities to certain specific industries—such as Indian textiles, Malayan rubber, New Zealand meat, Australian canned fruits—which they would not otherwise possess. Even though these industries are often peripheral to their countries' economies, they are sufficiently important, in terms of employment and the proceeds of exports, to warrant the governments in question wishing to preserve the advantages which they possess. In other words, the preference system means that most, if not all, Commonwealth members have an interest in the preservation of imperial preference. But this does not extend to its enlargement: in spite of the earnest pleas of Australia and New Zealand, which benefit most from preferences, the Prime Ministers have not felt inclined to suggest a general revision of the system. This is partly because the background of the existing system, with its "imperial" connections, is distasteful to the former colonies of administration; but it is mainly because the Prime Ministers recognize that to increase preferences among the Commonwealth countries might encourage reprisals from elsewhere, which would prejudice the markets which Commonwealth countries now have for their products in Europe and the Americas. The position is therefore largely one of stalemate: Britain has trimmed her preference arrangements with Australia and New Zealand, but otherwise the system remains much as it was, undirected, out of date, peripherally advantageous, but in no sense comprehensive. One might say that, while Commonwealth nations consider that they derive solid benefits from it, these benefits are not enough in themselves to explain membership of the Commonwealth, and not enough to make the members resist attractive offers of trade from countries outside the Commonwealth such as Japan and Germany.

British investment in the Commonwealth is a matter of considerable importance, whenever one considers economic relationships. Each member-nation has traditionally looked to Britain for a large part of its development capital, in most cases for the greater part of it. Britain is the only country in the Commonwealth which is a net long-term investor abroad. The Commonwealth members which are also members of the Sterling Area have been given special facilities for seeking investment from Britain: since 1945 they have had a preferential position on the London money market, no foreign governments being allowed to issue stock there; and the private sectors of their economies have benefited from the fact that Britain has operated no exchange control on the movement of capital to Sterling Area countries. In the 1950's colonies and member-nation governments borrowed £50 million a year in London. The normal private borrowing for investment in the Sterling Area has been running at a rate of about £50 million a year, and there has been substantial investment in Canada too.[1]

[1] The facts in this paragraph are taken from *Britain: An Official Handbook* (London, 1964), pp. 435–6.

The effect of such a connection upon Commonwealth members with ambitious programmes of development is obvious. They find borrowing elsewhere difficult, and investors elsewhere ignorant of conditions in their countries. The London money market, on the other hand, knows all about Malaya, West Africa, India, Ceylon, Australia, New Zealand and East Africa: it has been connected with economic development in these areas ever since there was any. So long as Britain has investible funds, and so long as British investors consider that their money is safe and will bring dividends in other parts of the Commonwealth, one can say that the interests of each Commonwealth country will be advanced by remaining within the Commonwealth. But there are two drawbacks to this point of view. One is that it presupposes a continual supply of British investible funds; and this may not prove to be true in all circumstances. The other is that it implies some sort of equality between Commonwealth members which is not, in fact, observed by the money market. British funds are available for investment in enterprises which seem likely to show a profit. They are readily available for factories in high-standard, boom countries like Canada and Australia, and for mining in South Africa, Canada, Australia and Zambia; they are less readily available for enterprises which seem to be mainly political in origin or to have little chance of showing clear returns. To a considerable extent, British investment is available for the "have" countries of the Commonwealth and not for the "have-nots". This position is alleviated for the dependencies by direct government loans and gifts, but not for all independent Commonwealth countries which have outgrown their colonial status.

One can say, then, that in so far as Commonwealth members have a favoured place in the money market, and while it is official British policy to encourage investment in the Commonwealth at the expense of investment elsewhere, the members of the Commonwealth have a clear common interest in retaining that status. But, again, the advantage may be only peripheral for them. If they have other sources of capital, or if the money they can get in London is insufficient for their needs, there is less point in being members of the Commonwealth.

We come now to the influence of the Sterling Area. As indicated earlier, the Sterling Area is not the same as the Commonwealth, but all Commonwealth members except Canada belong to it.

To the extent that the Area can be said to have any kind of controlling mechanism, it is provided by joint Commonwealth institutions. The system, as we saw, is one in which Britain acts as international banker for the members of the Area: they keep most of their international holdings in sterling, and Britain backs these holdings with the reserves of gold and convertible currencies for which she takes responsibility. The system was difficult to operate during the years immediately after World War II, when certain overseas members had very heavy "sterling balances" accumulated during the war; if these had been spent immediately, Britain would have had neither the goods nor the reserves of convertible currency to satisfy them. Moreover, the heavy outflow of U.S. gifts and loans had hardly begun, the United States was in surplus with the rest of the world, and there was a widespread "dollar shortage" or "dollar gap". Under such conditions it was necessary to ration the use of the reserves, and to make the Sterling Area much more a matter of control over spending than it is now. There was no central control in any binding sense, but the governments and central banks co-operated to restrict the spending of foreign currency, and investment outside the Sterling Area was frowned on. Each country was expected to try to balance its own external spending with its earnings and other receipts; the communiques of Prime Ministers' Meetings were speckled with adjurations to develop the earning capacity of the Commonwealth and save scarce foreign exchange. In the period of dollar shortage, the system worked to the advantage of all, since Sterling Area members which earned heavily in dollar areas (such as Malaya, Ghana and Nigeria with their sales of rubber, tin and cocoa) were satisfied to leave their dollar surpluses in the Sterling Area's pool, while getting equivalent value in imports from other sterling countries, especially Britain. As the 1950's wore on, the sterling balances were run down, Europe came back into the picture as a market and source of supply, and the United States increased its massive aid and investment abroad; the need for "control" of the Sterling Area became less and less. By the early 1960's, it was hardly being talked about at all.

The contemporary operations of the Sterling Area (now that sterling balances no longer complicate it as they did) can be seen on a year-to-year basis, as in the following:[1]

[1] From *The Economist*, November 14, 1964, p. 750.

Sterling Area: External Payments

(£ million)

	1959	1960	1961	1962	1963	First half 1963	First half 1964
Britain:							
Current account	+153	−258	−1	+115	+113	+162	−125
Long-term capital	−259	−188	+50	−107	−155	−73	−216
Balancing item	−67	+256	−29	+84	−111	−45	+85
Total	−173	−190	+20	+92	−153	+44	−256
of which: transactions with overseas sterling area	*+123*	*+245*	*+39*	*−9*	*+77*	*+51*	*+8*
Overseas Sterling Area:							
Current account	−226	−741	−486	−380	−372	−169	−98
Long-term capital	+566	+620	+574	+564	+671	+412	+454
Balancing item*	−7	−95	+60	+46	−18	−35	−161
Total	+333	−217	+148	+230	+281	+208	+195
of which: transactions with Britain	*−123*	*−245*	*−39*	*+9*	*−77*	*−51*	*−8*
Total Sterling Area	+160	−407	+168	+322	+128	+252	−61

* In payments with Britain; not computed separately for other areas.

During the period covered by this table, the reserves of gold and convertible currencies varied around the £1,000 million mark.[1]

The system works well, it will be seen, so long as either Britain or the Overseas Sterling Area returns a surplus on the year's transactions. If the whole Area is badly out, as in 1960, this is a warning sign that exports must be expanded and/or imports contracted; the system can stand one or two years like this, but two or three would deplete the reserves and remove whatever flexibility the system now has. It would be necessary to return to the stricter measures of the late 1940's and early 1950's. The wider the membership of the system, of course, the more chance there is of some section coming to the rescue of the rest by recording surpluses while they record dificits; it is one of the advantages of the sterling system that the members trade in a great variety of products and stand in varying relations to the United States as a giver of aid: if all the economies were the same, they would all go down or up together, and the system would work like a switchback. Nevertheless, it is broadly true that the Area is divided between Britain, an exporter of manufactures, and the overseas members, which are exporters of primary products; there is a tendency for their fortunes to be fairly uniform, while Britain's take the opposite course. When both sections are in deficit, danger signals are hoisted. But the danger is greatest when Britain herself is in genuine balance of payments difficulties, because Britain, as the base of the sterling system and the biggest single operator

[1] *Britain: An Official Handbook*, *op. cit.*, p. 434.

within it, is the custodian, not only of Sterling Area funds, but also of a large quantity of foreign funds, especially from Europe, which seek profits there. Once the London money market is disturbed by revelations of continued Sterling Area imbalance, these funds are likely to take flight, diminishing the reserves in the process, and reducing Britain's capacity to provide capital for the overseas members of the Sterling Area.

The sterling system would seem to work best in two contrasting situations. One is the situation which obtained during and after World War II, when all sterling earnings were pooled, strict and co-ordinated control was maintained over the flow of funds to foreign countries and the purchase of non-sterling goods, and British investment was largely confined to the Area. In these circumstances (which amount to a siege operation for currencies) the Area can be operated as something of a self-contained unit, provided the members are prepared to stick to it and obey the rules. The other situation is that in which full multi-lateralism prevails; sterling is strong, since both Britain and the overseas sterling countries are selling their goods at satisfactory prices and are receiving gifts, loans and investment from outside the Area; in consequence, no harm but only extra flexibility and opportunity accrue to the Sterling Area members from a *laissez-faire* approach to foreign transactions. In this latter situation, there may not be much Sterling Area to discuss; like the Cheshire Cat, it may vanish till all one sees is the smile. If, however, there is general and prolonged deficit for the Area as a whole, there will be a tendency to revert to the siege aspects of its management.

It is important to emphasize that the Area, as a recognizable institution, has grown from two circumstances: the nineteenth- and early twentieth-century British investment abroad, with the consequent close relationship between sterling and the other monetary systems of the member-countries; and the formalized arrangements of World War II, designed to conserve foreign currencies and use them for common purposes. It is unlikely that anyone would deliberately construct the sterling system now if he were starting from scratch. If he did, he would almost certainly not be able to include in it all the countries in it now. Political obstacles would prove too formidable. It is true of the Sterling Area, as of the Commonwealth, that much of it is due, not to deliberate choice, but simply to the perpetuation of existing arrangements because it would be fatiguing or otherwise troublesome to replace them. Negative agreement is a force in economic as in foreign policy. As the Commonwealth's independent members increase, so the membership of the Sterling Area becomes potentially more unruly. Co-ordination in the years immediately after the war was achieved in an atmosphere of strong faith in British leadership and experience. Now, as the newly independent countries become increasingly preoccupied with their own problems of development and receive more aid and advice from non-members of all kinds—and, it must be said, as Britain's own situation reveals more frequent weaknesses—it becomes the less likely that a future crisis could be handled with as much common loyalty to the Area as a group.

From these considerations I draw the conclusion that membership of the Sterling Area is a mixed blessing for all concerned. For Britain, which is the centre of the system, the fact that there is a Sterling Area facilitates overseas earnings in the form of payment for banking and foreign exchange services, for merchanting in commodities, for providing short-term credits, for shipping and chartering services and for insurance, all of which are services which she is accustomed to perform for other members of the Area (although she performs them for other countries too). They fit snugly into place in the City of London alongside the mechanism of the Area itself, as operated by the Treasury and the Bank of England. Britain gains prestige from the fact that her currency is the one in which the Area's transactions take place. Her exports have, moreover, a favoured position in Sterling Area countries, even where no question of imperial preference arises. In the past, they had an advantage over dollar goods, since each country in the Sterling Area exercised caution in buying from the dollar area. Thus, so long as Britain can provide a yearly surplus which will counteract the deficit of the rest of the Area, the British position may be advantageous. But there are certain drawbacks. First, if the overseas Sterling Area records a deficit with the rest of the world Britain must be sure of achieving a surplus, unless the reserves are to be broached or other help sought. Again, if the British are to retain their position as the sheet-anchor of the Sterling Area, Britain must continue to invest in the rest of the Sterling Area. But this may not always seem to the advantage of Britain; one can envisage a situation in which a British government might wish to institute a much higher level of domestic investment and be hampered by the need to invest elsewhere in the Area. Thirdly, there might be a fall in the proceeds of British exports, or in those of the exports of other members, or both, in which case it would be difficult to meet any increase in the demands for foreign currency on the part of the world's holders of sterling. These increased demands would come from two sources, from sterling countries covering the deficits in their balances of payments and from non-sterling countries flying from the pound. If every sterling holder made demands at once, the bank would break.

Membership may also prove a mixed blessing for the overseas members of the Sterling Area. As we have seen, they gain advantages so long as each preserves its balance of payments, and the Area as a whole does not experience a run on its reserves. Possible disadvantages arise if they accumulate sterling balances. If the other members keep their sterling balances intact, each individual member can draw as much as it wishes from its balance. But if it draws heavily in one year this may set up internal pressures to draw as heavily, or even more heavily, in the next year. This in turn may be manageable, provided the remaining members have a net surplus, or provided the member's drain on the central reserve is small in relation to the total. But no member has so big a balance that it could continue to draw down its balance indefinitely; to continue this process would land it in heavy deficit. If a number of members of the Sterling Area went on the spree in this manner at the same time, the end-point might be the breaking of the bank.

"The breaking of the bank" is a fanciful term which should perhaps not be used. What would happen is that Britain would be unable to provide foreign currency to meet the payments deficits of so many countries together; there would be general import restrictions throughout the Area; help would be requested from other countries and the International Monetary Fund. What would disappear is the full and free capacity to convert sterling by members of the Sterling Area. The Area might continue to serve a useful purpose by means of transferable accounts in terms of sterling, but its main attraction would have gone.

This long excursus upon the Sterling Area has been necessary in order to indicate what it is, what part is played in it by Britain and by the overseas member-nations of the Commonwealth, and what importance it has to the economies of its members. We must now try to relate it to the existence of the Commonwealth, and ask what effect membership of it has upon a country's wish to stay in the Commonwealth.

It is plain that a country can be in the Sterling Area and, presumably, exercise some influence upon its proceedings without being a member of the Commonwealth. Eire and Libya are both in this position. Neither seems alarmed at not being a member of the Commonwealth and not participating in meetings of Commonwealth Prime Ministers; and both customarily hold balances in sterling. Should we say, therefore, that being in the Commonwealth has no relation to being in the Sterling Area? I do not think so. What is important is not that some members of the Area are not in the Commonwealth, but that the major contributors to the Area's reserves are. With the exception of the oil states and South Africa, each major earner of gold and dollars in the Sterling Area is a member-nation of the Commonwealth. Its membership of the Area, and its behaviour as a trader, are matters of general Commonwealth interest and concern. In no case (except perhaps South Africa) is its trading position of such permanent strength as to allow it to disregard the views of the other members. Even the richest members might find that world prices turned against them. They might find that substantial development programmes could not be sustained, even with big accumulated balances. Since the Sterling Area has no controlling agency, and since the only places where its affairs are discussed at the highest level among its members are meetings of Finance and Prime Ministers, it is reasonable to assume that a country which is in the Sterling Area will find it an advantage to be represented at such meetings. This will be the case especially where the country's trading account is at all volatile, in the sense of being subject to sudden ups and downs. Mr. Nehru's frequent references to "economic reasons" for India's continuing to be a member of the Commonwealth were presumably meant to cover this kind of situation. Commonwealth countries have no other major multilateral trading area available, and none of them, except possibly Australia and Malaysia, can rely for long upon its exports to provide it with sufficient completely convertible currency to cover its import needs. Their economies have grown up within the assumptions of close trading and investment relations with Britain; the Sterling Area is the contemporary manifestation of this relationship. The extent to which each of them would ascribe its Commonwealth membership to its interest in the Sterling Area is very much a matter of conjecture. But I have little doubt that each would give it some credit.

If we take the three economic factors of imperial preference, British investment and Sterling Area membership together, we find that in each case Commonwealth members have interests which coincide. Broadly speaking, they are all interests which involve taking advantage of special relations with Britain. It is the British market that means most to Commonwealth industries benefiting from imperial preference. It is British investment which has been available on special terms to Commonwealth countries. It is the strength of sterling, the British currency, which provides the backing for the Sterling Area and such advantages as overseas members of the Commonwealth derive from it. Each Commonwealth member has an interest in preserving these special relations. It might do so by treaty or special agreement; even as a member of the Commonwealth it may seek a treaty to clarify its rights and opportunities. But the fact that the British government is concerned to extend special privileges to members of the Commonwealth, in order to retain existing links and to strengthen the notion that the Commonwealth is a going concern within which the members stand in a special sort of relationship to one another, must weigh with every government which is thinking either of staying in the Commonwealth or seeking membership of it on ceasing to be a British dependency. It is reasonable to assume that men like Mr. Kaunda, Mr. Nehru, Dr. Nkrumah and Tunku Abdul Rahman have weighed these advantages and seen that they can more readily be pursued within the Commonwealth than from outside it. It is important, however, to recognize that these advantages derive not from the association of each Commonwealth country with the rest, but mainly from its association with Britain. It is not difficult to see why this should be so; it is not British machiavellianism, designed to enslave countries which are nominally free, but the outcome of long-standing economic relationships. There is no reason why special relations in the fields of trade, investment and currency should be broken simply because a dependency has become a sovereign state. There is everything to be said for the continuance of mutually satisfying business. The special interests which have been developed through imperial preference, the tendency to assume that public and private investment will be forthcoming from Britain, the confidence in Britain as an international banker; these are not likely to be destroyed by a change of political status. We may expect, therefore, that in so far as Commonwealth membership helps to sustain them, and in so far as it imposes no new burdens or disadvantages, there will be a strong tendency for economic interest to demand Commonwealth membership—not as a solution for a country's problems but as a means of continuing profitable relationships.

The Springs of Action

This chapter has been devoted to seeing what common tendencies are revealed by the foreign policies and national interests of Commonwealth members, whether they seem to share common values and ideals and what economic ties they have in common. In discussing these we have been concerned to uncover the springs of action of the Commonwealth, to find out what makes it a going concern. We have seen, I think, that the assumption of common ideals and values can be sustained up to a point—the point of a degree of common culture among the leaders of a number of member-nations—but that it cannot be held to account for each country's membership of the Commonwealth, although it will go far to explain the sympathy which unites Britain with the former colonies of settlement. Parliamentary institutions, although common to all members, are diverse in their operation and do not embody dominant values; they are more likely to be shaped by the dominant values of the societies in which they operate. In discussing economic ties we saw that there are solid reasons, stemming from the long connection of most Commonwealth economies with Britain, for the closest possible links between the overseas members and Britain. In summarizing the approaches of member-nations to major problems of world politics, we saw that, although they have many divergent interests and find it difficult to unite on positive action to secure a common objective, they are characterized by a form of negative agreement which takes shape whenever something which they do not want to happen seems likely to happen. In this field, as in the economic field, the emphasis of British influence is thrown into the scale of common interests rather than into that of the interests of a section of the Commonwealth. British diplomacy, like British financial power, is directed towards as much consolidation of Commonwealth interests as can be achieved—towards the stressing of what the members have in common, rather than what they differ about.

My conclusion is that Commonwealth members retain or acquire membership because they consider it more in their interests to be in the Commonwealth than out of it; and that in this they are powerfully aided by the influence of Britain, which is employed in order to make membership of the Commonwealth as easy and profitable as it can be, without importing elements of obligation and responsibility which might make it seem unattractive. Primarily, the Commonwealth is a British interest. Unless it were so, the other members would not join together to carry on the kind of discussion and consultation which they undergo now. What they have in common is that they all wish to preserve the connection with Britain. They have different reasons for this, and there is no point in assuming that their reasons are all the same. To do so would be to make a mockery of the facts. But the fact that it is in the interests of each one to continue association with Britain, and in Britain's interests that this should be so, provides a nexus between them strong enough to make them see themselves not simply as engaged in friendly relations with Britain but as connected with one another. From the original nexus others have developed. The connections in diplomacy of Canada with India and of Australia with the Asian countries are connections which, arising from the original joint connection with Britain, can continue in their own right within the ambit of the Commonwealth.

All of this would be impossible if the conflicts between members of the Commonwealth were so great as to cancel out the agreement which each of them has developed with Britain and the degree of agreement which they have cultivated among themselves. But I have already suggested that, although some of the disagreements among Commonwealth members are serious and others are bitter, they have so far only in regard to South Africa overcome the negative agreement which, as sovereign states in the contemporary world, the members have discovered they share. Again the influence of Britain is observable. As I have suggested, the extent of negative agreement coincides to a considerable degree with the aims of British policy. If Britain had decided to choose between one set of Commonwealth countries and another, or if she had used her power consistently to support policies which were against the declared and understood interests of members, the force of negative agreement would have been destroyed by that of positive disagreement. I do not think this has happened. I think rather that British policy, except for entry to EEC and the Suez adventure, has been designed to placate, assist, encourage and support as many Commonwealth members as possible, and has increased the force of negative agreement. Such a process puts no stop to the development of national interests by individual Commonwealth members. Rather, it attempts to anticipate this development, assist it, and allow for its effects when calculating future policy. Again, with the exception of the Suez adventure, British policy seems to me to have accomplished this.

Given that the main springs of the Commonwealth in action are economic co-operation, negative agreement on certain issues of world politics, and the active encouragement of Commonwealth association by Britain, we can see that no one need be surprised at the persistance of the Commonwealth or at the fact that ex-colonies now wish to remain in it. It imposes no burdens. It provides contacts, opportunities, economic advantages, British goodwill and the sense of belonging. I have suggested that the sticking point, the stage of impossibility, would be the inclusion in the Commonwealth of a Communist government, bound into a Communist world system and responsible less to its own people and national interests than to the advancement of Communism as a political system. I do not believe that negative agreement could be present in such a case. Certainly I cannot see the obvious balance of relative advantage, which Commonwealth members enjoy at present, being preserved in association with a Communist state. But no Commonwealth member is Communist; and, as things stand, the Commonwealth can continue as a going concern.

How are we to classify it as an international entity? It has no written constitution like the United Nations and the specialized agencies; it can hardly be called an international organization. It imposes no military obligations, like NATO; it cannot be called an alliance. It does not come to decisions, and has no secretariat to attempt to carry them out, like the Organization of American States; although we often call it an international association, this will hardly do, since we think of an association as normally possessing rules and some sort of executive. The Headship of the Queen does not make it a Personal Union. We should not give it the rather contemptuous title of a study-group; in any case, its member-governments do not consciously engage in study of its common ends. It is plainly not a federation, nor is it a union, such as the French Union was meant to be. Its members are not even united by a common treaty of understanding. It is not a Zollverein. It is not a Community. In fact, it does not fit into any of the recognized international categories. Yet I have insisted that it is a going concern. Which name will suit it best? My own choice is to call it a *concert of convenience*. "Concert" conveys the idea of agreement, but not of any more unity of approach than the notion of negative agreement will stand. "Convenience" is essentially what holds the Commonwealth nations together, in so far as they can be said to be held together. They need consult nothing but their own convenience. Beyond this, no obligations are enjoined upon them. It is convenient to be in; it is convenient not to be out. It might one day become convenient to be out, in which case no difficulties would be raised. To call the Commonwealth a club is sometimes a useful metaphor, but carries overtones of membership dues and blackballing which are not suitable. To call it a family conjures up ideas of blood relationship and of mutual obligation which may fit some aspects of the Commonwealth relationship, but do not fit all. Both concert and convenience are words which might be misunderstood if taken singly; but put together to describe the Commonwealth they are capable of no misconstruction and do not mislead.

Chapter Fifteen

FUTURE POSSIBILITIES

As it stands in the middle of the 1960's, the Commonwealth is a concert of convenience between Britain and certain nations, all of which have been British dependencies and all of which have acquired national interests of their own. Its history indicates that it is a protean body, able to take on new forms and to respond to circumstances in ways which few other international entities can emulate. To speculate about its future is to ask for trouble, since it has so successfully resisted divination in the past. Nevertheless, the fact that the Commonwealth is so unusual and seems to have been so successful in adapting itself to change continues to invite speculation; and the purpose of this chapter is to examine some of the proposals which have been made in recent years, and some of the possibilities latent in the international situation, as these might affect the future of the Commonwealth. The proposals can be separated into those connected with the structure and membership of the Commonwealth and those concerned with its methods of operation. The possibilities latent in the international situation are those which might follow from changes in the positions of the major powers. Finally, there are possibilities of changed relationships within the Commonwealth itself, especially as they affect the position of Britain.

Changes in Structure and Membership

Changes suggested under this heading cannot easily be separated from those discussed under the next, since some of the new methods of operation which have been suggested have implications for the structure of the Commonwealth. The structure is so lacking in clear form, so much a matter of practice and not of theory, that almost any suggestion about what might be done with the Commonwealth is bound to affect the structure. Here I am concerned with two kinds of scheme for changing structure and membership which aim respectively at narrowing the effective membership of the Commonwealth and widening it.

At various times there have been suggestions that the Commonwealth should establish differential membership, by having perhaps "two tiers" of members, full and associate, or by having a core of tightly knit members surrounded by a number of others which, while having the same formal status, would not be involved in the close co-operation of those in the core. The "two-tier" idea was canvassed when it seemed possible that South Africa might refuse to countenance the admission of black states such as Ghana to full membership. When South Africa's attitude changed, the need for the idea lapsed. It was essentially a scheme for easing the path to independence of British dependencies which, for one reason or another, were unacceptable as fellow-members to the existing Commonwealth nations. No candidate for membership in the immediate future seems likely to be unacceptable in this way; so the "two-tier" idea is not likely to be resurrected on this ground. But it might return as a means of dealing with the problem of British colonies which, while anxious to acquire self-government, are not big enough to become sovereign states. Given full internal independence, but kept going by British subsidies and confined to British policy in international matters, their self-esteem might be soothed by being given associate membership of the Commonwealth. At the most, however, this would be a form of words. In any case, it is probable that the Commonwealth has now gone so far with membership for small communities that a country would have to be very small indeed to be refused entry. There was a time when no one envisaged full status for Malta or Cyprus, or Jamaica or Trinidad; in each case it is now a reality. Something may have to be done with the Falkland Islands and St. Helena, but the time has gone by for elaborate schemes for special status. The major nations might still resist the entry of representatives of minuscule communities, and the minuscule communities, in their turn, would probably resent the offer of associate membership (i.e. membership of the lower tier) if they could not be admitted to the reality of Prime Ministers' discussions. So it is likely that the "two-tier" system will not eventuate.

The other kind of scheme, which we may call here the "core" scheme, has been suggested unofficially at various times by Conservatives in Britain; the most open advocacy of it has come from Sir Eric Harrison, who took up the post of Australian High Commissioner in Britain in 1956. Sir Eric's theme[1] is that the

[1] The details which follow are from *Australian Newsletter* (London), December 13, 1956, and February 7, 1957, and *The Times*, December 6, 1956.

"British Commonwealth" is already present within the wider circle of "the Commonwealth", or, alternatively, that "the Commonwealth" has widened out beyond the "British Commonwealth" which is still present in something like its Statute of Westminster condition. The essence of the "British Commonwealth" is that it owes allegiance to the Crown and is populated by "British-speaking peoples" [*sic*]. Sir Eric Harrison has suggested that this "British Commonwealth" should have a permanent Committee of Co-ordination or a Secretariat which would have sufficient power to enable it to resolve the difficulties confronting the "British Commonwealth". It should be able to speak with one voice on external affairs, on defence, on finance, on immigration, on development and on other major matters. He does not think that any of the excluded parts of "the Commonwealth" would raise objections, for none of their own vital interests would in any way be endangered by the proposed close co-ordination. The object of the whole exercise would be to co-ordinate the resources—including manpower—of the "British Commonwealth". Sir Eric has not given particulars of which countries would be in the core and which would not, except to say that India would not.

The harshest justifiable criticism of this scheme would be that it looked very much like one for advancing the interests of Australia and New Zealand at the expense of other members of the Commonwealth, including Britain. Some British critics would maintain that, although it purported to improve the position of Britain, it would in fact mean that Britain was isolated from the non-British parts of the Commonwealth (including Canada as it seems, in addition to the Asian and African members) and was called upon to provide money, arms and men simply for the convenience of Australia and New Zealand. For it is quite evident that no other member of the Commonwealth would be prepared to accept Sir Eric Harrison's proposition that its interests were identical with those of Britain, Australia and New Zealand, and that it should subordinate its policies to those of a Committee of Co-ordination or a Secretariat in London. In this sense, the proposal looks like a scheme for forcing the British government to accept, in the name of the "British Commonwealth", responsibility for whatever demands might be made by Australia and New Zealand for trade, defence and immigration. In its assumption that the "Crown Commonwealth" [1] has a common set of interests which simply require co-ordination, the proposal overlooks the difficulties which arise in foreign policy and the divergent attitudes of the political parties about national interests—in Australia at least. Indeed, it has little to do with foreign policy, and seems mainly a scheme for attracting more British capital and preferential trade. It is hard to see any British government accepting such a proposal since this would mean destroying, or at any rate greatly weakening, the links which have been carefully made with Asia and Africa. In any case, British governments recognize a primary obligation to British dependencies rather than to Commonwealth members.

But it would be incomplete to leave Sir Eric Harrison's plan on this plane of criticism. While it is true that the plan is largely an attempt to assume an identity of interests which does not exist, in order to further the special interests of a section of the Commonwealth, it is also an example of the wistful concern of many people of British descent at the changes which have taken place in "the Empire". Many Australians, New Zealanders, British-connected Rhodesians, some Canadians and the white settlers of East Africa have often felt this concern; so do many people in Britain. But it is essentially a yearning for the past—and for a past which is idealized rather than historical. Ever since the first schemes for Imperial Federation were put forward there have been people who complained that the true interests of the Empire were being neglected, and that co-ordination of its resources was not being achieved. In all cases they have failed to recognize the conflict of interests between different parts of "the Empire" or "the Commonwealth"; they have failed to appreciate that some advantages derived from the association would disappear if the attempt were made to force the parts into agreement on a common set of interests; and they have put far too much weight on the "British" element in the total arrangement. As we have seen, the Commonwealth today is "British" only in the sense that British influence (cultural, institutional, economic) is to be found in each of the member-nations; the fact that a minority of the members are primarily British in stock is of much less importance. From

[1] The phrase used by Sir Robert Menzies, Sir Eric's Prime Minister: "Indeed, it might be more accurate to say that we have now a Crown Commonwealth within a total Commonwealth." (*The Times*, June 12, 1956.)

the standpoint of the British government, which is attempting to operate a system of external relations which includes not only the Commonwealth but also Europe, the United States and the Communist bloc, some of Britain's own most vociferously "British" dependencies—Kenya and Southern Rhodesia—have in fact been among her greatest sources of embarrassment. To equate national interests with racial origins is to leave out of account a whole range of interests which no British government can afford to neglect.

The "core" idea, which is intended to reduce the number of countries which are effective members of the Commonwealth, has something in common with the other kind of scheme sometimes suggested for changing the structure and membership of the Commonwealth. This is the "expansion" scheme, associated particularly with Hon. Patrick Maitland and the Expanding Commonwealth Group of Conservative and Unionist Members of Parliament.[1] While one looks to the restriction of Commonwealth membership and the other to its expansion, both wish to consolidate Britain's power and make the changed Commonwealth a more effective force in world affairs than it is now. The "expansion" scheme is, however, based upon a more contemporary notion of the Commonwealth than Sir Eric Harrison's. It assumes the existing decentralization of power within the Commonwealth, accepts as a fact the differential policies of the members, and even regards as valuable the recognition of divergence of interests. Its central view is that the Commonwealth "contains the seeds of a world system for which the 'middle Powers' are craving". The expansion to which it looks is to be achieved by admitting foreign countries to membership, provided their "nature and outlook" are in harmony with the character and interests of the existing Commonwealth. Mr. Maitland suggests that among these countries might eventually be Burma, the Sudan, Indonesia, France, Germany, Benelux and Turkey; these would first enter a form of Association with the Commonwealth, and later, if they wished, accede to it by becoming full members.

The advantage to these countries of joining the Commonwealth would be that "the Commonwealth differs from other inter-

[1] Mr. Maitland was a member, and one of the prime movers, of the Group. Quotations and references which follow are from Patrick Maitland, *Task for Giants* (London, 1957) and Conservative Political Centre, *The Expanding Commonwealth* (London, 1956). Neither should be regarded as an expression of policy on the part of the Conservative Party.

national groupings in that it has a common citizenship and its sovereign members can exchange secrets and consult together more intimately and more decisively than is possible for foreign States". The expansionists hope that continued consultation will lead to greater collaboration between the existing Commonwealth countries and to such obvious advantages in this collaboration as would make foreign countries realize the desirability of membership. They do not go so far as Sir Eric Harrison, and the Beaverbrook Press, in wishing to see co-ordination of economic effort directed from the centre; but they do envisage a considerable advance over the degree of co-operation which obtains at present.

One cogent criticism of such a scheme has been voiced by Mr. Patrick Gordon Walker,[1] as follows:

> "The Commonwealth is not an artificial creation nor a club that can be joined; it is a 'natural unit' and therefore has natural limits. It is made up of countries that have, for historical reasons, certain profound affinities one with another. Without the will and capacity to co-operate that spring from these affinities, the links of Commonwealth would become so vague and general as to be meaningless. It would not be enough, as is sometimes assumed, for a foreign country to have close natural links with Britain alone; to be a Member of the Commonwealth it would need to have similar affinities with India, Canada, Australia and all the other existing and future Members of the Commonwealth. With the possible exception of the United States, there is no foreign country that comes into this category. It is theoretically conceivable that countries like Israel or the Sudan or Burma that have had a close historical association with the British Empire might become Members, but it is very doubtful whether the bond of unity, once it has been snapped, can ever be restored."

As we have seen, the fact of association with Britain and the diffusion of certain cultural and institutional practices have much to do with the present cohesiveness of the Commonwealth. It is doubtful if any foreign country would feel inclined to associate itself so closely with countries which have so obviously been under British influence and control in the past; to do so would be to admit a certain priority (if not superiority) in British institutions which most of the countries on Mr. Maitland's list would not wish to admit. To ask for admission to the Commonwealth, a foreign

[1] P. C. Gordon Walker, "Policy for the Commonwealth", in T. E. M. McKitterick and Kenneth Younger (eds.), *Fabian International Essays* (London, 1957), pp. 190–1.

country would need to feel that quite tangible advantages which were available nowhere else would accrue to it. The proponents of the "expansion" scheme suggest that these would be found in common citizenship and in intimate consultation. But this is highly unlikely. As we have seen, there is in fact no common citizenship in the Commonwealth, except in so far as Britain recognizes the citizenship of each other member and gives conditional entry to their citizens. No other Commonwealth country does this; and until citizenship is *interchangeable* it is absurd to call it *common*. If France joined the Commonwealth, Frenchmen would be no nearer to citizen's rights in India than they are now. Consultation, as we saw, is interpreted in a Pickwickian way by the members of the Commonwealth. They provide as much or as little of it to one another as they feel inclined, and they do not consult if they consider that their vital interests will be endangered by doing so. These facts are perfectly plain to the Foreign Offices of countries outside the Commonwealth. Such countries would need to be offered much more than citizenship and consultation before they began to think of applying for membership.

The clinching reason why the idea of an Expanding Commonwealth is chimerical, however, is that it cannot give the countries in question what they are looking for—protection against attack and guaranteed economic advantages. They can get these from alliances and from *ad hoc* arrangements with Great Powers. Joining the Commonwealth would not advance them very far in their quest for security and prosperity. They would presumably get more favoured terms on the London money market, but their membership would not increase the total quantity of money available; it would simply decrease the quantity available for the existing members and the dependencies. The Commonwealth is not an alliance; they would get no increase in protection against attack. The Commonwealth is not a closed economic system; even if it were possible to bring them into the imperial preference system (which is doubtful), the advantages would be only marginal. There is, in fact, no clear reason for any foreign country to want to join the Commonwealth.

It might be stated in reply, of course, that if this argument applies to countries outside the Commonwealth it also applies to some of those within the Commonwealth, and that, in spite of this, they continue to remain members; if the argument is correct, why do they not secede? The answer is that there is a great deal of difference between making up your mind to leave something because you are not getting much out of it, and making up your mind to join something when you are aware that you will get very little out of it. In the first case, all the force of inertia is at work against leaving; there are existing ties of association which may not mean much, but have to be taken into account; and, in the instance of the Commonwealth, there is the additional fact that remaining a member costs you nothing. In the second case, the force of inertia is pulling the other way, against taking the step of applying for membership; ties of association are not evident, but must be sought for and manufactured; and joining may prove costly, in that your existing assumptions about international conduct and national pride may not fit in with those of the existing members. The two situations are not comparable.[1]

There is a further variant of the "expansion" idea which deserves attention here. It is sometimes suggested that, while there may be no point in suggesting to foreign countries that they might wish to join the Commonwealth, there is still some point in suggesting that they form some association *like* the Commonwealth. The Commonwealth, the argument runs, is a success because it imposes no obligation on its members, respects national sovereignty and yet enables the members to join in frank and free discussion of a kind which they do not find elsewhere. Other countries should learn the lesson of this.

The difficulty of this idea is that it neglects to recognize the force of Mr. Gordon Walker's point that the Commonwealth is a "natural unit". One does not need to accept the whole Aristotelian notion of change in order to recognize that the Commonwealth has grown and not been made. It is the outcome of policy, but of policy which was directed towards the particular needs of particular British colonies, not towards the creation of a new kind of international organization. The Commonwealth has happened; and it has happened because of the specific relationship between Britain and its successive members. As we have seen, there is a major difference between those which were colonies of settlement

[1] The point made in this paragraph applies with force to Mr. Guy Arnold's provocative scheme in *Towards Peace and a Multiracial Commonwealth* (London, 1964). He wishes to use the Commonwealth as a vehicle for British disengagement from alliances, and thus to create a common Commonwealth foreign policy. The Commonwealth is simply not capable of being made united enough for this.

and those which were colonies of administration; even so, we have also seen that an element of British organization, culture and institutional make-up is a common feature of all. The process of acquiring independence, whether gradually or suddenly, is the common experience which all Commonwealth members have shared; the influence of British culture, business and administration is the continuing element which they recognize in one another. To what group of foreign countries do these, or similar, features apply? The only cases directly analogous are those of colonial powers such as France, Spain, Holland and Portugal in relation to their former colonies. Only France has been in a position to apply the Commonwealth formula to some of her possessions and former possessions; and it seems unlikely that this will succeed. If we look for groups of existing sovereign states to which the pattern or formula might apply, we shall find none. All we can say to sovereign states is that they ought not to fight each other, and ought to consult now and then; this is what the Commonwealth model is reduced to if one takes out the historical element of dependency and the spread of culture and organization. To put it in such terms is to say no more than that sovereign states should respect each other as equals. It becomes an irritating platitude. I conclude, therefore, that it is a waste of time to urge the Commonwealth model on countries which have not had the historical experience common to Commonwealth countries.

Changes in Methods of Operation

If we assume that membership of the Commonwealth will continue to be confined to countries which have been British dependencies, and that the formal equality between members which now prevails will remain, we can still ask what changes may occur in the operation of Commonwealth institutions. Here we are faced with a great many suggestions. They can be divided into those which relate to the principles upon which the Commonwealth relationship is assumed to rest, those which are specifically concerned with the management of the Sterling Area, and those of a general economic character which look towards greater co-operation between the members.

As we have seen, it is difficult to find common principles, interests and values on which to base the Commonwealth relationship; it is easier to assume that the interests which the members have in common are those comprehended in negative agreement and in the overlay of British influence which each member bears. Even some form of parliamentary institutions is hardly sufficient to provide a principle of Commonwealth existence. So far, British governments have been cautious of suggesting that the Commonwealth should assert its support for anything more concrete than peace, prosperity and human happiness. This is because they know from experience that almost any concrete affirmation of belief is likely to cut across the interests (in terms of the domestic practices) of one member or another. However, although this caution is generally respected, one demand has been made with force, clarity and success—that the Commonwealth should declare its support for racial equality, and that the idea of a "multi-racial" association should thus be firmly established as the basis of Commonwealth connections. In 1956, this demand was voiced by K. M. Panikkar,[1] by the *New Statesman and Nation*, and by *The Economist*. In the opinion of the *New Statesman*, "today, it is the acceptance of human equality—not conceptions of strategy or law—that is the condition of Commonwealth survival";[2] the *Economist*, saying that "the outstanding problem of the new Commonwealth, as indeed at longer range of the world at large, is the problem of racial partnership",[3] considered that "it is more important that freedom should survive than that the Commonwealth should".[4] In each case there was a direct implication for South Africa. It was that if South Africa did not like a Commonwealth declaration of racial equality she should secede. This would amount to a vote of no confidence in her by the other Commonwealth members. From the Indian standpoint, it would be an endorsement of the complaints which India had made about South Africa at the United Nations since 1945. From the British standpoint, its utility was (and is) assumed to be that, with South Africa out of the Commonwealth, the way would be clearer for peaceful negotiation of independence for the remaining African colonies.

The 1956 suggestions came to nothing: it was still possible for Commonwealth countries to consider South Africa's behaviour a

[1] K. M. Panikkar, "Commonwealth Changes", in *Manchester Guardian*, June 18, 1956.
[2] "Does the Commonwealth Exist?", in *New Statesman and Nation*, June 30, 1956.
[3] "The Expanding Commonwealth", *The Economist*, April 7, 1956.
[4] "Commonwealth Fallacies", *The Economist*, July 14, 1956.

matter of domestic concern, and to reflect on what might happen to each of them if their own domestic concerns were made subject to some over-riding principle such as multi-racialism. This was the way in which the members of the Commonwealth had been accustomed to treat the South African situation for a decade; it was the way in which the earlier editions of this book argued about the unlikelihood of any Commonwealth declaration of racial equality. However, neither the customary Commonwealth view nor my analysis of its likely development could stand against the unexpected onrush of African independence, which precipitated the departure of South Africa and the affirmation of multi-racialism as a Commonwealth creed. It is instructive, however, to see how this affirmation came about, how far it has been taken, and what sort of precedent it seems to provide for other possible Commonwealth principles.

Multi-racialism as a principle made its appearance at the Prime Ministers' Conference *before* the one which saw South Africa's withdrawal, i.e. at the 1960 meeting, the communique from which contained the following:[1]

> "Whilst reaffirming the traditional practice that Commonwealth conferences do not discuss the internal affairs of member countries, Ministers availed themselves of Mr. Louw's presence in London to have informal discussions with him about the racial situation in South Africa. During these informal discussions Mr. Louw gave information and answered questions on the Union's policies, and other Ministers conveyed to him their views on the South African problem. *The Ministers emphasised that the Commonwealth itself is a multi-racial association* and expressed the need to ensure good relations between all member states and peoples of the Commonwealth."

It will be seen that on this occasion the principle was asserted by "Ministers", who in the context were presumably those from the countries which wished to express disapproval of *apartheid*.

The 1961 conference, from which South Africa finally withdrew, did not refer to the multi-racialism of the Commonwealth in its communique, except to say that Dr. Verwoerd came to his decision "in the light of the views expressed on behalf of other member governments and the indications of their future intentions regarding the racial policy of the Union government".[2] It is clear,

[1] *The Times*, May 14, 1960. (Emphasis added.)
[2] *Ibid.*, March 16, 1961.

however, that some of the Prime Ministers wanted a "Bill of Rights" propounded, and that Sir Robert Menzies for Australia opposed the idea.[1] He felt that it "could well lead to charges and counter-charges of breach". No doubt he had thoughts of possibly having to answer questions about White Australia or the position of New Guinea.

The 1964 conference, to which new African representatives came from Tanganyika, Sierra Leone, Uganda, Kenya and Malawi, did declare itself on racial issues. Its communique stated that "the Commonwealth has a particular role to play in the search for solutions to the inter-racial problems which are threatening the orderly development of mankind"; and the "Prime Ministers affirmed their belief that, for all Commonwealth governments, it should be an objective of policy to build in each country a structure of society which offers equal opportunity and non-discrimination for all its people, irrespective of race, colour or creed".[2] This requirement, presumably intended to apply in the immediate context to Southern Rhodesia, will in future govern the entry of new members; but it is phrased in such general terms, and could be used with telling effect against so many of the existing members, that it does not mean much in itself. Only if a coalition of members wished to pillory one of their number, or some aspiring member, would it be called into play; and in those conditions, as with the South African case, forms or words would be of little account alongside political passions.

Let us turn to proposals for some tribunal to advise or decide on matters at issue between Commonwealth members.[3] This proposal is frequently brought forward, with special reference to the issue of Kashmir. But it is subject to the same objection as all tribunals which attempt to apply voluntary arbitration between sovereign states, and do not have behind them the force of some international Leviathan. Members would refer to the tribunal only questions which they regarded as unimportant, in the sense of not affecting their vital interests. The tribunal would be given

[1] See his parliamentary report, reprinted in Nicholas Mansergh, *Documents and Speeches on Commonwealth Affairs 1952–1962* (London, 1963), p. 394.

[2] *The Times*, July 16, 1964.

[3] See K. M. Panikkar, *op. cit.*, where it is suggested that such a tribunal would be confined to justiciable issues, but "justiciable issues" are not defined. As a first stage, Mr. Panikkar suggests voluntary conciliation between members by "a panel of men with a record of distinguished services from different parts of the Commonwealth".

nothing of value to do; at the same time, brisk-minded persons throughout the Commonwealth would be continually calling upon it to settle disputes which the parties refused to refer to it. No meeting of Prime Ministers would be prepared to set up a tribunal with power, any more than they would be prepared to state general principles that were more than platitudes: in both cases they would fear the repercussions upon the national interests of their countries. The Commonwealth is not a super-state, and no foreseeable action can make it one. It is the members' jealously prized position as sovereign states that has so far overcome all attempts at providing common institutions with power.

The one case in which the members have been prepared to accept some sort of central direction—albeit of the gentlest and least coercive kind—has been that of the Sterling Area. "Direction" is hardly the word to use of a process which is essentially consultative and which, as we have seen, involves no sanctions. So long as the Sterling Area is roughly in balance in its yearly transactions with the rest of the world, nothing is heard of more elaborate organization of the Area's business. But when the reserves fall sharply, and when it looks as if the difficulties envisaged in the last chapter might develop, suggestions for tighter central control begin to appear in the British Press. They appear there, rather than elsewhere in the Commonwealth, because it is at times of stress that Britain's responsibilities as banker are most keenly felt. In normal times these responsibilities are an advantage: they seem to show how strong Britain is, and they lead to Sterling Area members using British facilities in a number of fields. But when things go wrong, Britain realizes that she has very small reserves and that a run on the bank could break it. At such times there are suggestions that the Area should have more central control, with the aim of making members keep within their incomes, and not embarrass sterling. There was a good deal of such agitation in 1952;[1] and although it diminished in the immediately following years, it appeared again in 1957. Indications were that the Sterling Area might again come under strain through a decline in earning power, and through heavy drawing on their sterling balances by newly independent states such as Ghana and Malaya. The suggestions included Mr. Peter Wiles's that the Area's gold reserve

[1] See, e.g. Mr. Hugh Gaitskell in *New Statesman and Nation*, December 29 1952.

should be distinguished from Britain's and deposited in a new central bank;[1] Mr. J. R. Sargent's that the management of the Area should be much less nervous of criticizing members, and should see that infringements of proposed claims on the reserves were "not just politely excused";[2] and the *Economist*'s that mild pressure should be brought to bear on countries whose policies were likely to plunge them into deficits, perhaps by control of capital movements to the offenders.[3] There were many such suggestions. These are chosen simply as examples. They amount to the expression of anxiety that some Area members with large sterling balances might go on the spree, and that Britain's general financial position would be affected by this action over which she had no effective control; in the end, it was pointed out, all Area members would suffer, but the immediate damage would be done to Britain with her sole responsibility for the Area's reserves.

The difficulty inherent in such suggestions is that they conflict with the essential basis of Commonwealth relations, which combines an absence of central direction with the utmost respect for national sovereignty. It is true that the Sterling Area is different from the Commonwealth, in that Canada does not belong to it and some non-Commonwealth countries do. But, as we have seen, the Area is operated largely as if it were a Commonwealth institution; in so far as it has had direction this has come from meetings of Commonwealth Prime Ministers and Finance Ministers. It would be possible to set up a Sterling Area organization by treaty without infringing any aspect of the Commonwealth's rules. But this would mean that the Commonwealth mystique, which the British government has so carefully fostered, would be removed from the Sterling Area, which would be revealed as simply a commercial enterprise. This, in itself, would be nothing to complain about; but it might not result in Britain's ultimate responsibility as banker being fully shared by the other members, and it would still call for some overall power of sanction to be vested in the management of the treaty organization. The only effective power would be that of control over the rate of release of the sterling balances of the members; but this is a form of control which Britain would be most reluctant to exercise unilaterally, and which

[1] Letter in *The Economist*, December 14, 1957.
[2] J. R. Sargent, "What Price the Sterling Area?" in *The Listener*, January 2, 1958.
[3] "Prime Ministers and the Pound", *The Economist*, June 22, 1957.

has now largely lost what force it may have had. In any case, from the British standpoint there are both advantages and disadvantages in sharing the ultimate responsibility for the Sterling Area. It would mean that members who went on the spree were restrained by the collective concern of their fellows; this is the case now, although the expression of that concern is less forceful than it might be under a system of formally shared responsibility. But it would also mean that Britain had put her financial power into commission; and this would certainly have its effect upon the much-prized reputation of the City as the source of financial wisdom. If Britain cannot be a banker on her own, men might say, what is the point of her trying to be a banker at all? Such possibilities would certainly occur to any British government which was thinking about control of the Area. Unless the situation were highly critical, such a government would probably decide to continue with the existing arrangements and hope for the best. In any case it would consider the situation not only in terms of Britain's financial situation but also in terms of the preservation of the Commonwealth. Whether rightly or not, the Commonwealth's assumptions of absolute national sovereignty have been made to apply to the Sterling Area; and to challenge them in the one case might look like challenging them in the other.

In the economic field, there remains the occasional suggestion that the Commonwealth ought to be organized as an economic unit, or that, at any rate, British investment ought to be confined within it and the members ought to make increasingly preferential arrangements among themselves in the field of trade. Many arguments have been used to support this general thesis. One is that the Commonwealth contains great undeveloped resources which can be developed co-operatively. Another is that the dollar shortage is a permanent feature of international life, and can be met only by extending trade and investment within the Sterling Area. A third is that Commonwealth countries are more stable politically than other "under-developed" countries, and should prove good investments. A fourth is the simple argument based upon kinship. A fifth is that if some scheme of this kind is not put into effect, the Commonwealth will succumb to the pressure of American investment. A sixth is that Britain and the overseas Commonwealth countries owe each other a kind of natural debt or obligation to take one another's goods.

Some of these arguments have achieved the dignity of being used in the communiques of Commonwealth conferences; but none has proved sufficiently strong to make the member-nations attempt the task. The reason is that each member has developed economic interests which could not be accommodated within a closed, or semi-closed, economic system. The essence of the idea, as it has been expounded over many years, is that there should be a division of labour between a manufacturing Britain and agricultural overseas countries. This allegedly natural dichotomy has been spoiled by the determination of the overseas countries to develop their own manufactures and the determination of Britain both to protect her own farmers and to take advantage of cheap food available in Europe and the Americas. Again, the idea depends upon some co-operative decision about those parts of the Commonwealth in which British capital can most worthily be invested; but any thorough-going acceptance of such co-operation would cut across Britain's interest in high returns, and would cause great jealousy among the sovereign states which were competing for the available funds. It is true that they compete now; but there is a great deal of difference between competing on the London money market and competing at a conference which has the power to decide where the money will go. One transaction is commercial, the other political; and the British government would not wish to introduce political struggle into such a contentious field, especially since there would certainly not be enough money to go round.

In general, however, the defects of this scheme are that it neglects the special interests which Commonwealth members have outside the Commonwealth, and that it does not appreciate how repugnant are suggestions for centralized control and co-operation of any kind. Canada, Australia, Zambia, Nigeria and India cannot sacrifice themselves to the stringencies of a closed economic system; neither can Britain. And none can see sufficient reason to do so. To think that they are likely to see sufficient reason is to mistake the whole nature of the Commonwealth connection.

To say this, however, is not to dismiss the whole notion of economic co-operation. It is only to dismiss the idea of centralized direction and closed opportunities. There will continue to be economic co-operation between Commonwealth members in future, but it is likely to be more of the Colombo than the Ottawa type—i.e. it will be technical aid and capital aid rather than a division of responsibilities in production and marketing. The Colombo Plan offers a model for arrangements which can develop between Britain, Canada and the West Indies, between Britain and the African members, and between Australia, New Zealand and the Asian countries.

Changes in External Relationships

Under this heading we may consider possibilities inherent in world politics, shifts which may occur in the relations of countries outside the Commonwealth with members of the Commonwealth. Speculation in this regard is usually pointless; but it is difficult to avoid asking what future relations may be expected between the Commonwealth and the United States, Europe and the Communist states.

Most Commonwealth members either have or would like to have close relations with the United States. Indeed, for some members —Britain, Canada and Australia—it is difficult to see any difference between the actual relationships with the United States and with another Commonwealth member. In fields such as citizenship there are differences, of course; in economic relations the differences are considerable. But in the field of foreign policy each of these three countries is as close to the United States as to one another. This is what made the Suez adventure so notable an event, not only in Anglo-American relations but in Commonwealth relations; it was difficult for the British, Canadian and Australian governments to adjust themselves to the realization that, for once, the connection between Britain and the United States had been broken. Other Commonwealth members do not have the same close relations with the United States, but none is constantly antipathetic to that country. India was the least popular Commonwealth country, in terms of American opinion; and Indian opinion is easily aroused against American policy. But relations between the two countries have notably improved since the Korean War, and they were never so bad as to call for withdrawal of diplomatic representatives or any of the other steps which signify acute differences between sovereign states. The African members, notably Ghana, have been in somewhat the same position, though India's is now friendlier than Ghana's.

We can expect this state of affairs to continue, and to be broken only by the unlikely event of a Commonwealth member going

Communist or actively ranging itself alongside the Communist bloc. There is the chance of this in Africa, but in terms of international alignment, the institutions and traditions of the Commonwealth members make it unlikely that they would wish to become Communist spheres of influence. But to say that they are likely to remain receptive to American influence, while retaining their freedom of action as sovereign states, is to invite the question: What sort of influence? Here we are faced with much confusion. There are two schools of thought in Commonwealth countries which, while they may agree on nothing else, are agreed on the undesirability of any extension of American economic and cultural influence into the Commonwealth. They are, respectively, the extreme Right (who think of the United States as an upstart, money-grubbing civilization which will corrupt the Commonwealth and replace good British traditions by bad American practices) and the extreme Left (who think of the United States as the vanguard of capitalist imperialism, and American culture as the last degenerate stage of capitalist moral decline). Both these schools of thought tend to represent American influence as taking the place of British influence to the detriment of the Commonwealth; they may go so far as to suggest that this infiltration is done with deliberate intent, or they may simply suggest that it is the nature of the American beast, but in either case they consider that the result is to be deplored.

To have discussion of the future of the Commonwealth bedevilled by these two kinds of demonology is most unfortunate; yet it is a fact that a good many such discussions in Britain take place in an atmosphere of prejudice inspired by one or the other. Both are fed by underlying British resentment at the decline of Britain as a Great Power and by anxiety about what the Americans will do next. But neither deserves to be taken as a guide to future Commonwealth relations with the United States, which will be influenced by two things over which the Commonwealth countries have no control: the increasing productivity of American industry and the fact that Americans speak English. Nobody could expect Commonwealth members to be unaffected by the richest country in the world, especially when that country is prepared to give help to free states which wish to hold out against Communist aggression or subversion. Nor could anyone of common sense fail to see that the link which the Commonwealth has in its use of English is a link joining it also to the United States, which has developed its own mature outgrowth of British culture and challenges the other English-speaking countries in education, literature, drama, business, religion, science and the other fields of endeavour in which communication is by way of language. To complain about the proliferation of American goods and American cultural products is to spit in the wind. When Commonwealth countries show their interest in both, they are not, in any sense, being "disloyal" to the Commonwealth; they are showing their awareness of the inventiveness and productivity of the United States, and they are consulting their own interests. American "influence" is the influence of what is technically the most advanced country of our time, the kind of influence which is inevitable in a period of constant intercommunication between countries.

Contrary to much of what is said on the extreme Right, American political influence is not directed against the Commonwealth. It is true that, during and immediately after World War II, there was considerable American suspicion of the Sterling Area and of Imperial Preference, and that some of this remains; but if it had been of consequence it would have prevented American aid to Britain and the Commonwealth countries under such schemes as the Anglo-American Loan, Marshall Aid and the Colombo Plan. In fact, Commonwealth countries have been able to receive all these kinds of help without sacrificing any of their mutual privileges and concessions. It is true that under GATT, which is largely of American inspiration, it is difficult, if not impossible, to raise the level of Imperial Preference; but most Commonwealth members do not want to raise it, since they see profitable trading opportunities outside the Commonwealth and fear that these might be denied to them in retaliation if they gave further privileges to one another. In the colonial field, the United States has been at times impatient, and at other times neutral, about British difficulties; but she has shown nothing but admiration for the Commonwealth as a means of solving the vexed question of a colonial power's relations with its ex-colonies, and has paid tribute to British sincerity in granting colonial independence. In the event, however, what matters is not what some people in the United States say, but what the United States government does. If we take a broad view of American policy as a whole, it has in no way been hostile to either the existence or the extension of the Commonwealth. It can be expected to show the same benevolence in the future. American economic and cultural influence will spread; but it will spread with the concurrence of Commonwealth members, who will eagerly seek it. It is unlikely that relations with the United States will affect the political shape of the Commonwealth, but they will certainly affect the policies and outlooks of individual members.

The question of the future relations of the Commonwealth and Europe is a teasing one. If Europe continues to be the collection of sovereign states which it is at present, there is no reason to expect that it will exert significant influence upon the Commonwealth. If the movement towards European political integration succeeds, however, the Commonwealth will be affected. The nature and extent of the effect would depend on how deeply Britain was involved in the integration scheme. It is difficult now to believe, as some people believed in the years immediately following World War II, that Britain might become part of a European federation. For reasons which have been described in Chapter Seven, no British government is likely to seek political integration with Europe. But the formation of the European Economic Community (or Common Market) by France, Italy, West Germany and Benelux has meant economic difficulties, not only for Britain but for the other Commonwealth members. If Britain had joined the Common Market the other Commonwealth countries would have been at a disadvantage, since Britain would no longer be able to grant them preferences, and they would be less able to sell their goods in Europe, since entry into some of the Common Market countries would be more difficult than before. If Britain remained outside the Common Market and no other arrangements were made, they would still be at a disadvantage, since their goods would still find entry into Europe more difficult, and Britain would be a poorer customer than before for their goods, since she too would find selling in Europe more difficult. Neither of these possibilities appealed to either Britain or the other Commonwealth members. It was on this account that Britain produced the plan for a European Free Trade Area, designed to get the best of both worlds—to retain preferential arrangements with the Commonwealth countries but to secure more favourable entry into European markets. Such a plan was not popular in Europe, especially in France; from the standpoint of the Common Market countries, the obviously desirable outcome would have been entry for their goods into Commonwealth markets on the same basis as Britain's. This would certainly have been the logical extension of a European Free Trade Area in which Britain participated. But it was resisted by both Britain and the other Commonwealth members, not because it would "break up the Commonwealth"—it would not have done so—but because it would have threatened a number of the interests which Commonwealth members have vested in the present incidence of the preference system. The African associates of European states, especially France, produce goods which would compete with goods from Commonwealth countries and British dependencies; European countries produce manufactures which would compete with British, and some overseas Commonwealth, manufactures. To say this is not to imply that in all cases the Commonwealth goods would be unable to compete satisfactorily; it is only to say that a sufficient number of Commonwealth producers would be incommoded to make the scheme unwelcome.

The future of Commonwealth relations with Europe is thus to be seen primarily in economic terms, and cannot be discerned until some accommodation is achieved between three sets of interests, those of the Common Market countries, of Britain, and of the Commonwealth countries which sell goods to Britain and to Europe. There is no full identity of interests between the Commonwealth countries, but all believe that they derive some benefit from the Imperial Preference system which would be reduced if that system were weakened by Britain's membership of the European Economic Community. The Free Trade Area scheme was acceptable to Commonwealth members because it seemed to preserve their existing privileges while leaving their opportunities unimpaired in Europe. Such an outcome would have been too good to be true. Whatever outcome does emerge, however, will not affect the basic relationship of Commonwealth members with one another. It may make economic life easier for some and harder for others, but it will not alter the advantages which members derive from the Sterling Area, from British investment, from their negative agreement in foreign policy and from the machinery of consultation. Europe will not affect these unless Britain becomes part of a European federal state.

The possibilities of changes in the Communist states affecting the Commonwealth must be seen in the general context of Communist politics in the world at large. There is nothing magical about the Commonwealth to insulate its members against world forces which affect free states at large. Those Commonwealth members which have entered the various alliances and coalitions of which the United States is a member must take their chance with the other committed states; the "non-aligned" members must take the same chances as non-Commonwealth countries like Burma, Indonesia and Egypt. It can be taken as axiomatic that non-Communist states are viewed by Communist leaders as either enemies or "neutrals" to be subjected to pressure, flattery and intimidation in the general service of their own world interests. To the Communist leaders, whether of Russia or China, Mr. Shastri and his counterparts are contemporary Chiang Kai Sheks and Kerenskys, representing national bourgeois revolutions which have managed to expel Western imperialist regimes but will in due course succumb to Communist revolutions or Communist military pressure. The Menzies and Pearson regimes are puppets of Washington, agents of American imperialism; the Labour leaders of the Commonwealth are social-fascists set to deceive the working classes of their countries in the interests of American capitalism. Such a view of Commonwealth leaders will not prevent the Russian and Chinese governments from concluding trade agreements with them (as in the case of Ceylon) or cordially assenting to platitudes (as in that of Ghana). But it may prevent them from taking Commonwealth leaders into their confidence; they cannot with any ease trust men who represent regimes which are either directly or indirectly capitalist, as they understand the term. The Commonwealth, in so far as it has any meaning for them at all, is simply a device to perpetuate British imperialism; it has no overtones of freedom, independence and willing co-operation, since these are things which, by definition, are not possible in the relations between major and minor capitalist states. The Communist powers can thus have no respect for the Commonwealth as a means of association between sovereign states. To them it is simply one of the many ways in which imperialism operates. As such, they will attack it; but this attack will be part of their general attack on non-Communist states' arrangements with one another. This means that any changes which the Commonwealth may experience as a result of Communist action will be changes which it shares with the rest of the non-Communist world—unless it is extremely unlucky and is singled out for special treatment. Even then, it is likely to be special treatment for particular members rather than for the whole, since there is no way in which the Communist powers could affect the whole, except by a Communist state becoming part of it. Under those conditions, I have suggested, the Commonwealth would suffer considerable change. But the eventuality is unlikely.

Changes in Leadership

As things stand, Britain is the most positive force in the Commonwealth. She is not, as is sometimes suggested, the "head" of the Commonwealth: this honour is reserved for the Queen, not for Britain. Nor is she, in any strict fashion, the "centre" of the Commonwealth: it has no centre if by this is meant a part round which the others revolve or from which their degrees of centrality to the association are measured. But she is certainly the member which devotes most time and attention to Commonwealth relations. This is to be expected, in view of that fact that all the other members were formerly her dependencies. It has been often stated in this book that British influence in the Commonwealth is pervasive and variegated, being expressed not only in the political sphere but also in business, culture, education, language and institutions. To a considerable extent, Britain has the initiative in Commonwealth relations; no change in the constitution of the Commonwealth is likely to take place without her consent. Also, as we have seen, Britain has the clearest interest of all members in maintaining and amplifying the scope of the Commonwealth. The position has been well put by *The Economist*: [1]

> "For Britain, the Commonwealth is a gentle let-down, a featherbed of fine phrases and outward forms, to ease the psychological impact of the loss—now approaching its last phase—of a powerful Empire. Yet the phrases and the forms can still symbolise something positive and valuable that can persist. The new ways of parting friends has prolonged Britain's influence in a way Holland might envy and France may soon sadly miss. It has given a short respite in which the adjustment can be made to the real loss of power, the consequences of which emerge nakedly from time to time, as, for example, at Abadan.

[1] "The Expanding Commonwealth", *op. cit.*

> It has preserved the friendship of former dependencies. And it has kept up Britain's stock in America, though at times the consequences of Britain's real loss of power have dismayed Americans."

For these reasons, British governments strive to preserve leadership in the Commonwealth, but to do so in ways which will not anger the nation-states which comprise it. This is not easy. Often British politicians and writers of editorials speak of "our Commonwealth" in ways which clearly indicate that they think of the Commonwealth as British property. References to the Commonwealth as a "family" often suggest that parental control is still in being. Yet this kind of assertion is the best way to break up the loose association which members have with one another. It is manifestly not in the British interest to claim jurisdiction, responsibility or any vestige of control over the Commonwealth; at the same time it is natural that British people should be behind-hand in their knowledge of constitutional changes, and should also be inclined to take pride in an association which is like nothing else on earth, but is obviously association with Britain. The fact that many British people claim a bigger part in Commonwealth affairs than the facts warrant is the obverse of the British government's determination to keep the Commonwealth a going concern. Both are minted in the same history.

There is no single competitor for leadership in the Commonwealth, although it is sometimes suggested that India might become one. This view is based upon the assumption that India sees great merits in the Commonwealth and would like to use its facilities to acquire the headship of the newer Commonwealth states. It is the case, however, that India finds that the Commonwealth relationship is not enough to assert this kind of leadership. She has little influence with the African states, since her row with China; she does not have it in regard to Malaysia, and in so far as she possesses it in regard to Ceylon her possession is not to be accounted for in Commonwealth terms. The remnants of colonialism which the Commonwealth has prevent India from exercising any sort of effective *leadership*; instead, she seeks *influence*, which she is able to exercise partly through her size, position and status in the world at large, and partly because Mr. Nehru was a Commonwealth Prime Minister for a longer continuous period than anyone else in the postwar period. Canada, Australia, New Zealand and Pakistan would not accept Indian leadership in the same way as they are prepared to accept British, but they are susceptible to suggestion and advice from India in varying degrees.

There is a possibility that the African members might try to use Commonwealth machinery as an annexe to the Organization of African Unity, in order to influence other Commonwealth members along the lines which anti-colonialism dictates in Africa. The African call for a Commonwealth secretariat at the 1964 Prime Ministers' conference was interpreted by some in this way: the secretariat, although located in London, might have an African head, and would highlight African problems. Whether this is true or not, there is little that African states can do to affect the policy of Britain, Canada, Australia and India through such a means that cannot be done now through the High Commissioners and Prime Ministers. In any case, they do not seem likely to agree for long enough to sustain a systematic campaign.

It is, in fact, difficult to see how Britain could be supplanted from leadership in the Commonwealth except by her own stupidity; and the outcome then would probably be the dissolution of the Commonwealth rather than the assumption of leadership by someone else. British stupidity would consist of insulting or interfering with Commonwealth members, backing one section of the membership against another, demanding promises which members could or would not keep, pursuing policies which vitally affected other members' interests but about which they had not been consulted, and claiming too loudly that the Commonwealth was a British invention and dependent upon British support. It is conceivable that circumstances might arise in which some of these actions were necessary in defence of British security; but in that case the Commonwealth would emerge from the situation in a very different condition from that which it enjoys now. So long as Britain wishes to retain a gentle, polite and moderately effective leadership of the disparate group of states which compose the existing concert of convenience, she must avoid these stupidities.

CONCLUSION

In so far as the Commonwealth is an international institution, its lineaments are now plain. It is based upon the free, unobliged association of sovereign states. They form a concert of convenience in which the prime consideration for each is its own interest. Their national interests have either clearly emerged or are in process of making themselves plain; there is agreement between members that each, within the ambit of the Commonwealth relationship, is entitled to define as domestic those matters which are to be no concern of the Commonwealth as a whole. National self-assertion is the aim of each one. Yet it is clear that a certain common element connects them. That element, it has been suggested, is the influence of their connection with Britain, as it has revealed itself in many fields beside the political. It does not go so far as a common set of values, but it is sufficiently embodied in institutions and modes of expression to make the business of consultation and discussion more congenial for some members than it might be with foreign countries. In addition, there are matters of policy on which members can agree, even if that process of agreement is more often negative than positive, in that they are more often united against some possible happening than in favour of one. They have economic links with Britain which they are not prepared to break, either because these are indissoluble parts of their own economies or because the facilities and opportunities which Britain provides are available nowhere else. They have agreed to differ on a variety of issues of foreign policy, but find that they are often opposed to the same things; the presence of a Communist state among them could disrupt the whole existing relationship.

To illuminate the differences between the Commonwealth and other forms of international association, one is forced back upon possibly misleading Aristotelian metaphors of natural growth and teleological change, if only in order to emphasize the fact that the Commonwealth is not a deliberate contrivance. When a country becomes a Commonwealth member it does so partly by an act of will, but mainly as the culmination of a process of growth and adaptation, the end of which is the status of a sovereign state. Commonwealth membership is, in a sense well understood in existing British dependencies, the mark of political maturity. The right to sit at a meeting of Commonwealth Prime Ministers is sought primarily because it shows that this maturity has been acknowledged by others who are known to possess it. This is presumably what Sir Keith Hancock meant when, in 1937, he wrote of the British Commonwealth as being "nothing else than the 'nature' of the British Empire defined, in Aristotelian fashion, by its end". It is why Mr. Gordon Walker uses the phrase "a natural unit" to describe the Commonwealth. And it justifies Professor Mansergh's usage:[1]

> "If the nature of the Commonwealth may be described teleologically its end is conceived to be the widening of a circle of self-governing peoples of differing cultural and racial origins with a community or a brotherhood of equal nations, linked by history, sharing some common interests and loyalties, membership of which is to the mutual advantage of all and which through the co-operation it seeks to promote brings, in the words of Pandit Nehru, 'a touch of healing' to an embittered world."

Each of these references is intended to stress the growth of the Commonwealth as the response to demands for self-government; and each invites the thought that, if self-government is the end, development beyond that point is uncertain but will presumably be influenced by the process by which the end was achieved. It may well be that convenience and a certain degree of mutual understanding are all that one can hope for in such circumstances, especially when one considers what has happened to the French and Dutch Empires and may well happen to the South African and Portuguese.

To this extent, in comparison with other ways of making friendships between colonial powers and their ex-colonies, the Commonwealth can be pleased with itself. But it is just as well to end on a note of caution and even scepticism, since writers and speakers on the Commonwealth are perpetually being pleased with themselves. "Commonwealth", as we use it now, has changed its meaning in its most significant particular, compared with its older usage in English. When John Healey used "commonwealth" to translate St. Augustine's and Cicero's *respublica*, and Hooker, Hobbes and Locke used the word, they all had in mind a collectivity organized for the public good, a State along the lines understood by T. H.

[1] Nicholas Mansergh, *The Name and Nature of the British Commonwealth* (Cambridge, 1954), p. 30.

Green rather than a sovereign state as understood, in their different ways, by Austin, Engels, Lenin and international lawyers. For hundreds of years, as Sir Keith Hancock has pointed out, "commonwealth" meant to Englishmen "the true society grounded upon the rule of law and the common good"; it could become "a programme in itself".[1] It was an aspiration rather than a fact, something to be aimed at even if never achieved; it was not a matter of convenience or shared selfish interest, but of common good, and it meant political organization directed to this end. But we have seen that the Commonwealth today is an institution whose members are reluctant to admit a common good, except in the most general and negative terms. They are in it for their mutual convenience, and because it shows their maturity. The nearest they come to common wealth is the British gold and currency reserve. This is not what the word meant in the past, and it is not what Lionel Curtis had in mind when he popularized the phrase "a Commonwealth of Nations". A commonwealth in the original sense is something which the present members of the Commonwealth do not desire, and could hardly attain if they did desire it. They want a limited Commonwealth, and that is what they have.

[1] Hancock, *Survey*, *op. cit.*, p. 58.

INDEX

Abyssinia, 44, 125, 139
Aden, 104, 110
Afghanistan, relations with Pakistan, 210–11, 214
Africa, and Britain, 186–7, 206–7, 288; pan-African independence movements, 187–9, 195–6, 200, 205, 207; contrast with Asia, 187, 190, 205; regional groupings, 188, 195, 197; relations with Commonwealth, 190–1, 200, 205–7, 260, 275, 296; Special Commonwealth African Assistance Plan, 193 n; High Commission Territories, 203; relations with the United States, 242; failure of Parliamentary government, 253–4; Communist prospects, 289
African Commission of Mediation, Conciliation and Arbitration, 189–90
African Development Bank, 189
African Unity, Organization for, 187–8, 192, 296
Afrikaner nationalism, 53–5, 203, 240, 255
Afro-Asian Peoples' Solidarity Organization, 189
Amery, L. S., 44 n
ANZUS, 169, 181, 250
Arnold, Guy, 279 n
Attlee, Lord, 12, 66
Australia, national sentiment in, 19–20, 160; growth of navy, 26; and Chanak crisis, 36; war with Japan, 46; schemes for Commonwealth co-operation, 47–8, 50; Asian relations, 89, 168–9, 171–6, 178–9, 269, 288; comparison with New Zealand, 157–9, 167, 180, 182; relations with Indonesia, 159, 164, 170–1, 179; interests and policies, 159–79, 242, 253, 255, 257, 266, 283, 287; relations with Britain, 160–1, 166, 172–3, 175–8, 248, 288; and the United States, 164, 167–70, 173, 175, 177–8, 242, 288; and New Guinea, 164, 171, 179, 235, 246; and the Commonwealth, 167–8, 176–9, 258–60, 275, 287, 295; comparison with Canada, 179; 1944 agreement with New Zealand, 184; interest in Africa, 204–6; aid to Malaysia, 221, 223; and schemes for altering structure of the Commonwealth, 273–4
Australian Labour Party, 33, 160–1, 167, 169–71, 173–5, 178
Avon, Lord (Sir Anthony Eden), 65, 112, 180
Awolowo, O., 192
Ayub Khan, 212
Azikiwe, N., 192

Baghdad Pact, 213
Bajpai, Sir G. S., 137, 150
Balewa, Sir A. T., 189
Balfour Report of 1926, 11, 37
Ball, W. Macmahon, 173
Bandaranaike, S. W. R. D., 217–18, 242
Bandung Conference, 217–18, 144–5, 208
Bank of England, 77–8
Beaverbrook press, 157, 277
Bell, Sir Francis, 180
Borden, Sir Robert, 32, 37
British Commonwealth of Nations, use of term, 11, 13–15, 202; Statute of Westminster, 13–14; status in war and foreign affairs, 40–4; Sir Eric Harrison on, 273–4, 277
British Empire, use of term, 11; relation to Commonwealth, 11–14, representation at Versailles, 34; and at Washington, 35; British interests, 102–3, 114–15; yearnings for return to, 275
British Guiana, 232–3
Burma, 149, 252, 276

Callard, Keith, 209 n, 212 n
Canada, national sentiment in, 19–20; relations with the United States, 19, 23, 119–34, 242, 288; constitution, 23–4 n, 131; and Chanak crisis, 36; and declaration of war in 1939, 45; French-Canadian attitudes, 54, 122–3, 125, 128, 131, 240; interests and policies, 118–34, 242, 257, 287; as pioneer of Dominion status, 118, 124; importance of Commonwealth to, 124, 129, 131, 259, 269, 274–5, 287, 295; Asian relations, 132; interest in Africa, 206; and NATO, 250
Casey, Lord, 166, 169, 174, 178
Castro, Fidel, 231
CENTO, 208, 214
Central Office of Information, 10 n, 252 n
Ceylon, national sentiment in, 20; interests and policies, 114, 217–20, 224, 242; relations with India, 149, 217–19; and the United Kingdom, 217, 220, 256; and the Commonwealth, 217, 220, 225, 260; at Bandung Conference, 217–18; internal politics, 219; relations with the United States, 242
Chanak crisis, 36–8
Chifley, J. B., 178, 184
China, 96, 100, 104–5, 110, 121, 129, 139, 149–51, 153, 157, 161, 164, 174–5, 178, 183, 196, 206, 210, 214–15, 218, 222–5, 243, 249, 293
Chou En-lai, 147
Churchill, Sir Winston, 46, 112
Colombo Plan, 78, 164, 170–2, 175, 183, 218, 287–8, 290
Colonies, difference from sovereign states, 9, 12–13, 23; British policy towards, 19, 22–4, 103; the "two-tier" idea, 273
Commonwealth African Assistance Plan, 77
Commonwealth Air Transport Council, 174
Commonwealth Corporation, 78
Commonwealth Development Finance Co. Ltd., 78
Commonwealth Economic Conference, 53, 69
Commonwealth Economic Consultative Council, 77
Commonwealth Liaison Committee, 75

Commonwealth of Nations (see also Members of), definition, 9–10; nomenclature, 11–15; nature and functions as an international association, 48–9, 51, 239–71, 297–9; non-British aspect, 52–5; limitations of, 84, 298–9; importance to the United Kingdom, 113–15; multi-racialism, 200, 281–3; expansion of, 226, 276; classification of members' interests, 239–46; British culture in, 255–7; proposals for changes in, 272–96; leadership of, 294–6
Commonwealth Parliamentary Association, 79
Commonwealth Prime Ministers' meetings, 13, 48, 50, 53, 55, 67–71, 151, 204, 207, 215, 232, 250, 261, 282–3, 296; Southern Rhodesia not invited, 62, 199–200
Commonwealth Relations Office, 12, 63, 69, 71–2
Commonwealth Scientific Conference, 75
Commonwealth Secretariat, 43, 79, 274, 296
Commonwealth Shipping Committee, 74
Commonwealth Telecommunications Board, 74
Commonwealth Trade and Economic Conference, 77
Communism, 94–5, 103, 105, 128–30, 153, 157, 167, 170, 173–5, 189–90, 206, 213–14, 221, 233, 242–4, 246–7, 249–50, 270, 288–9, 292–4
Congo Republic, 189, 196
Consultation within the Commonwealth, 67–73, 112
Convention People's Party, 194
Cooper, Duff, 42 n
Creighton, D. G., 124 n
Crowe, Sir Eyre, 102 n
Crown, in Malaysia, 15, 54; in British Commonwealth of Nations, 40, 274; in relation to a republic in the Commonwealth, 53, 61; functions in the Commonwealth, 56–8, 270
Cunningham, J. K., 183 n
Current Affairs Bulletin, 163 n
Curtin, John, 47
Curtis, Lionel, 27–8, 202
Cyprus, and Britain, 103–4, 113, 226–7, 288–9; treaty with Greece and Turkey, 227, 229; and the Commonwealth, 227–8, 273; UN mediation, 228; the *Enosis* aim, 229; relations with the United States, 243

Defence in the Commonwealth, 25, 39, 42–4, 48–9, 78–9, 105, 110, 116, 128–31, 155, 169, 177, 179, 181, 184, 193, 197, 221–3, 225
Diefenbaker, John, 134
Dollar shortage in the Commonwealth, 261, 286
Dominions, use of term, 15; official grant of name to self-governing colonies, 24; effects of World War I upon, 31; status defined, 37–8, 43; relation to Britain in foreign policy, 39–44; effects of World War II upon, 44–51, 181, 202
Dulles, J. F., 109, 112, 247
Durham Report, 23, 124

East African federation, 197
Economist, The, 261 n, 281, 285, 294
Eden, Sir Anthony, see Lord Avon

Eire, 42, 58, 60, 252, 266
Entry into the Commonwealth, 60–2, 276–80
Europe, the eclipse of, 92; Britain's relations with, 105–7, 291; and the Commonwealth, 276, 278, 280, 291–2
European Defence Community, 69, 92
European Economic Community (Common Market), 92, 185, 270, 291–2
European Free Trade Association (EFTA), 291–2
Evatt, H. V., 166–7, 173–5, 178, 182
Expanding Commonwealth Group, 276
Expulsion from Commonwealth, 62–3

Falkland Islands, 273
Fiji, 233
Foreign policy, connection with national interest, 90; of new states, 94
Formosa, 97, 108, 129, 149, 175, 183
Franks, Sir Oliver, 73 n
Fraser, Peter, 184

Gaitskell, Hugh, 284
Gandhism, 139–40
GATT, 182, 290
George VI, 14, 51
Ghana, national sentiment in, 20; relations with the Commonwealth, 54, 194–5, 207; and South Africa, 61, 273; interests and policies, 101, 114, 188, 242, 255; independence of, 186; relations with Nigeria, 192, 195, 251; and the United Kingdom, 193–5; and the United States, 242–3, 261, 288; and the Sterling Area, 261, 284
Gibraltar, 113
Goa, 149
Gordon Walker, P. C., 57 n, 277, 279, 298
Governors-General, 22 n, 58, 71–2, 211–12
Guiana, British, 232–3

Hall, H. Duncan, 34 n, 43–4
Hancock, Sir Keith, 7, 11, 13, 298–9
Harrison, Sir Eric, 273–4, 277
Harvey, Heather J., 48 n
Hasluck, Paul, 40 n, 41 n
Hegel, G. W. F., 86–7
Hertzog, J. B. M., 203
High Commissioners, 71–2, 182, 184
High Commission Territories in southern Africa, 203–4
Holland, S. G., 180–1
Holyoake, K., 182
Hughes, W. M., 32

Imperial Conference, 24, 29, 37–8, 40–1, 51, 63, 68, 72
Imperial Federation, 28, 275
Imperial Preference, 25, 29 30, 43, 77, 106, 155, 172, 182, 257–9, 267, 286, 290, 292
Imperial War Cabinet, 32, 36
India, relations with Indonesia, 14, 149; national sentiment in, 20, 139–40; and Pakistan, 51, 135–6, 138, 208–10, 213–14, 216–17, 251; Kashmir question, 51, 69, 148, 152, 155, 209–10, 213–15; decision to become a republic, 53, 61; and the Commonwealth, 53, 151–6, 216, 258, 260, 269, 287;

and South Africa, 72, 141, 146–8, 152, 155, 203, 251, 281; and China, 132, 139, 149–51, 153, 243, 293; member of League of Nations, 135; interests and policies, 135–56, 242, 245, 287; at Bandung Conference, 144–5; non-alignment policy, 144, 150–1, 154, 249; relations with Burma, Ceylon and Goa, 149, 217–19; at 1964 Cairo conference, 150; military aid from United Kingdom and United States, 150, 242–3; Sterling Area, 155; links with Australia, 169, 179; relations with Britain, 216, 256; and the United States, 242, 250, 288; and the U.S.S.R., 293; and Commonwealth leadership, 295
Indian National Congress, 135–7, 139–42, 209
Indian Ocean defence, 225
Indo-China, 96–7, 108, 112, 129, 175
Indonesia, Indian view of and relations with, 14, 149; comparison and relations with Australia, 159, 164, 170–1, 179; confrontation of Malaysia, 170–1, 223–5; Pakistani support of, 214; relations with Commonwealth, 276
International Monetary Fund, 265

Jagan, Cheddi, 233
Jamaica, 229–32, 273
Jebb, Richard, 14, 29
Jinnah, M., 209, 212

Kahin, G. McT., 145 n
Kashmir, 51, 69, 148, 152, 155, 209–10, 214–15, 217, 283
Kaunda, K. D., 267
Keith, A. Berriedale, 35 n, 38 n
Kenya, independence of, 186; role in pan-Africanism, 195–6; comparison and relations with Tanganyika and Uganda, 195–7; relations with United Kingdom, 197–8, 245, 276; dispute with Somalia, 197; and Indian Ocean defence, 225
Kenyatta, Jomo, 196, 197
Korea, 97, 108, 112, 149
Kotelawala, Sir John, 217, 221

Laurier, Sir Wilfrid, 26
League of Nations, Dominions as members of, 34, 125, 135, 183
Libya, 266
Lloyd George, David, 35
Lloyd, Selwyn, 180
Locarno Treaty, 38
Louw, F., 282

Macdonald, Sir John, 123
Mackenzie King, W. L., 13, 37, 47, 48, 125–6, 128
Macmillan, Harold, 248
Maitland, Hon. Patrick, 276
Malan, D. F., 203, 255
Malawi, 199
Malaya, status of, 15; and the Commonwealth, 54, 245, 258, 260, 284; Communist rebellion in, 221; defence agreement with Britain, 223; interests and policies, 256; relations with the United States, 261; and the Sterling Area, 261
Malaysia, Crown's relation to, 15; defence agreement with Britain, 110, 221–5; Indonesian confrontation of, 170–1, 223–5; Australian and New Zealand military aid to, 170–1, 179, 184, 221, 223; contrast with India and Pakistan, 221; relations with the Commonwealth, 221–5; interests and policies, 221–4, 242, 266; Chinese population and relations with China, 222; relations with the United States, 242; anti-communism, 243
Malta, 113, 273
Malvern, Lord (Sir Godfrey Huggins), 68
Manila Treaty, 169
Mansergh, Nicholas, 7, 12 n, 41, 48 n, 51 n, 65, 193, 202 n, 228, 283, 298
Maude, Angus, 41 n
Members of the Commonwealth, treated as sovereign states, 9, 114; dependencies of, 9; use of term, 15; divergent national interests of, 49–50, 54, 275; rights of, 58–63; common interests of, 70, 267–8; classification of, 239–52; disputes between, 251, 269; economic ties of, 257–68, 286–7
Menon, Krishna, 141
Menzies, Sir Robert, 64–7, 71, 166, 168, 173, 182, 255, 275 n, 283
Middle East, British policy in, 108–10, 181, 227–9
Milner, Lord, 202
Mirza, Iskander, 212
Mohammed, Ghulam, 212
Morris-Jones, W. H., 253
Munich Conference, 41–2, 181
Muslim League, 209, 212

Nash, Walter, 182
National interest, concept of, 83–92; connection with foreign policy, 90
Nationality in the Commonwealth, 74
National sentiment, growth of, in the Commonwealth, 19–21, 29, 33–4, 86–7, 134, 139
NATO, 98, 105, 116, 127–8, 131, 134, 250
Nehru, Jawaharlal, 134, 136, 139–41, 144–9, 245, 266–7, 295
Nepal, 220
New Guinea (Australian), 9, 164, 171, 235, 246, 283
New Statesman and Nation, 281
New Zealand, national sentiment in, 20; and Chanak crisis, 36; war with Japan, 46; comparison with Australia, 157–9, 167, 180, 182; interests and policies, 180–5, 242, 253, 257; links with Britain, 180–5, 248; relations with the United States, 181, 242; diplomatic activity, 181–2; at the United Nations, 181, 183, 261; relations with Asia, 183, 288; and the Commonwealth, 183–4, 258–60; 1944 agreement with Australia, 184; aid to Malaysia, 184, 221, 223; relations with South Africa, 204–5; interest in Africa, 206; and Samoa, 234–6
Nicolson, Sir Harold, 87, 117
Nigeria, independence, 186; interests and policies, 191, 287; relations with Ghana, 192, 195, 251; and the United Kingdom, 192–3; and Sterling Area, 261, 287

Nkrumah, Kwame, 188–9, 193–4, 242, 255, 267
Noon, Malik Firoz Khan, 210
Nuclear weapons, 98, 107, 110, 116, 130, 151
Nyerere, Julius, 189, 196, 198

Organization for African Unity, 187–8, 192, 296
Ottawa agreements of 1932, 43, 77, 287

Pacific area, 233–4
Pacific War Council, 46
PAFMECSA, 189
Pakistan, national sentiment in, 20; republican status, 54; Kashmir issue at Prime Ministers' meetings, 51, 69; relations with India, 51, 135–6, 138, 208–10, 213–14, 216–17, 251, 295; and Bandung Conference, 208; relations with Afghanistan, 210–11, 214; and the United States, 210, 213–14, 216, 242–3; and China, 210, 214–15; interests and policies, 211–17, 242, 255; internal politics, 211–12, 252; and the Commonwealth, 211, 215–17, 225; support of Indonesia, 214
Panch Sheela, 147
Panikkar, K. M., 138, 141, 281, 283 n
Papua, 9, 24, 235
Parliamentary institutions in the Commonwealth, 212–13, 240, 252–7, 268
Pearson, Lester, 65, 127–8, 133
Powell, J. Enoch, 41 n
Privy Council, Judicial Committee of the, 74

Queensland, 24

Rahman, Tunku Abdul, 222, 267
Reid, Escott, 127
Rhodes, Cecil, 24
Rhodesia and Nyasaland, Federation of, presence of Prime Minister at Commonwealth meetings, 62, 68–9; interests and policies, 196; British attitude to, 198; collapse of Federation, 198, 241; relations with South Africa, 204; comparison with West Indies Federation, 231; relations with the Commonwealth, 245
Rhodesia (Southern), independence issue, 61–2, 186–7, 199–200, 283; relations with South Africa, 199; and the Commonwealth, 275–6
Roosevelt, F. D., 48
Round Table groups, 28
Royal Institute of International Affairs, 11

St. Helena, 273
St. Laurent, Louis, 14, 133
Samoa, 183, 234–6
Sandys, Duncan, 177
Sargent, J. R., 285
Savage, M. J., 180
SCAAP, 193 n
SEATO, 97, 105, 169–71, 175, 179, 181, 183, 208, 213–15
Secession of members of the Commonwealth, 58–60
Sierra Leone, 186
Simonstown naval base, 204–5
Smith, Ian, 199
Smith, Sidney E., 134
Smuts, J. C., 13, 33, 37, 44, 47, 48, 202–3
Soekarno, A., 223
Somalia, dispute with Kenya, 197
Sorel, Georges, 143, 209
South Africa, national sentiment in, 19–20, 53–5, 203, 255; and Chanak crisis, 36; effects of World War II upon, 44; attitude to new members of Commonwealth, 55, 61, 245, 273; withdrawal from Commonwealth, 62, 186, 202, 204–5, 281–2; Apartheid issue, 63, 204, 269, 281–3; relations with India, 72, 141, 146–8, 152, 155, 203–4, 251, 281; and Tanganyika, 198; and Federation of Rhodesia and Nyasaland, 199, 204; and the United Kingdom, 203–5, 260; contribution to the Commonwealth, 202; interests and policies, 202–5, 245, 252, 257; the High Commission Territories' dispute, 203–4; relations with the United States, 250
South-west Africa, 246
Statute of Westminster, 13–14, 38, 40, 45, 48, 53, 274
Sterling Area, 52, 69, 70, 75–6, 155, 260–3, 284–6, 290
Strijdom, J. G., 255
Sudan, 276
Suez action of 1956, 64–7, 98, 108–9, 112, 133–4, 152, 173, 270, 288
Suhrawardy, H. S., 255
Sunday Times, 65

Tanganyika, attitude to South Africa, 62, 198; independence of, 186; role in pan-Africanism, 195–6; comparison and co-operation with Kenya and Uganda, 195–7; union with Zanzibar, 196, 207; relations with the United Kingdom, 197–8; and Commonwealth membership, 198; and Indian Ocean defence, 225
Tanzania, 186, 195 n, 196–7
Templewood, Lord, 41
Times, The, 49
Trinidad, 229–32, 273
Turkey, 227–9, 276

Uganda, independence of, 186; role in pan-Africanism, 195–6; comparison and co-operation with Kenya and Tanganyika, 195–7; relations with the United Kingdom, 197–8
Under-developed countries, foreign policy of, 95; appeal of communism to, 94–6, 100; protectionist policy of, 99
Underhill, Frank, 125 n
United Arab Republic, 196
United Kingdom, colonial policy, 19, 22–4 103; unilateral Suez action in 1956, 64–7; interests and policies, 66, 84–5, 99, 102–17; Cyprus policy, 103–4, 113, 226–7, 288–9; China's effect on Asian policy of, 104; relations with the United States, 104–5, 107–11, 130, 249, 289; and Europe, 105–7, 291–2; and the Commonwealth, 106, 111, 113–15, 160–1, 166, 172–8, 180–2, 192–3, 225; and Ghana and Nigeria, 114, 192–5; and the

Sterling Area, 115, 259–65, 267, 284–6; investment in the Commonwealth, 177, 203, 206, 240, 259–60, 264, 267–8, 286–7; policy and interests in Africa, 186, 206; relations with Kenya, Tanganyika and Uganda, 197; and the Federation of Rhodesia and Nyasaland, 198; disputes with South Africa over High Commission Territories, 203–4; relations with India, 216; defence agreement with Malaysia, 221–3; position in the Commonwealth, 241, 248, 255–6, 268–71, 274–6, 284, 294–6; and Imperial Preference, 258–9
United Nations, 73, 90–1, 127, 134, 148, 156, 173–4, 181, 183, 204, 210, 214–15, 218, 228, 234, 245–6
United States of America, and World War II, 46; intervention in world affairs, 96–7; British attitudes towards, 97, 104–5, 107–11, 130, 289; relations with the Commonwealth, 97, 242–4, 250, 261–2, 286, 288–90; and Canada, 97, 119–34; and Australia, 164, 170, 173, 175, 177–8; and New Zealand, 181; and Pakistan, 214; and Ghana, 288; and India, 288
Union of Soviet Socialist Republics, 96, 100, 107, 109–10, 121, 127, 149–50, 153, 196, 206, 210, 215, 218, 293

Verwoerd, H. F., 282

West Indies, and the United Kingdom, 241, 288
West Indies, Federation of the, 230–1
White Australia policy, 161–2, 283
Wiles, Peter, 284
Wood, F. L. W., 180
World War I, effects on Dominions, 31, 124–5, 161
World War II, effects on Dominions, 44–51, 181, 202; effects on Commonwealth relations, 51–2

Zambia, 199, 200, 260, 287
Zanzibar, independence of, 186; 1963 revolt in, 196, 206–7; union with Tanganyika, 196, 207
Zimmern, Alfred, 44 n
Zinkin, Taya, 153